JESUS &
JELLIED EELS

making sense of my life

Laurie Green

Brimstone Press

Acknowledgements

I wish to thank Mel Thompson of Brimstone Press for his invaluable guidance in bringing the book to publication and David Moloney of DLT for his additional encouragement. Philip Painter has expertly proofed the text, and for the cover, Newham Heritage Service has given permission to use their photograph of East Ham High Street where I grew up. My thanks are also due to Vicki my wife, Dr Philip Need and Graham Hamer for reading early drafts, and to Rowan Williams for allowing me to quote from his publication. Other friends have offered their photographs, although most are from my own collection. Biblical quotations are mainly from DLT's Revised New Jerusalem Bible although I've occasionally offered my own translation or paraphrase.

As I've told my story, I've sometimes found it appropriate to change the names. But my fullest thanks are nevertheless due to all those I've mentioned for it is they who have made my life so rich and fulfilling.

ISBN-13:   978-1906 38590 3

First published by Brimstone Press
© Laurie Green 2022
www.lauriegreen.org

www.brimstone-press.com
Brimstone Press is a not-for-profit,
self-publishing cooperative.

I affectionately dedicate this book to my children, grandchildren and those who come after, so they can better understand a little of how my unusual life contributed to how I turned out – for better or worse. The book is also a 'thank you' to Vicki my wife who has put up with me through almost all my years.

Contents

The unusual enterprise
Building confidence
Moving the church on
What next?

All Saints Poplar
Religion in Poplar
Getting physical
All Saints faces the challenge
God and Jesus?
In for a big surprise

Finding my way
After the waiting, the reality
Sharing the workload
Supporting the good work of the parishes
The Church International
Being part of the team
Special urban needs
Grace abounding
Enlarging my responsibilities

Getting ready to leave
A home of our own
A personal breakthrough
Three fulfilling initiatives
The glories of India
A world full of religions
Exploring the beyond
The overwhelming depth of it all

AN INTRODUCTORY WARNING

I first drafted this book as my attempt to fathom how on earth an East End lad like me ended up as a bishop in the established Church of England. But that draft prompted so much reflection on my part that I've kept coming back to it, adding paragraphs and deleting some of the nonsense. I suppose reflecting on our past always makes us do this, but unlike a written text, in real life we don't have the privilege of going back and putting our mistakes right: we just have to find ways of living with them. But as I've cast my mind back, it's occurred to me that human memory, even at its best, is rarely to be trusted. Some marriage counsellors, when helping people who are contemplating divorce, ask them to write down an account of what is happening in their relationship and to seal it away for the future. Some years later they're asked to unseal the envelope and read afresh that contemporary account, only to find that it annoyingly clashes with how they now remember what happened. During the intervening period it has been necessary for them to find a way to deal with the horrendous dislocation of their life, and quite unconsciously we human beings do that by reinterpreting and even reinventing past events to help ourselves along life's challenging pathways.

Napoleon is said to have proclaimed: 'all history is fiction,' for it has to be acknowledged that history is always selection, presentation and interpretation. It is never a complete and unbiased account of the events it relates. There is of course a whole philosophical argument to be had as to whether our history writes us or we write history. Is history just a meaningless series of events and the human mind, fearful of meaninglessness, finds a way to thread the events together into meaningful story? Or is there something in the dynamic process of events that actually has purpose and meaning which the human mind then delights in uncovering? Either way, the human mind is clearly an agent of great creativity, not just a recording machine.

To all this you may well respond: 'So much for autobiography,' except that this surely is the very point of writing any biography in the first place – we intentionally set out not merely to present facts but to interpret and search for coherence and meaning. A biography tries to dig down to see what makes the person in question tick, not merely tell us what they had for breakfast each day. And this in part explains why I set about writing this book. It was in order to find out for myself what really makes me tick. This is why I've kept coming back to the text, adding in reflections as aspects of my life have become clearer to me after mulling them over. It's been proving a fascinating exploration, teaching me about myself, but also bringing into much sharper focus just how important to me have been those around me.

The event which prompted me to begin writing was the occasion of my mother's funeral. As so often occurs at such gatherings, my sister and I were reminiscing on the events of my mum's life and on overhearing our conversation, our daughters Rebecca and Hannah exclaimed: 'but we never knew any of this before!' When we pop our clogs, we take all our experiences with us, and it's often only when a dear one dies that we realise how little we know about the earlier life of those whom we have loved. I promised our girls, then and there, that I'd write something for the family scrapbook, and so it all began.

Soon after that, I heard on the car radio a panel of celebrities being asked what period of history they would have liked most to have lived through. To my surprise, the final panellist answered: 'the last eighty years, because they seem to have encompassed the most astonishing kaleidoscope of events.' And as one of those who have lived through that period, I have to agree. My generation has experienced the abject poverty of those post-war years of rationing when the world tried to claw its way back from the devastation of two world wars largely engendered by the upsurge of nationalism. We've played our part in revolutions in popular culture, and been in on the birth of some of the most creative and inventive pop music and jazz; we've experienced a liberation of ordinary people from many a confinement, and enjoyed the optimism of what Prime Minister Harold Wilson called, in its earliest days: 'the White Heat of technology.' We've lived through and taken part in the Flower-Power Hippie revolution, the sudden move from productive industry to consumer-led economics and monetarism, trodden the road from Empire to Europeanism and then the descent back into Nationalism, and even been consumed by the advent of television and computer technology. The age of individualism has been given a turbo-boost by the invention of the personal smartphone, but in its turn that little device has introduced each of us to a wide world beyond our imaginations, and we've learnt to call that 'globalisation'. We've seen bloody war, Cold War, the fall of the Berlin Wall, environmental depletion, Polio and Covid outbreaks, Brexit, Putin, three monarchs, and so much more. And the silly thing is that I've lived through all seventy and more years of this abundant historical era without always registering just how earth-shattering a period it has been. All this has been the defining backdrop to what these pages record and, in very large measure, these momentous historical and cultural shifts have shaped the way I and my generation view the world, even though we rarely recognise the fact. Perhaps this exercise will help me understand some of that as I continue to write and reflect. For the present I'm still here, at least for a while, seeking to learn from all that has been, and still enjoying and savouring every moment of what each new today brings.

Before plunging in, may I finally own up to the inevitable fact that an autobiography by its very nature, revolves around the author. Therefore I'm feeling very embarrassed at the thought of it being read. I did my best to guard the reader from the worst excesses of my self-indulgence by seeking to give an account of what went wrong as well as right and of the situation and people around me as I passed on my way. But what emerged as I wrote were inevitably realisations of how these events and individuals affected me, fashioned me and led me to develop a faith to live by. I hope therefore that the reader will forgive me if there's still too much 'auto' in this auto-biography.

Anyway, there we are, and here we go.

CHAPTER 1

EAST ENDERS

On Saturday 22 January 2011, I climbed up into the bulky modern pulpit, sipped at the water that the Cathedral verger had provided, and began. I was saying farewell to the Diocese of Chelmsford and to hundreds of dear friends that I'd come to know over my years there in the extraordinary county of Essex and in East London. For eighteen years I had served there as the Bishop of Bradwell and I was now handing on the mantle and retiring with Vicki to the south coast town of Bexhill. So what was I to say? I remembered being told by a wise priest many years before that all of us really only have one sermon in us and that we preach it over and over in a thousand different ways. So I felt that this was the moment when I needed to come clean and state what I thought the substance of my one sermon really was. I put it this way: 'Whoever we are, there are those times in all our lives when we sense that there is a mystery – a deep mystery about this world and about being alive in it. And if we give it our very fullest attention, then it dawns on us that this mystery is intimately in love with us. In other words, that the Divine loves you and me to bits. And if that's true for you and me, then God must love all those around us equally.' Of course I could appreciate that for some that might have sounded like sentimental twaddle, so I went on to explain what I meant in less romantic and more down to earth terms.

I have to admit that I was able to say I felt love all around me because while others live their whole lives beset by deprivation and misery, and I had occasionally seen that misery first hand through the years, I had been one of the lucky ones, having been born surrounded by love – although it was certainly not in a time nor a place as resplendent as that moment in the glorious cathedral in Essex.

I had not been the first child of my cockney parents, Laura and Len Green. In 1941, as the night-time bombing of the East End of London was reaching its devastating peak, a little girl was conceived who would be born on 7 November of that year. This was my sister, Barbara Vivienne Green, known to me always as Babs. My aunt told me that, although the family were not church-goers, her name was adopted from the wife of a local vicar who hosted meetings of the Young Communist League in his vicarage, and, since many of our family were ardent communists, that sounds quite plausible – but who can now be sure? Our dad had been a promising pupil at his local school, but when his ever-eccentric mother Ruby heard he was on the brink of winning a scholarship, he was whisked down the road to the gates of Victoria Dock. So, at the age of only thirteen, he was made to sign on as a ship's cabin boy bound for New Zealand – and he remained a sailor for many years thereafter. Our mother's family lived in the East End's Canning Town but she had relations who had owned a fish and chip shop on Steep Hill in Lincoln. It was to their retirement bungalow in Lincolnshire that she would take her precious baby Barbara for short breaks away from the terrifying London bombings. Things became so dangerous however that eventually Babs was evacuated with her Nanny Green to a Suffolk village. There the local folk were oblivious to the desolation back home where every night was filled with the dread of the Luftwaffe's bombing 'blitz'.

It was only after Babs was born, that a very reluctant USA joined in the war, the Soviet Union began to push back the German lines, and we began to make progress across northern Africa and into Italy. Babs still remembers that, as the bombing eased, her mum would take her down to Dover to stay in a room over the shop at 11 High Street where Laura's friend Sylvia lived. Laura would take Babs down to the shore to wave to Len who was skippering vessels across the Channel, ferrying our troops back and forth. As he brought the craft up the beach, men exhausted by the fighting came off the boat, tussling Bab's hair as they went by, leaving her daddy still on board. He was only able to wave his goodbye before turning his boat around and heading back out to sea carrying replacement troops intent on Hitler's final defeat. Although only a toddler, Babs vividly remembers her tears of disappointment as her daddy went off once more, but Len must have come ashore sometimes to stay at number 11 because it was there in March 1945 that a baby was conceived who was to become Yours Truly, born on Boxing Day of the same year. By that time, Hitler was no more.

Like many of their generation, Laura and Len had first met at their local dancehall, Len standing out from the others by being dressed immaculately in the very latest fashion, brought back from one of his many seafaring trips to New York. Laura was renowned for having quirky premonitions about the future and, as soon as he walked on to the dance floor, she told the friend sitting next to her that he was the man she would marry, this despite the fact that she was already engaged to someone else! Len found this out when walking Laura home after the dance. He asked if he could examine the engagement ring and as soon as it was put into his hand, he threw it over a wall, casually remarking, 'well, you're not engaged anymore, so that's OK.' Apparently, Laura was not at all fazed by this and they just strolled on home.

When not at sea, Len lived with his parents, his father being licensee at the famous dockers' pub, the Galleons, while his mum had grown up at Becton Gas Works Cottages. She was never a woman to have young boys under her feet who were not paying their way and that's probably why Len and his younger brother had both been sent away to sea. It nevertheless turned out to be a life he enjoyed, taking him to New Zealand, Canada and the United States. However, it was South America, and Argentina in particular, that he really loved. It was there that he learnt to play the accordion and dance the Argentine Tango. In all those years Len and his brother Arthur only met up once and that was in an

Argentinian gaol after being arrested for taking part in a bare-knuckle fight in one of the Latino gaming rings. Sometimes I would catch him off-guard and he would mention machine guns and the like, but then he would deny he'd said anything at all. The only thing I learnt for sure was that in the bare-knuckle ring he had been known as the Star Kid, named after the Star Line shipping company.

Len & his brother
just in from
Argentina

Laura was determined on a church wedding, but they didn't have money enough for the banns to be read for both addresses so the marriage register has them both living at her family address in Portland Road, Canning Town. The service took place in 1935 at Holy Trinity Church, just along the Barking Road from his father's first pub in Rathbone Market. Fifty years later, dad always liked to tell us that he walked down the aisle with his bride saying to himself: 'This will never last!' When the church was hit by one of Hitler's bombs, he rejoiced in the knowledge that the marriage register must have gone up in smoke! The couple were lucky enough to find two upstairs rooms to rent in Ruskin Avenue, and so began their long relationship with London's East Ham.

Their marriage brought together two families who were deeply rooted in London's East End cockney culture. The prevailing winds of most cities of the northern hemisphere blow across to the east, carrying with them the smoke and dirt of the city, and this is why the east side of most cities is where you'll find the cheaper housing and the city's working class. In London, the east also looked out to the sea and therefore was the preferred site for the docks and the early ship-building industry along the Thames. The Elizabethans relegated certain 'dirty' trades to the area just beyond the Tower of London – what's now called Tower Hamlets – and it was here that the distinctive cockney culture grew up. Back then, locals largely depended for cheap food on the abundant eel stocks of the estuary and even Shakespeare mentions this when he has King Lear's fool shout, 'Cry to it, Nuncle, as the cockney did to the eels when she put 'em i' th' paste alive.' We were always blessed with copious quantities of jellied eels, cockles and mussels because during our childhood, mum worked at the jellied eel factory at the top of our street. We were exceedingly proud of our ancient cockney culture with its distinctive language and songs. It's all gone now, but it was sturdy and strong all through the years of my youth. From the very earliest days, cargoes of enormous value from all around the world would be unloaded at the London Docks and taken upriver to adorn the houses of the rich. Meanwhile, on the outgoing tides, the detritus and sewage of the city flowed past those labouring in the eastern dockyards. But despite being excluded from enjoying the imported wealth they were handling every day, they knew they belonged to a local culture which had become strong and resilient, empowered by recurrent influxes of new migrants, especially the Jews at Whitechapel, the Chinese in Limehouse and the French Huguenots at Spitalfields. The East End always housed the obscenely poor who lived as best they could from employment in small exploitative businesses and were, from time to time, decimated by outbreaks of cholera and plague. Dickens had walked these streets to find fascinating characters a-plenty, from the foul Bill Sikes to the homely Sam Weller, all representing the challenges and joys of the cockney world, with its eels, its own language and its very own way of life.

So it was that my cockney mum had grown up in abject poverty, her abusive father having deserted his wife Elsie and their six young children. Laura, as the oldest child, had to care for her five siblings while her mother took what work she could find. This was an arrangement which suited her mother quite well for she never was a one to attend to chores of any kind. So it was that almost everything was left for Laura to manage from a very young age. They all crammed into one upstairs room, and a shared communal water-tap, which was made to serve all the families in the crumbling tenement, was down in the yard. Laura treasured her time at school because it offered a refuge from the bleak world she inhabited. But as soon as she was old enough, she was sent out to work as a 'nippy' – a waitress nipping from table to table taking orders from the wealthy customers. At the outbreak of war, wealthier folk moved away from the constant bombing, leaving their London properties for rent, and this gave young Laura the opportunity to grab one such home. She moved first into a little terraced house in Cheltenham Gardens, taking with her her mother and young siblings, and later, when Babs was born, into a larger house on the other side of the railway at 128 Browning Road. In this way, she was able to keep the family well-housed, and more important still, together. Goodness knows how she organised all this, but although diminutive in stature, she was and remained always a cockney force of nature.

Laura and Len were to live in that same house for the rest of their married life together and it was there that I was born into the world. Barbara clearly remembers that on that day she had been taken for a walk by her dad when Uncle Peter came cycling furiously up the road shouting that it had happened! Dad scooped her up into his arms and ran like the wind to arrive back at the house where I had just been born. In fact the birth had proved to be a hit and miss affair. Laura had already lost one child in 1937 when baby Colin had only lived for one hour, and this time it was my turn to cause concern, weighing in at 9 pounds 7 ounces to my diminutive mum. For a poor couple, my problematic birth proved to be a financial challenge too, it being prior to the advent of the National Health Service. Laura had already decided on my name, for as a child there had been only one book in her house: *Little Women* by Louisa May Alcott. She had fallen in love with Laurie who was the young boy in the story, so the decision was a foregone conclusion. My father's middle name was added in and so I was registered for my war-time ID card as 'Laurence Alexander Green' and, as was expected of all families, baptised soon thereafter at our local St Barnabas church by the new vicar, Mr Porter.

Full House

The house was full to bursting and to this day I've never figured out how all the family, at least ten of us, fitted in. Mum's five siblings were all there and by the time I was toddling they were all courting. After the stipulated periods of engagement, each was married at St Barnabas Church, which was just across the road from our home. My uncles were mostly navy men – Syd serving in the *Andrew* (the Royal Navy) for 21 years and marrying Joan, a Wren (the Women's Royal Naval Service). Uncle David married a clippy, clipping bus-tickets as a bus conductor. It was in this role she acquired the name Mick, because she was repeatedly called upon to sort out any fist fights among the passengers. But while Mick had the right hook of a professional, to us she was just our great big cuddly aunt with a great big smile and voice to match. In our neighbourhood everyone had to share their bedroom with others, so in the middle of our front bedroom stood mum and dad's double bed with my cot in the corner next to

Bab's make-shift bed, with a canvas screen around us to provide at least a modicum of privacy for our parents. We had a separate window, so Babs and I could look down on to the street below, where each evening the corner lamppost attracted the local lads and lassies enjoying one another's company. As I gazed, I dreamt of one day being old enough to join that exciting gang of youngsters. When we're young we constantly yearn to grow up and when old we look back nostalgically. What a lot of time we waste not savouring the present moment.

It's only now when I study the data or see contemporary news footage that I appreciate just how hard it must have been for our parents to make ends meet. It was a period of financial struggle coupled with stringent rationing and very high unemployment. But we had no inkling of our poverty, because all the people we knew locally shared exactly the same predicament and there was no television to show us how the other half lived. In some ways the need to share and not to waste a thing had brought us all even more closely together and despite the odds, we children had wonderfully happy times, oblivious of the concerns that dogged our parents as they looked for work or juggled the pennies. Only much later did we learn that mum had often gone without food herself to ensure that we were well-nourished.

The war had cost Britain more than we could know, for the fight against Hitler had meant six years of 'total war' which left Britain on her knees. Drained of energy, money and infrastructure, she had looked to her wealthy cousins across the ocean for support. Churchill was half American himself, but at the end of the war he lost power to the socialist Labour Party. Although many were shocked to see Churchill, the strong wartime leader, depart from office, his previous track record in peacetime had been lamentable and so while remaining a war-time hero in the eyes of the British people they now mistrusted his intended policies, especially his objections to the introduction of what was now being called the 'Welfare State'. This was a term coined by the then

Archbishop of Canterbury William Temple, in contrast to what he termed Hitler's 'Power State'. It won the support of the British electorate who believed that since pulling together for the common good had won the war, it stood to reason that the same could win the peace. There was a new optimism in the air and a determination to make Britain into something significantly better, and that was the promise of Labour's brand new government.

However, with Britain's war debt amounting to 250 per cent of its own GDP, the difficulty for any government was that the country was bust, and added to that, the Americans, to whom Labour looked for financial help, despised their socialism. Only one week after dropping the atomic bomb on Nagasaki, President Truman brought to an end the Lend-Lease programme which during the war had provided the financial scaffolding of our nation. The UK government sent a delegation headed by its economics wizard, John Maynard Keynes, to ask its ally for a loan, but on arrival at the White House they were kept waiting in the corridor. The best Keynes was able to secure was a miserly loan spread over a whole fifty-year period, and that on condition that sterling was made freely exchangeable for dollars. This ensured that the American financial system would from now on dominate internationally. As a consequence, there was an immediate run on sterling as pounds were freely exchanged for dollars, forcing our currency to be devalued. Britain was left in deep trouble, and so was its promised socialist programme. All the plans were scuppered until the US realised that Europe was so impoverished that it might feel forced to turn instead towards the Soviet bloc for support, thus securing for the Soviets a financial and political hold on the whole continent. So America instituted its generous Marshall Plan to help Europe back on its feet as a bulwark against the Soviets. The necessary inclusion of the UK in the programme certainly helped, but by then it was already perilously indebted and fragile.

All this meant that growing up immediately after the war in our poorer part of London had its downside. No toys, few sweets, rarely any fruit, and of course what houses remained were full to bursting and agonisingly cold because coal was strictly rationed and central heating unheard of. Like many other local families, we collected coal dust and mixed it with cement to give it solidity. Along with very tightly-rolled old newspaper, this made reasonable briquettes for the fire. Other newspaper was torn carefully into squares, gathered up on a string and hung in the loo as a substitute for toilet paper. The toilet was cold too being outdoors, and in winter we hung up a little oil lamp to keep the water from freezing, but without much success. Most of us therefore were thankful for the 'gazunder' – the chamber pot under the bed – but everyone tried to skive off the consequent slopping-out duties the following morning. We were lucky enough to have a bathroom upstairs in our house, but it was not usable due to bomb damage. Even when the pipes were eventually operable, the thought of carrying all those saucepans of hot water up the stairs in such freezing cold conditions was clearly not as enticing as bringing the tin bath in from the garden shed, placing it in front of the open fire and pouring in hot water straight from a steaming kettle. Even then it was such a palaver and so expensive to heat all that water that bath night only came round once a week. Then the argument would rage about who would go last! Having played in the street all day, I was so filthy that I was usually made to take the last dip into what was by then very sinister-looking, tepid water.

In the evenings when dad was still at work, we'd huddle round the fire to play our part in bringing a little more income into the household by stripping wire coat-hangers or sorting used egg-boxes for which we'd be paid piecework rates. Working every evening until bedtime meant that we could raise enough family money through the winter to pay for a week-long summer holiday which for us was at the Bognor Regis caravan park. Uncle George would lend us his old Commer van and dad would bolt two coach-seats into the back for Babs and me, making it possible to transport the four of us in style, along with all our provisions for the week. It always seemed to rain, but what an adventure to look forward to each year!

Mum and Dad
Babs and me
on holiday
at Bognor

Dad meanwhile took what work he could find. He had been taught to drive by a wealthy Egyptian lady in Alexandria about whom he never divulged any details, although an old sepia photo of the car remains tantalisingly mysterious. With no driving test system then in place, driving was a rare skill and so he luckily landed a job driving for Jack Cohen's 'Victor Values', the forerunner of Tesco's. Having badly dented the front wing of the lorry and demolishing a headlight, he returned from his first run expecting immediate dismissal. To his surprise, the yard manager simply observed, 'oh, everyone does that first time out.' Perhaps that was not such a foolhardy remark when we remember that back then heavy goods vehicles had only rudimentary brakes and no assisted steering, demanding immense strength to accomplish even the simplest manoeuvre. Eventually he landed a steady job driving London buses and worked for London Transport till he retired in 1977, never once being asked to take a driving test.

Babs and I delighted in dad's fund of stories, especially those from his earliest days as a young cabin boy. One of his duties had been to take a mug of tea every evening from the galley to the captain on the bridge, but was always chastised for spilling it on the way. The cook had to explain how it was done.

'What you do son, is take a good swig of tea before you climb the ladders up to the bridge and, before you give it to the old man, spit it back in the mug. That's what we all do.' When we were naughty dad would threaten us with his belt but would call mum in to do the deed lest he forgot his strength and hurt us unduly. So when the cry went up: 'come here and hit these kids!' we knew our ears would be smarting for the rest of the day. But for all that, their love for us was beyond question and remained rock solid all their days. Dad would sometimes take us to the all-in wrestling at the town hall, or even disappear with me into the snooker hall which was accessed through a mysterious hidden doorway at the side of a dingy shop, which made me feel that I was being admitted to the inner sanctum of male adulthood. When at last the time arrived when he presented me with my first open 'cut-throat' razor and taught me to shave with it, I knew I'd arrived.

My Uncle Joe

Being able to defend yourself was an essential requirement on the streets, but it was not only dad who taught me to fight. Laura's mother, whom we happily called 'Nan Upstairs', was keen to assure me that 'in this world, you've got to be able to use your dukes,' and gave both me and my sister some very useful hints. Fighting was not, however, the main focus of the education I received from my Nan. One of my very earliest memories is of knocking on her door at the top of the stairs each morning, wrapped in my little blue dressing gown. Mum and dad were already at work so Nan would usher me in and sit me up at her little table for my breakfast. Once finished, she would bring out one of her many scrap-books into which she had diligently pasted newspaper cuttings of the exploits of her hero, the man I got to know as my Uncle Joe. It was he, I learnt, who had led his people to freedom and after that had liberated Europe from the clutches of the evil Hitler. Nan explained to me that Uncle Joe was such a 'man of steel' that in their own language his people had nicknamed him 'Stalin'. Years later, when I heard of the dreadful things he had done to his people, Nan still stuck to her guns, arguing that if he had not been so ruthless, the Soviet Union would never have been transformed from serfdom to a fully industrialised nation in such short time. It was that rapid development which enabled him to attack Hitler from the east, saving us from facing the full might of the Nazi military machine by ourselves. That would clearly have resulted in the occupation of Britain by Hitler's evil regime. I still wondered if it required Stalin to inflict so much cruelty and suffering upon his people to achieve his ends, but I was canny enough to know that you never argued with Nan Upstairs.

Nan had been an East End suffragette alongside Sylvia Pankhurst, the socialist member of that esteemed family, had taken part in the famous Battle of Cable Street against the fascists, and had been an early supporter of the Marie Stopes family planning clinics. For this latter activity she had paid dearly at home, being beaten by her Roman Catholic husband for daring to mention contraception. Her father had instilled a passionate socialism in her as a child and, at the age of five, had taken her along to the now famous national strike rally for the Dockers' Tanner in 1889. It later turned out that her father had also been a member of the London City Missionaries to Coalies, 'offering the Gospel of word and action to the poor labourers' in the dockyards. So in keeping with the family tradition, my Nan encouraged me to follow in his courageous, socialist footsteps, never dreaming then that I'd eventually follow his example in other ways too.

I never met my maternal grandfather who bore the name Sydney after the Australian city in which he was born. There is a memorial stone there dating back to 1891 when Submariner Corporal John McKee, his father, on attachment from the Royal Engineers, inadvertently connected the wrong cable to a detonator and blew his ship out of Sydney harbour. This makes mine one of the few Brits who can claim that his ancestors were deported *from* Australia! Grandfather Sydney continued the same destructive tradition on return to England and took to drink and violence, which steadily ripped the family apart. Nan would say to me, 'everyone said I'd married a drunk, but I always knew it was a disease – and now they all know it's true cos they call it alcu-olism.' Nan, like all the family, spoke with a decidedly cockney accent, but that belied her intelligence and her fervent intent on self-education. She even managed to learn some rudimentary Russian from her rented radio and proudly took me to the Soviet Union exhibition when, some years later, it arrived in London. I still treasure the vinyl albums she bought me there, including, *The Soviet Army in Song* and a commemorative recording of Yuri Gagarin's first manned journey into space.

Nan Upstairs was certainly not the easiest person to have in the house – my dad called her 'the original antibody' – but when disputes arose, my family always sent me ahead to sort it out because for some unknown reason, in my Nan's eyes I could do no wrong. She didn't care much for the church and when eventually I was ordained into its ministry she asked me, 'how much do you earn?' I told her the trifling figure that was my stipend, to which she responded in good socialist style, 'that's not much, but it's only fair, because you don't produce anything do you.' On the other hand, although an ardent Stalinist, she would always share with me her very deep home-spun philosophy, summed up in her oft-repeated mantra: 'if there was no Supreme Being, there wouldn't even be nuffin.' She'd come to the conclusion, not only that for things to exist there had to be a Supreme Being as she called it, but even for there to be no thing, there would have to be a Supreme Being to make even that negativity possible. I have often wondered whether it was Nan's perceptive conviction of there being something beyond what we see that in turn led me towards having a decisively formative experience as a child. I was just a young lad from the East End streets, but I very distinctly remember standing alone at our front lace-curtained window, looking out into some distant beyond, and being overcome with a very certain assurance that there was a depth, some awesome meaning beyond and yet within, and that one day I was going to engage with that and find in it my own destiny. I was not able to articulate the experience at the time, but it was so vivid that it left an indelible imprint on my life as a consequence. At the time I thought that I must be the only person to have had such a poignant moment, and it was only later that I was to learn that many shared such an experience. For my ordination present Nan Upstairs bought me a Bible, which surprised everyone except me. She even wrote in it for me, and although the book itself has long since fallen apart, I still keep the signed frontispiece as a memento, in her honour.

After he had deserted the family in an alcoholic rage, it had long been assumed that Nan's husband Sydney had died. But many years later, out of the blue, I received a very moving letter from New Zealand. It informed me that, because as a Roman Catholic he had not believed in divorce, he decided not to mention his former marriage when he married yet again! His abusive behaviour continued on however and his new wife was made to raise for him a further family of six children in Wimborne, Dorset. The photos we were then sent of our newly-acquired aunts and uncles from around the world were of people who were almost the spitting image of those I'd grown up with in the East End. Despite Sydney's harsh hand, they proved to be yet more lovely aunts and uncles with whom we've happily kept in touch ever since.

Because toys were hard to come by, parents turned their hand to making them for us and so it was that for my tenth birthday, dad presented me with what was to become my pride and joy – a 'jigger'. It was essentially four wheels attached to a wooden box with a swivelling front axle to enable it to be steered. Smiffy, my best school friend, would push me at breakneck speed round the busy streets, resulting in many a near miss and howls from justifiably complaining pedestrians. To be frank, as we grew older we were often up to no good, stealing from local shops in order to prove our bravado and vandalising property just for the thrill of the chase. Later still, Smiffy went off to prison and I completely lost touch with him, whereas my earlier pavement escapades only earnt me a long scar down my leg, but from which I still accrued great prestige in the gang.

But back in those earlier years, when it was still quite new, I found the jigger ideal for transporting the family laundry to the 'bag-wash' factory each week. I would return with the big white bag of washing smelling clean and fresh – altogether different from the very unpleasant pong on the outward journey! It's easy to forget that life then was indeed a smelly affair, most of us only able to bathe once a week, the winter coal fires and oil heaters distributing stinking fumes around the house and no man prepared to wear 'that sissy deodorant stuff.' Today we expend a lot of energy defending ourselves from the truth about being human, but that generation had witnessed the gassings of the Holocaust, the callous bombing of civilians and the sudden death of family and friends. They knew that although humanity has the propensity to soar like angels, we also at times, really stink.

A fast-changing world

Surprisingly for siblings, my sister Barbara and I were always close friends. As we grew older and our aunts and uncles fled the coop, there was room enough for me to sleep downstairs on the sofa, while Babs, from the age of thirteen, had always to share with our female lodgers in a room which was separated off from mine by a heavy wooden partition. It could not have been easy in her adolescent years to have to share with older women. However, the income from the lodgers was essential to the household budget and they were always lovely people who shared fully in the life of the family, central to which was a passion for music. During his seafaring years dad had brought back from New York many jazz records made of fragile shellac which revolved at 78 revolutions per minute. Babs played a mean piano, but a stomach-curdling squeaky violin, and I toyed with dad's accordion and learnt to knock out a tune on the piano. It was at that time that Rock n' Roll music began arriving on the scene from America, along with another new phenomenon – the 'Teenager'. Babs was now allowed to wear a very widely flared skirt in 'shocking pink' and I donned luminous yellow nylon socks. Until then, shopping had only been concerned with the essentials of life. But suddenly we began to see in the shop windows items which were quite unnecessary, but which attracted the eye delightfully, especially after a generation-long period of drab austerity. It was the beginning of the 'Age of Acquisition', and it was to turn our world upside down.

It's difficult to describe adequately just what a profound change this was to the way we lived our lives and the expectations we harboured about the future. Perhaps we should have taken more care to consider what these changes would do to us all in the longer term, but we were too overwhelmed to bother with that. We were thrilled to be finding that our life as working-class people with our timeless tradition of 'make do and mend', was suddenly opening up to the possibility that we too could enjoy possessions that would delight us and promised to save us from much of the drudgery of everyday housework. It also did wonders to lift the spirits, and gave everyone a feeling that work could now result in a lot more than just getting by. However, this new Age of Acquisition immediately brought with it a new and pernicious form of debt for the many who were tempted to live on the 'never-never' – receiving goods straight away for the payment of a small affordable deposit, even when there was little hope of covering the ongoing payments. It was the dawn of an economic system that would eventually entice even careful savers into debt. Additionally, the sudden acquisition of the new commodities engendered envy and competition among neighbours who had previously never bothered to lock their doors and had habitually shared whatever they had. I remember being very disappointed with my parents when they told me we could not afford to have the cushioned plastic floor covering that I'd seen in a friend's house, although I'd never given a thought to such 'luxuries' before. It was just the beginning of the breakdown of shared community living and the advent of a new individualism that eventually would transform Britain.

Life at the heart of a culture

Perhaps it was precisely because we had an inkling that our time-honoured cockney culture was becoming prey to the new that we hung on to it so passionately while it still wrapped itself cosily around us. And it was that culture which had, through the generations, turned our drab world into vibrant Technicolor® when we gathered for our cockney parties – and there were parties galore! The front room was where I slept on the sofa, but its heavy partitions could be folded back to reveal Barbara's bedroom, creating quite a large space for dancing. The back kitchen table would heave with sandwiches and cakes brought in by the women of the family and full beer crates would be piled high by the men. Family and friends crowded into the house all dressed to the nines and the singing and dancing would begin, so that for just a while all the problems could be forgotten. Some of us would be expected to knock out a tune on the 'old Joanna' and would be well provided with drinks while we did so. The family rule however was to keep Uncle Beaky away from the piano at all costs, for he was the only person in the world who believed that he could play the thing! He would sneak to the piano when no one was looking and hammer at the keyboard until he fell off the stool.

I was surrounded at parties by lots of exciting cousins, including one teenage girl with rat-tailed hair who since a baby had been affectionately known by all as 'Stinker'! I never did learn her real name. As the family became more lubricated so individuals would be persuaded to offer their party pieces, Uncle Syd's usually being somewhat risqué and dad offering a tango or two on his accordion. But his mother, our Nanny

Green, was an eccentric party-piece every moment of her life. I remember her suddenly appearing at one family gathering dressed as a bus conductor in black trouser-suit and flat hat, carrying a ticket machine, demanding that we each pay for a ticket to occupy our seat. We were never sure with Nanny Green whether she was joking or not, so we all had to fork out our tuppences. She once turned up at a party having waddled all along the high street dressed in a bulky fur coat and hat, wearing a gorilla mask, boasting that she had not had to ask anyone to step aside for her on the way. After all the crazy turns, we'd continue singing our cockney songs with outstretched arms, crooning with an endearing passion as we gazed adoringly into the faces of those around us. It all helped to create a bond of family and cultural solidarity which was unshakable. The dancing always included a communal conga all round the house and out into the street so that all the neighbours could join in the fun. Everyone instinctively knew the order in which the songs had to be sung and as the evening drew to a close we would hang on tightly to one another and begin singing 'Knees up Mother Brown', which was literally a 'knees up' dance – up as far as you could manage without falling over, although someone always did. Before going home we'd sink back into the armchairs or on to the settee and call for Uncle Eddie to sing us something special. He was a very fine musician with a glorious operatic voice and, as he serenaded us with an aria or two, woe betide anyone who interrupted the concentrated attention. It was early morning before everyone dispersed to their own homes, many quite local, leaving the room to be reassembled and for me to make up my bed on the sofa. They are happy memories of a culture which gradually faded away under the pressure of the new. It left me with an abiding interest in what exactly constitutes a culture, how it functions to bring people together or force us apart, and how we might or might not discern God at the very heart of it. But more of that later.

Mum & Babs singing the old cockney songs

Early challenges

Given that few families had a telephone and social media did not yet exist, girls and boys therefore had no virtual friends, but still managed to accrue many real ones. And the place to meet up was either at the Saturday Morning Pictures, where hundreds of screaming children would pile into the local cinema for cartoons and cowboys, or at Drews Dance Studio on the Romford Road. Mum and dad were superb ballroom dancers and taught Babs and me at a very early age, so my ability to cope with all the latest dance steps meant that I was never short of partners and friends. I was therefore always having fun socially, but schooling was an altogether different matter, for I'd soon come to realise that I was finding it almost impossible to read, and my arithmetic was just as bad. To hide my shame from the nearly fifty other children in my class, I therefore adopted the role of Jack the Lad, joking and generally playing the fool to steer attention away from my scholarly inadequacies. I'm sorry now to admit that I much enjoyed the role, but largely to the detriment of others who were forever being distracted from their lessons. I must have been about ten years old when my father was eventually summoned to the school to talk about my misbehaviour, but he had the nous to perceive the underlying cause of the problem and so did his best to encourage me to read and calculate, but alas to no avail. I was useless, and at the end of every week there came the inevitable caning for being unable to recite my 'times tables' or pass the week's spelling test. It was all just too difficult for me and so it came as no surprise when I failed my Eleven Plus Exam, which at the age of eleven determined whether a child would move on to the Grammar School or be assigned to the Secondary Modern in Cornwell Road. The latter had the grim and unfair reputation as a refuge for budding hooligans and criminals. East Ham Borough Council was however solidly controlled by the Labour Party who were spending huge sums on the education of its local children, and that provision made it possible for dunces like me to be given a second opportunity to sit the exam, and by a whisker, I just managed to squeeze a pass. It was just as well because, had I gone to the other school, I would have made a lousy criminal.

Despite the fact that the Eleven Plus largely resulted in segregating working-class children from those destined for 'higher things', my Stalinist grandmother was pleased as punch that I had passed because, as she put it, 'they'll try taking everything else away from you, but they won't be able to take your education!' What perhaps she had also spotted was the fact that although I was a dunce when it came to reading, I was already well able to hold my own in the tough argumentation and discussion which was all around me at home. For among the members of my family politics was not just an excuse for interesting coffee-table chatter, but was that which could determine whether our everyday lives would be constrained or liberated. Our discussions were, therefore, passionate and heated. It was within that atmosphere that I developed an acute class-consciousness and was taught a raft of socialist theory. Dad taught me all he knew about Marx's theory of dialectical materialism, arguing that wealth-creating capitalism was bound to throw up its inner contradictions of poverty and alienation so that when those trapped by those pressures rose up against the wealthy, the new righteous synthesis would come to birth – the glorious socialist society. As I listened to my dad, I absorbed these theories and the passion of class-consciousness that went with them, convinced that creativity was born, not of polite cheesy agreement, but the cut and thrust of conflict. So it was that the family always expected me to be challenging and questioning, but I'm sure that those from outside our circle therefore found me rather rough-cut and aggressive.

Most members of my extended family had belonged to the Young Communist League, so politically they were all quite astute, but because their meetings took place at a local vicarage, my parents were not too bothered when I began to take some interest in things religious. Marx himself was the grandson of an eminent rabbi of Trier city, and I'm apt to think that much of Karl's early thinking was derived initially from an unconscious religious bias, although he would never have admitted it. He had certainly inherited the same passion for the freedom of the alienated that he must have imbibed as a child on hearing of his own people's Exodus from slavery in Egypt. Additionally, every Jew had a clear conviction that God demanded that we express our belief by our actions – by obeying God's Commandments – and so Marx became involved not only in theoretical philosophy, but in active politics. And finally, while his forebears looked forward to a new 'promised land', he too yearned for a promised future of proletarian socialism. For Judaism, as for Marx, history had a purpose.

But despite having inherited so much from his believing forebears, Marx believed that religion was a hoax. It was something used by the powerful to lull the poor into thinking that a better world could only be achieved in the hereafter, as the reward for not complaining about this life, but shutting up and working hard for the capitalist masters. Religion was 'the opium of the people,' he said – sending them to sleep so that they never asked why it was that such injustice had been visited upon them. He saw his task as waking society from its stupor, like a latter-day prophet casting off the works of religion and applying the analytical scalpel of Enlightenment rationality.

Although the communists hammered atheism into its adherents, that harsh antagonism towards the church was not evident in my family. My dad had even thought it important to give the Bible its chance, and so had set about reading it from the beginning to its end. Unfortunately he did not get far before he encountered very obvious self-contradictions in the text which he couldn't fathom, and so gave up on the exercise. Neither was he much enamoured of the common picture of God as an old man in the sky, a kind of human being, only bigger and better and living in outer space, beyond the clouds. My more staunchly committed communist friends thought religion was not merely irrelevant, but dangerous, in that it implied that scientific evidence should be discounted. Some even felt vindicated when the Russians, on jetting the first man into space, had broadcast to the world that nowhere up there had they seen anything of this so-called God.

Mum and dad were not communist purists, quite admiring the social and pastoral commitment of the local clergy, and so sent Babs and me to Sunday School each Sunday afternoon. All parents did the same during those years because it was their one chance in the week to have their bedroom to themselves. The Sunday Schools were therefore full to bursting. There seemed to be hundreds of us, my lovely teacher being Miss Olive Parsons, a single lady with a cheery smile and a small, pink, feathery hat. Many years later I was to visit Olive in hospital where she had been taken in her final months. With my bishop's retinue in train I was ushered into the ward by the sister who whispered, 'I don't think she'll recognise you any longer, she's very muddled.' But on spotting me, Olive sat straight up in the bed and exclaimed, 'Oh I remember you! All you ever did in Sunday School was slide up and down the pew whistling a happy tune. I knew you'd never take any of it in!' The entourage around me giggled nervously, but I knew she was right.

CHAPTER 2

JESUS AND JELLIED EELS

My move up from primary school in 1956 marked a very significant break for me, but everything around me was changing too. I remember that Miss Wing, our primary school teacher, had unfurled a huge wall-map of the world on which a quarter of the landmass was coloured pink to indicate the extent of the British Empire. 'The pink parts of the world belong to us,' she had naively proclaimed. But the truth of it was that already in 1947, India had won her autonomy, much to the annoyance of Churchill who feared that it would prompt other nations to seek independence from their British overlords. Despite the truth of that prediction, seeing the leaders of the British Empire's nations parading through London in honour of the new queen's coronation had created the illusion in the hearts of onlookers that Cecil Rhodes' dictum was still valid that: 'to be born an Englishman is to have won first prize in the lottery of life.' And, at that impressionable age, I had swallowed that assumption of natural superiority along with all my contemporaries. After all, we were told that we Brits had just won a world war, mostly by ourselves, we'd conquered Mount Everest and run the four-minute mile before anyone else. To our blinkered eyes, everything looked rosy.

By the time I arrived at my new school, East Ham Grammar School for Boys, rationing had at last ended, the Festival of Britain had given the population a sense that we were in the vanguard of progress, the Civil Rights Movement was rocking the USA and American pop music was rocking the UK. Only five years before, we'd been listening to people like Mario Lanza singing melodious ballads, but now Elvis the Pelvis Presley was amazing us with his first UK number one, 'All Shook Up!' and Lonny Donegan's 'Puttin' on the Style' and

Tommy Steele's 'Singing the Blues' were not far behind. Our local streets still only saw the occasional private car amidst the horse-drawn carts, but homes were beginning to harbour washing machines and a few black and white televisions. The age of austerity was retreating to such an extent that when the owners of our rented home decided to offer it for sale at £960, my mother was keen to try for it. Dad was extremely reluctant, resolved that home ownership was not for the likes of us, but mum, as ever, convinced him that if he worked even more overtime and she took on an additional job, it might just be manageable. The times were certainly changing and there was such optimism in the air after all those years of military strife and uncertainty, that in 1957 Prime Minister Harold Macmillan led his Conservative party back to Westminster with his proud boast to the British people that, 'You've never had it so good!'

Learning the language

My going to the grammar school seemed to impress the whole family, but the fact that my parents managed to rustle up enough money to purchase the expensive uniform still astonishes me. However, it's simply another reminder of how refined the budgeting skills of the poor can be. On arrival at my new school, I immediately realised that I was going to struggle because my reading problems were now compounded by the need to learn a different form of English altogether. Out went our everyday slang, and in came consonants and a completely new vocabulary along with rules of grammar that defied my understanding. It was all designed to instil into us the syntax and accent which were accepted in 'polite society' and enable us to better ourselves in a Britain which still frowned upon working class or even regional accents. It was assumed that without the clipped pronunciation and well-articulated sentences of the BBC announcer, we were going nowhere.

On the streets, my first language had actually been body language and the occasional grunt rather than the spoken word, and I still pride myself on being able to interpret the faintest movement of a hand or shoulder. In order to remain secure on a city street, it's quite important to be able to read visual signs instantaneously, and in those days our distinctive cockney accents also helped us to distinguish who was one of us and therefore to be trusted, and those others who were suspect. Often, inclusion was reinforced by our habit of turning each statement into a question – you know what I mean? – so that the listener was constantly invited into a relationship with the speaker – wasn't he. We also used little linguistic devices to make our verbal descriptions less abstract and more concrete so, for example, I would never describe myself as simply answering a question, but I would preface it by adding, 'so I turned round and said.' The gospels use precisely the same device when they describe Jesus as 'turning around' or 'lifting his eyes' before he speaks. It's no wonder the language in which the New Testament was originally written was called not 'classical' Greek but 'common' Greek – the language of the more common people. When we conversed, we often unconsciously utilised the well-documented rhyming slang, but there were many other esoteric cockney word systems too, said to have arisen in order to evade the comprehension of outsiders, especially the police. I'm sure though, that much of our slang, and rhyming slang in particular, was originally developed to bring humour and delight into an everyday life which could otherwise be somewhat lack-lustre. Indeed, such word-play was one of the special gifts of that culture and quickfire humour was essential to survival, for as they said, 'you've got to laugh or you'd cry – wouldn't you?'

When I at last gained the rank of 'teenager' I went in search of some after-school employment at a barber's shop that had newly opened on East Ham High Street. I ventured in to find the owner, David Firestone, having his lunchbreak and trying to open a bottle of beer without a bottle opener. I explained that my boy-scout belt would do the job nicely and, fitting the bottle-top into the belt's clasp, began to wrestle with it until the cap came flying off, spraying the bubbling contents of the bottle all across his new reception desk, thoroughly drenching all the hairdressing certificates that he had laid out ready for framing. After mopping up as best I could with my grubby handkerchief I still had the temerity to ask him for a job. He sniffed, smiled, and took me on despite my being legally too young to take employment. I greatly enjoyed the work, learning not only to sweep up hair and make the tea, but also to strop an open razor properly, shampoo and blow-dry hair and even, eventually, to offer the occasional haircut. This after-school employment brought in some pocket money to call my own, but, because David was Jewish like so many of the local shopkeepers, he did not trade on Saturdays, for that was Shabbat – the Sabbath. So I still needed to find additional weekend work to fill the gap.

Henry, the jovial patriarch of the large Jewish household living across the road offered to take me on full time and teach me the rag-and-bone trade but dad was keen for me to continue on at school. Luckily, mum by then had secured regular work at Grick's Jellied Eel Factory, just five minutes' walk from our home, and it was there that she managed to find me work to fill my Saturdays. So it was that I became a qualified 'jellied eel basher', a job title alluded to by Shakespeare, when in King Lear (again), he remarked that the cockney 'knapped em o' th' coxcombs with a stick, and cried, "Down, wantons, down!"' It was a crude method to stun the fish before they were cooked, although nowadays the job is done using electricity.

Fortunately, most of the work to which I was assigned was winkle-bottling and stocking the vast refrigeration room. This meant the rather dangerous job of gutting and chopping those slithery creatures was left to the professionals. I was, however, responsible for taking steaming mugs of tea into the cold gutting shed and there I would stand gazing at the eels, still wriggling around in their ice-packed crates ready for gutting. I had the distinct impression that these strange creatures were staring back at me, looking me in the eye and daring me to behold their extraordinary mystery. No one has yet been able to breed edible eels in captivity so we had to rely on their natural return to the Sargasso Sea some four thousand miles away where these snake-like fish spawn and then die. The fertile eggs then float up towards the surface and are carried back to Europe on the oceanic currents. Over that two-year journey the egg is transformed into a transparent worm-like being which, on reaching fresh water, begins to make its way upstream, becoming what is known to us as the yellow eel. That river journey alone takes up to twenty years to complete. Over time, its eyes slowly enlarge up to ten times their original size and its body darkens as it grows to become the curious adult eel we all know and love. But although we have all this information about the eel, the most mysterious part of the story is that no one has actually seen an adult eel in the Sargasso Sea. So the question remains: what on earth are we to believe about these strange creatures? The whole saga of the eel is an enigma, leaving us not only to bemoan its impending extinction, but also the mysterious purpose of our own perplexing existence as just another speck in the ebb and flow of a mysterious natural world. Nan Upstairs had started me thinking that there must be depths of being beyond merely what we see, and this eel, I felt sure, was looking back at me and asking what I thought about the enigmatic mystery of this beguiling universe.

The jellied eel factory was not, however, very receptive to such romantic speculation and these fascinating creatures were destined to go the way of all flesh and be chopped up into bite-sized chunks. Perhaps that's the only way we have of dealing with mystery – we cut it down into bits which we can more easily digest, control or belittle. These chunks were then stewed by our excellent Irish cook in his enormous aluminium pots before being ladled into tubs and topped up with glistening gelatine. The contents of the tubs were then left to cool, ready to be transported all across east London as the cockneys' traditional and defining delicacy. I enjoyed the work despite the smell, which invaded every fibre of my clothing. It was only disguised on weekdays by the stink of the cheap perfumed shampoo that we used at the hairdressers. Either way, I got some strange looks.

New discoveries

Dad's brother Uncle Arthur was the proud owner of a television. Since he lived upstairs in a house just across the road, we'd venture over to join his family for our favourite programmes. One Sunday night, while watching *Sunday Night at the London Palladium*, an entertainment extravaganza hosted by a very young Bruce Forsyth, I fell very seriously in love – with the guitar! Jon Pertwee, the actor and comedian, after telling a few jokes, produced a guitar with which to accompany his comedy song. I noticed that in order to play the few chords he needed, he only used two fingers: it all looked so easy! Whilst I also had two fingers and a vast collection of songs in my head, as yet I had no guitar. That lack was easily remedied by the acquisition of a very basic instrument bought from a school friend for a meagre sum. The rusty steel strings cut into my fingers and the instrument refused to hold its tuning, but with the aid of an old copy of *A Tune a Day*, written by Bert Weedon, a near neighbour, I was soon making headway. After a few months I was able to impress my dad to the extent that he took me along to the local music shop and bought me my first proper Spanish guitar. I was in heaven.

That guitar stayed
with me for years

Speaking of heaven, I also began to notice that the boys who
were reading well and getting good marks at school seemed to
be much attracted to church-going. And so it dawned on me
that if I went along too, my reading problems might be eased.
But that was not the only questionable motive for my interest.
I was now spending each day in a boys-only school, but I'd
noticed a particularly attractive young girl was a member of the
church youth club, entry to which was allowed only to those
who turned up for the Sunday evening service. I thought it was
worth a shot and so I steeled myself and went along in a
sceptical and somewhat suspicious mood, sitting myself in the
very back row. I fully expected to have to endure what I
considered religious nonsense about Adam and Eve and 'pie
in the sky when you die,' but when the vicar climbed into the
pulpit I was somewhat taken aback. I had been ready to
ridicule his every word, but he began to talk about the tough
reality of suffering and how love alone is the creative power
which can transform evil into good, and at the heart of it all
was what he called the supreme mystery of God. I couldn't
quite grasp how he'd arrived at that conclusion, but his words

reminded me of that supreme being that my Stalinist Nan had always acknowledged. It also brought back my experience as a child of gazing out from my window and sensing that in the world there was some deeper meaning. The sermon also alluded to the importance of justice and caring for the downtrodden – and that chimed in very well with the political concerns I'd become accustomed to at home. Although I was not convinced by all the vicar's words, what he said seemed to be borne out by the atmosphere in the church that evening when I'd received such a warm, unconditional welcome from members of the congregation. At political party meetings I'd certainly felt the togetherness of 'comrades' but that was conditional upon affiliation. Here no one asked what I believed, they just thrust a cup of tea into my hand, showed me where the cakes were and told me the youth club started at seven that evening. It was a wholehearted acceptance, not dependent upon who I was or what I was. I'm sure that what every human being is most in need of is to be accepted and loved unconditionally, and it was a tiny glimpse of that which I'd experienced at the end of that service. The promise in the sermon and the open attitude of the people were such that it prompted me to go along the next Sunday evening to see if I had been imagining things.

As the weeks and months went by, those first impressions were steadily confirmed. But there was much else besides which impressed me about these people. For a start it was clear that the god that I did not believe in was not believed in by those Christians either. The notion of some big person up in the sky was rubbish for them too, as was the belief that if you asked God for something you would always get exactly what you wanted, as if God was there at your beck and call. The god they believed in had a lot more going for him than that. Their view of the Bible too seemed more sensible when they suggested that to expect people of pre-scientific times to express their experience of God in modern scientific terms was ridiculous. So the ancient writers of the Bible had therefore used the terms and symbols of their day to tell of their astonishing experience of the presence of God. On hearing all this I realised I'd need to rethink all that I'd assumed about Christianity if I were to do these people and their faith justice. I had already begun to turn away from Marxism, having been disillusioned with it when comparing Marx's fine theories with how abysmally communist leaders treated their own people, so I was open to fresh thinking. I'd been very pleased to learn from the folk at the church, that St Barnabas, after whom the building was dedicated, had been a member of the earliest church where they'd held all their possessions in common so that 'there was not a needy person among them' (Acts 4: 34). It seemed then that the earliest converts, on the basis of their time with Jesus, had adopted a sort of socialism, and that certainly appealed to me. So, although my understanding of the Christian faith at that age must have been very rudimentary, I had a growing conviction that whatever it was that these Christians had, I wanted some too. I have to admit however that this conviction was strongly reinforced by the fact that the girls at the church were clearly much more attractive than I'd even imagined.

Being a young teenager in this brave new post-war world was full of adventure and excitement. During school holidays I'd take on extra work, helping out at Nanny Green's jewellery stall in East Ham market. It was here that I received my first lessons in how to sell anything to anybody. 'My goodness, that looks beautiful on you love! It suits you so well, I'll tell you what. If you promise not to tell anyone else, I'll let you have it at a special price.' They went away extra happy, although they'd paid exactly the same as everyone else. Having spent my first wage on a present for mum, a cockney obligation, I saved my earnings carefully because it only cost about four pounds for a foot-passenger return ticket on the ferry to Belgium. I went with my school chum Peter down to the docks on the bus, crossed the Channel, and took to the road, hitch-hiking our way as far as Austria and Italy. Reminders of the horrors and heroics of the war were still everywhere evident, but two fifteen-year-old English lads sporting a Union

Jack had no problem cadging lifts. Peter and I were smitten with the loveliness of the spacious medieval town centres slowly being restored to their pre-war glory. But we took care to be wary of the dangers in the less salubrious back-streets into which we sometimes found ourselves decanted on arrival in the industrial cities we visited. In these impoverished areas, the devastation of war had left indelible scars and it was here, for the first time, I witnessed beggars on the streets, some carrying emaciated children, others displaying amputations. Some were obviously after snatching what little we carried with us, but one way and another we would always scrape through and eventually arrived back safely, more worldly wise.

Fearful realisations

Back at school my problems were increasing as I came to the realisation that my learning difficulties went a lot deeper than merely spelling and reading. For my music homework, one week I was required to learn the names and dates of twenty world-famous composers in readiness for a test that Friday, and so a friend, Gerald, offered to help me revise. We sat on the roundabout in Plashet Park as he prompted me with each name. By the end of the afternoon, while Gerald had them off pat, I could not remember a single one! The reading problems I'd first encountered at junior school were obviously compounded by some sort of memory deficiency, but that didn't make much sense when on the other hand I could recite the words of countless songs without a hiccup. I stumbled along somehow, devising all sorts of learning tricks as I went, but the situation was neatly summed up by my history master who returned my essay on which he had written, 'Top marks for fiction, for history, none!'

On other fronts all was going exceedingly well. I was always surrounded by friends and in the swim of the social life at school, at church and on the streets, and yet I had the gnawing sense that a section of my brain simply refused to function as it should. I became scared because it felt like the early onset of dementia, although close friends became used to my odd forgetfulness and even today my daughters are always forgiving when I muddle their names. In polite company I still live with a secret panic going on in my head as I cast about for the words I need in order to make coherent sense – even though nobody seems to notice. I think that back then it was perhaps this profound word-blindness that made me want to hit out at those who had no difficulties with conversation, or those indeed who appeared relaxed in environments which intimidated me. I became very competitive and enjoyed team sports such as rugby, but when individually tested, my fear of failure would easily turn to unwarranted anger. In discussion, I would find myself trying to score points rather than dig down to the truth, my frustrated anger lurking only just beneath the surface, ready to intrude unpleasantly at any unguarded moment. I experienced it as pent-up energy and knew it had to be harnessed and transformed into something more positive if it were to conform more properly to the Christianity I was now beginning to affirm. As it turned out, that was to be achieved only years later.

A new direction

I had become increasingly happy at our local church and joined one of the many groups preparing for confirmation which would allow me then to participate in receiving the communion of the bread and wine with the adults. The six-months course consisted of regular weekly meetings led by one of the many assistant curates, Richard Bray, who took us carefully through the chapters of a small confirmation book written by the vicar Nigel Oram Porter, whose initials resulted in him being affectionately known by all as 'Nop'. Looking back through that confirmation book today, I'm still impressed by its breadth and thoroughness. This meant that by the end of the course we were able to make an informed decision about whether or not we wanted to go forward to our confirmation by the bishop. Three weeks prior to the great day, we all gathered outside the church, waiting to be called in one at a time to be interviewed by Nop in the Lady chapel. There, we assumed, he would test us on our knowledge of the faith. But when it came to my turn, he sat me down, looked intently at me and asked: 'well, if you're going to take Christianity seriously, you'd better tell me what you're going to do about it. I already know what you think, but what will you do?' In reply I was surprised to hear myself saying that I thought I should offer myself for ordination and become a vicar. I don't recall having a very clear idea of what that meant, but since he had put me on the spot, it seemed to me that he deserved a robust answer. Since God was important to him, and now to me, then following in Nop's footsteps seemed to be the obvious consequence. My answer had come as a great surprise to me, but apparently not to him, as he calmly responded by putting my name down to attend some local meetings where I could get to know what ordination was all about. I readily agreed and left the church with a rather odd feeling – but there's no getting away from it that becoming a vicar *is indeed* rather odd!

The confirmation service turned out to be quite an experience. The key moment came when each candidate went forward to kneel before the bishop as he laid his hands on our head, and prayed that God's Spirit would dwell in us and guide us in our lives. He explained that when he was just a lad he had himself knelt in front of a bishop for this same thing to happen to him, and that bishop had had the same experience of the 'laying on of hands' when he had been confirmed years before that. And this chain went all the way back to the moment when Jesus had laid his hands on his followers and prayed that they would be inspired by God's Spirit. So this touch had been handed on through generations, initiated by Jesus himself, as an outward expression of being touched by God's Spirit. I remember that 'laying on of hands' as a very empowering moment and I found it hard to fathom how such a one as me could have been invited to experience such a profound moment for myself. Little did I know then that one day others would kneel as I laid my hands on their heads with that special prayer and, as their bishop, pass on that touch to the generations that would come after.

One thing that terrified me at the thought of becoming a vicar was the realisation that a great deal of the role appeared to involve reading aloud in church. Clergy would read their way through the service, read their sermon from the pulpit, and read at many other meetings too, or so it appeared to me. I was only too aware that it was necessary therefore to address my difficulties with the language. It happened that my friend, Carol Armon, had a touch-typing course, given to her by her father, and she was more than happy to lend it to me. It was the churchwarden, Ernie Fenn, who owned the typewriter shop in the High Street, and he equipped me with an ancient manual machine. I set it up on the kitchen table and in no time I was hammering away at the heavy keys. At first I had to learn the tricky business of inserting the paper, setting up the margins and using carbon paper to make copies without leaving inky smudges all over my work. It was quite tiring on the hands, and the constant clacking of the keys and ringing of the return bell made an agonising din. As I progressed however, I found not only that I was developing quite a useful speed that would serve me well in later life, but it made me concentrate more distinctly on each letter and word as I typed. The unexpected by-product of this concentration was that I began to discern how words were constructed and that certainly improved my spelling and made reading a lot easier too.

I was also beginning to realise that diagrams and charts or even pictures were really valuable for me in prompting my memory, and I began to use them extensively to assist my learning. It was a struggle, but such tricks as these were helping me to get by. I was confident about the singing aspect of the vicar's role for I loved music, sang with my guitar, and was pleased to join the church choir where Peter Burness, the young choir master and organist, took me under his wing, and built up my self-confidence.

Coach choir outing (I'm with arms crossed)

I didn't mind being lampooned at school for becoming a Christian, but was annoyed that they assumed I believed the nonsense that they mistakenly thought Christianity was all about. My family, however, were really taken aback at the thought that after all their hard work to support me through my education I might end up 'going into the church'. For them it appeared as something of a waste. Their concern was tempered a little, however, when they came to know some of my new church friends and saw for themselves that their faith in no way lessened their preparedness to engage with life's issues. Gerald Elvin was a fine example. On one hand he had been the one to instruct me in how to prepare the altar for the church service but he also played double bass at the dances my parents attended and at election time invited me to help canvass door to door for the Labour Party. And Gerald was just typical of the many they met from St Barnabas whose Christian faith energised them for a very full and committed life. Some years later, David and Phyllis Halstead, who had been so supportive of me, became their close friends too, and mum and dad even became confirmed Christians – but that was some years hence.

When asked today why it was that I eventually decided that ordination was to be the way forward for me, I usually reply that I'd heard that a vicar only had to work one day a week. But that the truth turned out differently – we only get *paid* for one day a week! The true reason, however, was complex and remains very difficult to explain. This is complicated by the fact that the reasons have changed and developed over the fifty and more years of my ordained life. I suspect that at that young age, dressing up and looking important came into it somewhere, but what attracted me most were the superb role models who were around at St Barnabas. The clergy and lay leaders were erudite, honest, dynamic people of stature, models of commitment and great fun to boot. Even more important was the fact that I had, by dint of discussion and personal reflection, become convinced that God was real, that Jesus was something more than just a special person and that the Holy Spirit was a power to be reckoned with. It had by now dawned on me that God was the meaning deep down at the heart of things, creatively holding everything together. It was an unshakable conviction that the world had purpose and meaning, not only at the scientific level, and that was exciting enough, but also at a level which made science itself reasonable and possible. Sometimes I found it simpler to say, 'God is Love making everything possible', but whatever words I used, they could never do any of it proper justice. The sticking point was that this whole God thing had become a very real experience for me, akin to that sixth sense that Nan Upstairs seemed to have acquired, although she pictured it in a very different way. I read much later in life, that a famous theologian called Austin Farrer had offered himself for ordination because it would demand that he address the all-important God question every day. And if I became a vicar, I too would have to wrestle with the God thing every day of my life, rather than become distracted by lesser matters and float by it in careless oblivion. In the last analysis it felt, as it still feels today, that it was a decision that was out of my hands. I simply had to do it because if I didn't then I would never become me; for it was God who had fashioned the 'me' that he was hoping I'd become. So despite all the very good reasons why I felt it an inappropriate job for me, and although I tried to convince myself that it was just my imagination playing tricks, I can only say that at that time I somehow knew that this was what I was made for. I felt that God was doing the deciding, and had all the time been catching me by hook or by crook – even by alerting me to how lovely the girls were at the youth club!

Life at St Barnabas had taught me that being a Christian did not preclude fun. And I was certainly enjoying life to the full, surrounded by music, all-night parties and good friends galore, whilst constantly indulging in new hobbies and interests – life was a ball! But it was then that I suddenly realised that exams were ahead, and it was imperative that I pass them if my dreams were not to end in tatters. Study of this sort was rather alien to our home, and although the family tried to help, I just wasn't able to settle amidst the constant interruption of chatter, radio and housework, and in our one quiet room there was nowhere to rest my books except on the floor. In order to study, I needed to learn the art of prolonged self-discipline, but there were so many fascinating distractions! When mum saw how much I wanted to study, she did what she thought best and bought me a pack of quality Russian cigarettes. I didn't smoke at the time, but she counselled that if I persevered they would calm my mind and help me concentrate. I puffed away until I was smoking like a cocoa-tin but it didn't help. As the time of examinations approached, the school ran a series of mock exams to give us an impression of how our final results might turn out. It appeared that my determination was paying dividends in all subjects, apart from maths and English, both of which I was destined to fail miserably.

A maths pass would be essential if I were to be allowed to proceed to the next stage of study. By good fortune, my Uncle Eddie, he with the amazing voice, on hearing that I had flunked the test, suggested I pop up to his house for a few extra lessons. He was a born maths teacher and soon diagnosed my problem, suggesting that since I couldn't hold any of the figures in my head, that I show all my working-out, even the simplest addition, in the margin of the paper. With that advice, and a few other pointers from my uncle, I sat the official examinations and much to everyone's surprise I attained top grades in maths and even scraped by in English Language. I had moved one small step closer to my goal.

My other subjects included, I remember, Economics and British Constitution (the option nearest to politics). But I had known from the first that I would never pass the French examination, largely thanks to the French teacher who drank heavily, and who liked to humiliate his pupils rather than bother to teach them. I had, therefore, opted to substitute Religious Education for French, at which he had guffawed with laughter and yelled across the classroom: 'you'll just end up as a religious bus driver!' Given my dad's job, that made me furious – although I managed to curb my tongue, knowing the beating he'd give me if I uttered a word. Our school days can make or break us, and he wasn't going to break me! He had, however, lodged in my psyche a heart-felt concern about how we can be deskilled by adverse learning experiences. Although I didn't know it then, that interest in educational process was to prove a very central factor in much of my future life's work.

Sixth Form fun

On the morning of my seventeenth birthday, and for ten weeks thereafter, the snow fell and the ice set in, bringing much of Britain to a standstill. Factories and shops had to close and domestic lockdown resulted, some nine months later, in a baby boom. Philip Larkin famously interpreted that to mean that 'sexual intercourse began in 1963.' For me, it signalled a transition from a routinised timetable to the much more expansive life of the sixth-former. Our Art teacher Melvyn Sykes Robinson, had in the past played trombone with the Temperance Seven, a highly successful jazz band. He took a group of us under his wing, calling us the Barking Creek Stompers, named after a very muddy trickle of water that skirted around the school playing field. We would pile into his ancient black, left-hand drive saloon and head off to play gigs at lesser-known jazz clubs. I'd bought a decrepit banjo in a Clapham Junction pub which gave the rhythm section a powerfully authentic stomping flavour as we played 'Beal Street Blues' and other classics. We were also paid reasonably well too and always managed to come home sober, although it was noticeable that Mr Robinson's car would occasionally nudge the kerb on the homeward journey. He played piano in our group, while John 'the Tweasel' Garlick blew the horn and on trombone there was Paul Hurst, who later had the dubious pleasure of becoming a specialist in Hurst's disease!

Despite the fascination of traditional jazz, I never really took to the banjo, for it was the guitar that continued to be my passion. I saved up enough to take a few classical guitar lessons, and Stan Edelman, a school mate who played superb modern jazz guitar, introduced me to his lush chord progressions, so tender and subtle. But it was then that the craze for British folk song took off, and that was the path I chose to follow, singing my first songs in an East Ham folk club hidden in a damp sweaty cellar below a local snack bar. The club had been set up by another class mate, Barrie Keeffe, who also introduced me to a love of theatre and strong coffee. He took leading rôles in all the school plays and went on to become an esteemed playwright for TV and the London stage. Another sixth form friend, Malcolm McVicar, rose to become Vice-Chancellor of Lancaster University, while Keith Gurry eventually played violin with the BBC Symphony Orchestra, and John

Carrington founded Cellnet, later called O2, and was instrumental in creating the GSM digital standard for Europe. But back then we were just a bunch of East End classmates having a great time, lucky enough to be picking up a good school education along the way. When four of us were invited to edit the rather staid and boring school magazine, the *Esthameian*, we immediately set about subverting it by introducing a page of quotations drawn from our classroom experiences. The history master, for example, was quoted as having observed, 'perhaps Johnson, you'd like to go further with Marie Antoinette than you would with Louis XVI?' Serious pieces were interspersed with cartoons and poems, one of which ran, 'There was a headmaster called Whitely, Who, in spite of his age was quite spritely. He could flourish a cane, with considerable pain, Though still do it very politely.' We were astonished that, although a disciplinarian, Dr Whitely, our headmaster was game enough to let us get away with it all, and we loved him for it.

The hope of things to come

Amidst all this frivolity I nevertheless managed to find time to study for the advanced level papers which would allow me to pass on to the next step of my intended journey towards ordination by attaining a university place. Many of my classmates were also hoping to get to university, although it would be a family first for most of us since only about four per cent of all school leavers at that time managed to obtain a place. Lads from an area like ours were certainly not expected to be among them. In my ignorance, I only knew of one college where theology was taught, and that was King's College London, and so I wrote for a prospectus. It landed on my doormat almost the next day, a slim, grey, lifeless booklet of concentrated text which frightened the living daylights out of me. The miniscule typeface seemed designed to attract only those with remarkably good eyesight, and the content, which covered the intricate complexities of the syllabus, was intelligible only to those who already knew the meaning of its specialised theological words and academic phrases. Not a single picture or graphic was there to relieve my agony. I nevertheless filled in the enclosed application form, and was both amazed and terrified to receive an invitation to attend for interview.

One of the things that most worried me about that impending interview was that the Christianity that I now espoused was radically different from what I heard from other Christians who were not members at St Barnabas. I already appreciated that while many church-goers were beyond thinking of God as 'up there' in the sky, most still thought of God as 'out there' in some metaphysical space apart, but I was experiencing what I took to be God in the here and now. I'd heard clergy urge their congregation to, 'come aside, forget the worries of the world and meet God,' which made me think they were using this 'God out there' business as an escape from the world's issues. It was using religion as the 'opium of the people' just as Marx had asserted.

I'd talked all my worries through with Nop, my vicar, who told me that a new book had just been published which might help me think this through for myself prior to attending the interview at King's. He'd already introduced me to the letters of the German pastor, Dietrich Bonhoeffer, which he'd written from his Flossenburg prison cell as he awaited execution at the hands of Hitler's Nazis. He'd written of the possibility of a Christianity without all the trappings of the religious theoretical and institutional paraphernalia that had been turning modern people off Christianity for so long. Nop had also helped me to look at the work of his favourite biblical scholar, Rudolf Bultmann, who encouraged his students to get under the skin of the mythical language used in the Bible and reinterpret that in language and concepts that better suited our modern era. But the trouble with the book Nop was now encouraging me to read was that it was so controversial and popular that it was difficult getting hold of a copy. By the time

I got my hands on one, it was already in its fourth printing and its first year was not yet out.

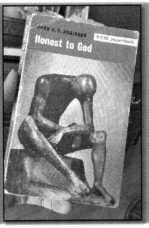

NOP and that book!

The writer, John Robinson, was another biblical scholar who had been made Bishop of Woolwich only four years earlier. It was, therefore, barely conceivable that his little book about God could be rocking the nation. The national press headlined it as so controversial as to be verging on heresy, but as Robinson explained, he was only making public what a range of top flight theologians had been saying about God for some time. It was his hope that by sharing this thinking with the British church at large it would encourage us all to think more carefully about our faith – hence the title, *Honest to God.* My copy cost three shillings and sixpence, and although now tattered and torn it still has pride of place on my bookshelf. It made an enormous impact on me, and convinced me that although I had a long way to go in my understanding of it, I was far from alone in my interpretation of the Christian faith.

Robinson was adamant that God was not some supernatural entity out at the margins of the world, but right at its heart as the 'Ground of our Being'. This was a phrase that had been coined first by Meister Eckhart, a medieval mystic, and latterly by Paul Tillich, an influential American-German thinker. It emphasised that the fundamental reality of God can, to some extent, be experienced by us all, maybe when contemplating a work of art or nature, or when we fall in love or face a great tragedy and feel overwhelmed by the depths of what we experience. The Christian had been taken to a deeper appreciation of what that experience was all about by the man Jesus, who had been so in touch with that Ground of Being that he was utterly transparent to it – and indeed was the very expression of that deep mystery. So if you wanted to see God, the Ground of our Being, you would need to look at Jesus and not dream up some phantom 'out there' who was keeping a beady eye on us from a distance. John Robinson went much deeper into the philosophy surrounding this notion of the Ground of our Being than I was able to understand, and his take on how the Bible should be understood was also very challenging for one so new to it all. It would take me many years of experience, concentrated study and reflection before I was ever able to get my head around what he was explaining. But despite the fact that I then only half understood it, reading Robinson's *Honest to God* left me feeling that it was perfectly rational to think about the faith in the radical ways that were being encouraged at my own St Barnabas church. My ideas might be verging on the heretical, but at least I was in good company. After all, had not Jesus himself taught us to push at the boundaries of human understanding – 'to ask, seek and knock' – promising that if we did so we would find answers, and the door would be opened to us (Matt 7: 7-8). On reading *Honest to God*, I became even more excited by the wonders and relevance of the Christian faith. Yet I had to acknowledge that if John Robinson, a bishop, was being hounded for what he was writing, then I too would certainly have to face difficult challenges in future from those who still espoused what I took to be a far too simplistic view of the profound mystery of God and the Christian faith.

I was barely eighteen when I was summoned by the national church authorities to attend what they termed a 'Selection Conference', at which they would decide whether or not I could proceed to theological training. Nop explained that he had recommended me to them, and they had therefore gathered reports and references from a wide range of others who knew me well. Of the three-day gathering I have only a blurred recollection of pipe-smoking clerical interviewers and a barrage of what I took to be rather churchy questions. It was organised by a church department still referred to as CACTM, even though it had long since been rebranded as CACM, the Central Advisory Council for the Ministry. I joined fifteen or so other young men who all appeared to me to be rather middle class, neat and nice. Being so very young my answers in interview must have been naïve in the extreme, but I kept my head down and smiled politely. Only a few days later, I was informed that the conference selectors had decided that I could now proceed to train for ordination, so another hurdle was behind me.

Crossing the threshold

Towards the end of my final school year, it was a matter of knuckling down and studying hard for our Advanced level examinations, John Carrington and I finding the town hall reference library an ideal place for silent revision together. The added bonus was that for our lunch break we could easily slip across to the opposite corner of the town hall square and disappear into the Denmark Arms for a sausage roll and a pint. But once having lived through the trauma of sitting those final school exams, I was then free to prepare myself for the crucial interview at King's College. So for some weeks I read the *Guardian* newspaper from cover to cover every day in the hope of giving a good account of myself if I were asked about current affairs. I remember 'mugging up' on the increasing tensions in Vietnam where monks had been burning themselves to death in protest against the French occupation of their country, and in Mississippi the oppressed Black community were preparing for 'Freedom Summer' – a whole raft of creative initiatives designed to give them a voice and to press for full voting rights. Came the morning of the crucial interview, I dressed in my best jacket and tie and made my way on the London Underground to arrive at the college in great trepidation and with hours to spare.

King's stands on the Strand overlooking the Thames, its architect, William Chambers, having also designed the adjacent Somerset House. King's College, which was named after its first patron, King George IV, was an imposing grey stone building with a grand entrance hall where a uniformed porter directed me to 'C' corridor at the top of a great flight of stone steps, flanked by imposing marble statues. Thankfully, the Dean's door stood open and so I ventured in, to find myself in a large reception room in which sat the Dean's secretary who instructed me to sit and wait. I remained there for what felt like an age, quaking silently, until a heavy oak door was opened and I was ushered into the inner sanctum. But it was there that a very pleasant surprise awaited me, for in his book-lined study and distanced from his imposing desk, sat the tall wiry figure of Dean Sydney Evans, relaxing in his leather armchair, bidding me to come and join him 'for our little chat.' He wore an immaculate, if somewhat dated, suit, academic gown and a winning smile. He had neat black hair, enigmatic, piercing eyes and an effortless air of authority which said, 'all is well', and although it was for me a totally alien environment, I found myself oddly at ease in his delightful company. My week of mugging up the news served me not at all, for instead, he touched immediately upon my most vulnerable weakness by asking what contemporary novels I had been reading. I was thus taken completely off guard, for the only novels I'd ever tried to read were those given as my examination set texts plus a slim horror called *Camp on Blood*

Island. I managed to stumble along whilst he helpfully, and I think knowingly, penned a list of contemporary novels and advised me to read them in order to better understand the complexities of our modern times. I assured him that I would do so, hoping all the while not to disclose the fact that I felt an alien in a foreign and forbidding environment.

I had been hoping that the Dean might be prepared to accept me for the college's own AKC diploma course, having realised from the prospectus booklet that the degree courses on offer were probably beyond my grasp. But by now the Dean was already in full flow, describing the scope of the Bachelor of Divinity syllabus, so I dared not interrupt him. I had done surprisingly well in my ordinary level exams and my teachers were predicting reasonable advanced level grades, and I sensed that it was on that basis that he had already added my name to his BD list. He told me that I would be studying for the AKC diploma *alongside* my degree work. By taking on that additional task, I would cover all the qualifications necessary to offer for ordination without having to obtain any further qualifications later. I sat dumbfounded as he continued to explain that after my degree I would join the other King's graduates at a college in Wiltshire for a further year before moving on to ordination. Then, whilst I was reduced to nods and smiles, he snapped his folder closed to indicate that the matter of which course I was to follow had all been settled. He relaxed back into his armchair and shared the news that the Church of England authorities had recently decided that no ordinands were to be allowed to go directly from school to college and thence into ordained life without at least one year out in the world of work. It later occurred to me that it was therefore the Church of England which had invented what is now commonly known as the student 'gap year', except that whilst today the emphasis is on using that year to have fun, I was being told to go out and earn a living. I readily agreed to a year away from academia, but it struck me too that it would be an opportunity for yet more adventures.

I had walked into the college building concerned about answering questions to do with theology and current affairs but had experienced instead three quarters of an hour during which my life had been spun around and given a direction that would profoundly affect the rest of my life. Dean Sydney Evans then breathed a very relaxed sigh which had the magical effect of calming reassurance, whilst making clear that the interview had come to its end. I swallowed, smiled, and said thank you. I came out of the interview and walked back down the Strand in a daze.

CHAPTER 3

STRIKING OUT

As I approached the end of my schooling I had the task of working out how I was to spend my gap year in response to Dean Sydney Evan's directive. The intention was not, as some interpret the gap year today, an opportunity to experience a year of travel and enjoyment, but rather to dig deep into the harsh world that ordinary, hard-working people were experiencing year in and year out. Fortunately for me, although my year was to entail much hard work, there was lots of fun besides!

My attention was drawn to a newspaper advert that was offering a year's experience in an entirely new venture in the back streets of Birmingham where young men were invited to help establish a Christian commune and work in the local neighbourhood. The commune would offer opportunities for discussion and community living and was to be supported by the Church's diocesan youth service. The more I read, the more intrigued I became, so having booked a place, I packed my bags and made my way to Birmingham, Britain's second largest city. And it was this heavily industrialised city that was destined to play an extremely significant part in my life, not only for that one gap year, but for many years to come.

Living in community

Birmingham may have advertised itself as 'the heart of the nation,' which, geographically speaking, was nearly true. But the clapped-out bus which took me from the city centre out to the red light district of Balsall Heath, spoke of a city that was miles behind the progress being made in the south of England. I lugged my suitcase round the corner and into Edgbaston

Road where I was hailed by a slight figure walking towards me – it was Sid Lockley, who was to be the leader of the new project. Sid must have recognised me from the photo I'd sent with my application. As he was rushing off to see the cricket at the local ground, he explained that in the kitchen I'd find some food ready to heat up. He then pointed out the vast red-brick building that had once been a vicarage, but which now bore a freshly painted name board proclaiming it to be the Edgbaston Community House. The project had been established with a dual purpose: so that young people like me could experience communal life whilst engaging with the local community, and also so that by pooling our wages we could finance the commune and play host to a range of Birmingham charities. It would save them considerable rental costs, but more importantly, by housing the charities together in our one building, it would encourage them to work together in a more integrated manner.

The old rambling house had a vast kitchen where I hungrily devoured my first meal and then found my way to the room that was to be my bedroom for the year. It was the first time I'd had a proper bed of my own, having always slept on a sofa at home. Therefore, although the enormous high-ceilinged room was sparsely furnished, for me it was very heaven. During those first weeks it began to dawn on me that I felt a great sense of relief at coming away from my extended East End family. Although I could not have wished for a more loving upbringing, I was now released to make my own way in the world and find out a little more of who I was. Extended families bring many benefits, but they can also confine us by imposing conformist expectations upon us, thus precluding the exploration of wider horizons. I was now experiencing an almost visceral sensation of freedom at being in a place where I was free to grow up and leave my childhood behind me – although none of us of course ever detach ourselves entirely from our childhood, nor perhaps should we. But the year 1964 was certainly a time for exploration, for it was the year in which Jean Shrimpton wore the first mini-skirt, the Rolling

Stones released '(I can't get no) Satisfaction', BBC2 was being launched, Martin Luther King was introducing the world to the Civil Rights Movement and the first US ground troops were arriving in Vietnam. I was determined to begin playing my part in this exciting and dangerous new world where there were issues to face, wrongs to be righted and a lot of fun to be had.

The other lads joining the Birmingham commune were many and varied, most staying only a few months rather than the full year. Chris had fallen in love with a young woman who occasionally popped in to cook for us, and although coming from a strict Baptist background, he was hopelessly addicted to nicotine. We therefore relegated him and his cigarettes to a separate bedroom where he acquired the habit of sleeping in on Saturday mornings instead of attending to his allotted household chores. The only way to rouse him was to lodge a cigarette between his lips, light it and hold his nose. When this didn't have the desired effect, we would 'escort' the sleeping Christopher to the bathroom where a cold shower and wet pyjamas were guaranteed to bring him round. His only continuing concern seemed to be that his cigarette had become too soggy to re-light.

Learning about learning

The one volunteer who stayed longest, and became a life-long friend, was Peter Watsham, a bright spark whose father owned the cinema at his hometown of Henley-on-Thames. Peter and I had the very good fortune to be employed together at Monyhull Hospital which had been founded in 1908, 'for the purpose of the provision and maintenance of Homes for the reception and treatment of sane epileptics and feebleminded persons.' For most of its life it had been a very grim workhouse-like institution, but in recent years a thoroughly radical vision had been brought to the hospital by Dr Herbert C. Günzburg, the consultant psychologist who was now in charge. I was to work as a personal aide to Dr John Locking who was convinced that the key to a patient's future development lay in what he was calling 'process learning'. He hoped that by discovering what the very first elements of learning were, and only moving the students on to the next step after they had fully mastered the first, we might be able to progress them, step by tiny step, up a ladder of learning until they could manage tasks which they had never found possible before. In this way they could eventually move out into the world and live an independent, although assisted, life. Whilst John sat chewing his pencil and building his ground-breaking theories, our task was to act as his practical helpers. We would draw up charts and build gadgets according to his specifications so that we could test each stage of his developing theory directly with small groups of patients in a little classroom Dr Günzburg had set aside for the purpose.

Cyril and Dennis
students at Monyhull

I was to read much later in life that Günzburg was considered internationally to be one of the most creative leaders and teachers in the field of intellectual impairment who was, for the first time, bringing the classroom into the hospital and building teams where psychiatrists and psychologists would work together. He was modelling the whole institution on his dictum that, 'every experience, activity and personal relationship should be regarded as having therapeutic potential for the patient.' This meant that the whole place was becoming a hive of radical thinking. An elderly retired doctor had even chosen to live on campus, teaching Esperanto to the patients and staging hospital dances. At these he would encourage patients to enjoy dancing together – dancing himself with everyone in turn. In those days this was all thought to be slightly dotty, but I suspect he was a saint and way ahead of his time. What I was learning from that team of doctors was that every human being is a child of God, and what's more, should always be treated as such no matter the circumstances. It was a truth that had in no way permeated into the British culture of the day, nor had it been properly recognised within the church. In the latter case this was despite the fact that in the New Testament St Paul had written, 'there is no longer Jew or Greek, no longer slave or free, there is no longer male or female – for you are all one in Christ Jesus' (Gal 3:28). At Monyhull Hospital the team was already putting this principle into practice in recognising every patient as a full and deserving member of society, even when the wider society preferred to lock such men and women away from the common gaze. But it never dawned on me to apply this same principle to my own church which still discriminated against women, even when clearly called and gifted for ordained ministry. I was enjoying God's call to me whilst denying that God was as equally gracious to others. I was still labouring under the youthful illusion that life was all about me, and the church in some ways reinforced that myopic delusion by assuming that the Christian faith was mostly about itself.

As I look back now, I realise that during that year, Monyhull Hospital was introducing me to myself in a whole variety of ways. My main place of work was at a desk which my immediate boss, John Locking, had set up for me in one corner of his large office. To help me understand something of his developing theories he would feed me books about psychology together with the works of Freud, Adler and Jung, and I found to my surprise that I devoured them with relish. One day however, having looked quizzically at me for some time, John suddenly stood up at his desk and pronounced: 'I've just realised that however much you disguise it, you are clearly dyslexic!' At that time the word 'dyslexia' was heard only in professional circles and was not common currency as it is today, and so at first I assumed that he'd just heaped some nasty insult upon me. But my anger rapidly subsided as he systematically explained what dyslexia was, and how it affected different people in a great variety of ways. As he did so, I felt that at last here was somebody who understood what I had been wrestling with all my life; it was as if he was telling me my life story. Explaining that dyslexia was in fact a catch-all term for a complex syndrome of symptoms, he set about offering me a barrage of tests which proved his initial diagnosis to be correct. He was intrigued to observe the battery of skills I had unconsciously developed over the years to help me manage the difficulties. But his tests also convinced him that my problematic birth experience had probably resulted in certain cognitive malfunctions, thus accounting for the interminable battle for words constantly raging within me. His explanations didn't of themselves make it easier for me to manage, but at last I had a handle on what had been troubling me for so long, and that came as a great relief.

All the world's a stage

Whilst searching the library for more books by Freud, I happened upon what looked like a fun read. It was all about Franz Mesmer, an eighteenth-century German doctor, who had given his name to mesmerism or what we now know as hypnosis. One evening Peter and I decided to give it a try, during which I happened to suggest to the hypnotised Peter that he make my breakfast the next morning. When next day he presented me with breakfast in bed we were both taken aback! And when Peter was informed that he'd been acting in response to my prompting, he made me vow never to suggest anything like that again. We consigned the book about Mesmer to the waste bin. That episode did however bring home to me just how malleable and controllable is the human mind. Peter is a highly intelligent and self-aware person and yet, given the right stimulus, it had proved possible to convince him to do something which, although not alien to his generous personality, was nevertheless not an action which had been prompted of his own volition. I'd already been learning how much we are controlled by our cultural and linguistic environments, but this experience demonstrated how clever 'subliminal' advertising or publicity can convince the public to buy or vote in accordance with the will of the advertiser. For an individual or group to withstand the onslaught of these mind-controlling forces or cultural assumptions and arrive at an independent judgement takes immense courage and not a little stubbornness.

Living alongside us in the Community House was one of the most endearing characters I'd ever chanced to meet. Malcolm Goldsmith was just finishing his years as assistant curate at the Balsall Heath church just nearby, where he'd founded the Balsall Heath Association. He had set up its headquarters in an old toy shop at 91 Court Road in the heart of an unimaginably deprived area, and there his team offered local people personal advice and worked hard to build up community solidarity. Balsall Heath was then famous as the red light district of the city. The shop therefore provided confidential pregnancy advice along with educational opportunities, help with housing problems, and much more. Malcolm had also emphasised the importance of acknowledging the many faiths of Balsall Heath, encouraging them to work together, sometimes in the face of heavy racist opposition. With his Yorkshire humour and rollicking laughter, he left me with many memories to savour. But I treasure most of all how he demonstrated that a local church congregation can be in evident solidarity with the community around it, and additionally, how important it is to underpin that with careful theological reflection on the issues it raises. He always maintained that his own theological abilities were meagre, but with his great buddy Nev Chamberlain (who later became Bishop of Brechin), he produced a monthly broadsheet of theological reflections on various topics of concern, such as youth unemployment and racism, together with truly fascinating articles about relevant prayer and ecumenism. It made me realise just how staid, churchy and inward-looking many other churches had become. Indeed, once Malcolm and Nev had moved off to their next posts, I would go along on Sundays to other neighbouring churches, but never once did I find anywhere radical or challenging enough to claim it as my spiritual home for the rest of the year. So, whilst life at the house and in the hospital continued to ask so much of me and challenge me to engage life's issues to the full, the local churches seemed to be living in their own irrelevant world: a self-defeating stance and at odds with what a vibrant Christianity could be.

One evening as I was strumming along and singing my songs in Sid's sitting room, a visitor to the house invited me to go along with him to a folk club in Solihull to meet a special friend, and suggested that I bring my guitar along. His friend turned out to be a tall and sinewy folk singer called Dave Ward - Spike to his friends - and he and I immediately formed a bond which has lasted a lifetime. Dave and I began to share our songs and sing regularly together at the B Flat Folk Club which gathered in the back room of the Mason's Arms pub in Solihull. Our singing duo became so popular that we were soon invited to become the club's resident hosts, welcoming other singers to the stage - including one newcomer who went by the name of Jasper Carrott, later to become a household name. Dave would take the lead vocal and my guitar and voice added the accompanying harmonies. There being just the two of us we toyed with calling ourselves 'The Bifocals' but luckily decided against it. We became quite popular at other clubs too, and when we teamed up with Doug

Law, who played a mean five-string banjo, we were soon touring as special guests on the West Midlands folk circuit.

With Dave & Doug
at the Bb Folk Club

We enjoyed the acclaim and especially the adoration of the young women in the audiences. Folk clubs at that time were totally acoustic experiences with not a microphone in sight, so in the larger venues, any singer who had a weak stage presence or could not project their voice stood no chance of being heard. Dave, however, was a born entertainer and taught me the techniques of holding a crowd's attention with just a look and a gesture. He had an extraordinary stage presence, so that when we were singing our songs you could hear a pin drop and even people ordering their drinks at the bar would do so in whispers. We shared a stage with some of the great names of the time. On one occasion we were invited to warm up the audience for Jake Thackray, by then a regular TV star. We also thoroughly enjoyed meeting Paul Simon, then still touring the UK by himself, who shared with me a few tips on finger-style folk guitar.

Ever before taking up his career as a schoolteacher, Dave had met Janice who was still a student at Hereford Teacher

Training College. So I often joined him, and a gang of his friends, to journey across to Hereford where we would camp near the college and eat in the refectory with the students. Dave and I often performed for them at college events, and I suppose it was inevitable that I should take up with another of the female students studying there. Over time our relationship became really quite serious. We all had great times together, on one occasion being broadcast by Welsh TV (Tellywelly) as we played a novelty game of rugby against the female students. This was well before any women's rugby was on the horizon and the intention was to dress up in crazy costumes, have a good laugh and raise a lot of money for charity. To ensure the score would draw level at the end of the game, the lads picked up the college's smallest female player and, with the ball still in her arms, ran her up-field and dropped her over the goal line for their finishing try. We thought that a very gallant gesture when, much to our amazement, a female player then picked up the ball with a superior sniff, placed it carefully, and expertly scored a winning conversion. The final whistle blew and we all collapsed in howls of laughter. We should have realised there and then that women's rugby was to have a very successful and serious future.

Interesting company

Back at the Birmingham house our commune was constantly receiving visitors who would come to investigate how our community experiment was progressing. The Bishop of Birmingham sat down to a meal with us and shared his remarkable wisdom and warmth. Leonard Wilson had been Bishop of Singapore during the war. He was arrested by the Japanese invaders and sent to the infamous Changi prisoner of war camp where he and others had undergone interrogation and brutal torture. It was extraordinary that by the end of the war he had inspired some of his torturers to become Christians. During the meal we asked him about his work for the decriminalisation of homosexual acts, and his campaign for the end of the death penalty which at that time was still on the statute book in the UK. He was also an ardent early supporter of the ordination of women, and it was such a sadness that he never lived to see the ordination of his own daughter, Susan Cole-King, when it was at last allowed many years later.

Another radical clerical visitor came in the form of Nick Stacey who stood, sipping sherry with his back to Sid's fire, and told us about his parish church in Woolwich. Despite his rather superior *Boys' Own* manner, what he was actually attempting to do in his Thameside parish was intriguing. He reordered the interior of the church in order to be of real service to those with dire needs in the community, and built around himself an inspiring and committed team of workers. It sounded a little top-down and patronising, but he was still streets ahead of those C of E clerics who were content with business as usual. I learnt later that soon after his visit to us, Nick Stacey left church ministry in despair, realising that his experiment had failed to touch the real needs of the marginalised people of Woolwich. His visit challenged me to wonder if I would find working for the church the uphill struggle against the inertia that Nick had experienced. There were, however, some shining exceptions to that gloomy picture, and I was saved from throwing in the towel by meeting some of them almost immediately afterwards.

Sid gloried in his Ford Consul Classic, and one Sunday drove Peter and me to a church in Smethwick to meet the parish priest, Donald Tytler. Donald and his people were proving once again that the church did not have to live in the past, nor concern itself only with its own survival and well-being. He had the laity fully involved in all church decision-making, ran a full programme of Christian education, and together they had turned their church hall over to serving the community's needs in all sorts of innovative ways. There was one disconcerting factor however, for I found that I could not tear my eye away from Donald's right arm which he constantly held at an odd angle. In later years, when I got to know him as a close friend, he related that he had been an instructor in the army. He had been demonstrating the best technique for throwing hand grenades when one day he pulled out the pin and threw the pin instead of the grenade, thus losing not just his right hand but most of his arm. In later years Donald was made bishop, but always retained his rascally charm and humour, becoming affectionately known to his friends as 'the one-armed bandit'. He very much disliked sanctuary creepers as he called those assistants at the altar who fawned over visiting bishops. He boasted that, on one occasion, he became so angered by the fussing around by a particularly unctuous server that when he reached out to Donald at an important moment to take the bishop's staff from him, Donald surreptitiously unclipped his false arm, thus letting the poor man walk away with the crozier with a hand and arm still attached!

We often had the great pleasure of welcoming Charles Parker to the house, a man who was to prove very important to Britain's understanding of its own cultural history. There now exists in Birmingham's magnificent Central Library the Charles Parker Archive consisting of more than five thousand hours of taped recordings and reams of research papers all relating to the cultural history of Britain in the 50s, 60s and 70s. He was utterly charming, and gave me a number of songs he had written which he hoped I'd enjoy singing, neither of us knowing then that years later I would perform one of them, 'No Room for Jesus', on Broadway at a New York Christmas concert. It was Charles Parker who made me yet more conscious of how folk song had been a vehicle for oppressed and forgotten groups of people to voice their needs and encourage them to fight for their rights. Later, of course, the whole world of folk music would be taken over by commercial interests which changed it quite radically so that the singer, rather than the song, was brought to the fore. Charles Parker's archive speaks vividly of an earlier story.

Who needs the church?

As the year in Birmingham raced by I found my time being eaten up by my work at Monyhull Hospital, singing on the folk circuit, and on free weekends, racing down to Hereford with Dave to visit our girlfriends. As I look back I realise that little by little I was drifting away from regular church attendance. I was trying to read the occasional theological book, but that was only to prepare myself for my future studies rather than to enhance my faith and understanding. The worship services I had attended in local churches seemed detached from the world in which I was finding excitement and challenge. If it had not been for that earlier decision of mine to follow the call towards ordination, I would have paid services no more attention. I suspect that, like the vast majority of British people, I would have simply drifted away from the church, even though I still felt passionately about the life of Jesus, the Man for Others. I was also sure in my mind that the fascinating world around me was underpinned by the presence of God. So if I had been lucky enough to venture into a church where the members had welcomed me into their fellowship it may have been different. But on those occasions when I popped along, they had never said 'hello', and the boring services had never encouraged me to go back.

What particularly annoyed me was how often churches assumed that the Holy Spirit of God only works through religion – and through the Christian Church in particular. That seemed such a blinkered view, especially when the gospels tell us how the curtain in the Jerusalem temple, which was supposed to separate the secular world from the sacred world was, at the crucifixion of Jesus, torn from top to bottom (Matt 27: 51). This symbolised that, in Jesus, God is never separated from the non-religious, secular world, nor from its secular people. God's Spirit is alive and active in every sphere. And I was meeting what I took to be Spirit-inspired people, many not religious in the slightest, who were offering diligent care and love to those around them. Others were contributing to the wellbeing of all through the arts, science, architecture, or simply their commitment to the routines of a life well lived. So surely the Holy Spirit was alive in them too? And this thought was reinforced once again by the Bible itself which speaks of God's Spirit being there at creation, breathing life into every single living thing and inspiring all humankind. St Paul seemed to have been aware of this because when he first preached to the Athenians, he assured them that although they knew nothing of church or synagogue, they were already aware of God, 'since it is in him that we live and move and have our being' (Acts 17:28). And that had to be why I was meeting so many beautiful non-church people who were alive with God's Spirit.

But although I'd been unable to find a local church where the services were alive to that 'spiritedness', I still felt convinced that religion had an important part to play in helping us all to remain mindful of the wonder around us and not to take it for granted. I could see how the Christian faith – if interpreted correctly – could point people to the divine origin of the 'spiritedness' that I saw all around me in Birmingham. The church's buildings, its music, its liturgies, its Gospels and its community all serve the function of orientating us towards a deeper awareness and understanding of what lies at the heart of our experience and which is so evident in the goodness and creativity of those around us. Many people say they are spiritual but not religious, but the Christian faith, if allowed to be its true self, can guide spiritual people into the realisation that, as Gerard Manley Hopkins famously observed: 'The world is charged with the grandeur of *God*,' and that awareness can lead to unimaginable joy. So while the church doesn't have a monopoly on the Spirit's self-revelation, it does help us into deeper awareness and greater spiritual maturity.

I suspect that I'd been rather spoilt by my formative experiences at St Barnabas back in East Ham where I'd been surrounded by inspiring people who had found the Christian religion had given them a language to express what it was that was driving them, and it was clearly taking them a lot deeper into its mystery. It was that which had impressed me, and as I registered at the time, although I didn't know what it was that they had, I knew I wanted some of it. But in Birmingham, none of the nearby churches seemed to be alive in that way, nor playing its full part in engaging with society. Or perhaps I was so full of myself that I didn't really give them a chance.

Hitting the road

That year away from the confines of my family culture had opened worlds to me that otherwise I would never have contemplated. So it was quite an emotional wrench when the time came to say goodbye to the city of Birmingham, for what I thought was the last time. It was my singing buddy's mum who helped me make the break by inviting me to their home, sitting me down in pride of place at the table on a chair she had extravagantly decorated for the purpose, and feeding me a meal the like of which I'd not tasted in a very long time. With much singing and laughter Dave and his family sent me back home to the Smoke, as they called it, although it seemed to me ironic that Brummies should call London the Smoke when I'd just coughed my way through a deep Birmingham winter. I'd come to love that city, but I still enjoyed getting away from it occasionally, and especially when we all journeyed down to Hereford at weekends, not least because it was there that my relationship with my girlfriend was flourishing. It was a time when it was expected that any relationship that became at all serious would inevitably lead to marriage and to prepare for that, all young couples would become engaged. So before I left for London we did just that, expecting to put the seal on it some years later. She then remained in Hereford to complete her teacher training and I took the train from Birmingham's Snow Hill station back to the capital city.

I arrived back in East London in the summer of 1965 just as the capital was revelling in the songs of a brand new musical, *The Sound of Music*, and at the same time mourning the death of Sir Winston Churchill. But I was brought up sharp by the realisation that while my generous student grant would pay for my forthcoming college fees, the cost of digs in the centre of London would still be completely beyond my reach. It was therefore back to the sofa at Browning Road for me. The room was now equipped with a simple pull-down bureau where I could write my essays, and because I would be catching an early train each morning and getting home late each evening, it meant my parents would not have to suffer my intrusion into their peace too much. They were in any case still very supportive of my home-coming.

Before starting at King's College there was still a month or two of summer remaining, and so I made contact with an old school pal, Malcolm Jones, and together we walked up to the railway station, jumped aboard and took off on another adventure. We hitch-hiked across Europe and made our way to what was then Yugoslavia where our visas were carefully scrutinised before we were allowed to cross into the first communist state either of us had ever visited. We set out in sweltering heat to locate the Brotherhood and Unity Highway which ran the length of the country, expecting to find a smart and spacious motorway. Instead we were confronted by a dust-laden, narrow two-way road across what looked like semi-desert. Our first stop was Ljubljana, the pleasant state capital of Slovenia, after which we continued to hitch-hike our way eastward into Croatia and its filthy industrial capital, Zagreb. The next leg of our journey was very challenging, for rarely would a car stop to pick us up as we stood by the road amidst the filth and dust, breathing in the toxic fumes from the clouds of diesel exhaust that followed each ancient, heavy-laden lorry on its way to Belgrade. Realising that this was becoming too much for us, we devised a new trick. We'd noticed that these old trucks would tend to stall on any steep incline, so we would seek out a nearby steep hill, take up our stand at its summit and when a truck came near to stalling, we'd clamber up into the cab, quite unbidden, close the door behind us and cheerfully wish the driver hello. On no occasion were they ever fazed by this ruse and after perhaps muttering a little, would pull out their bottle of homemade lemonade and offer us a swig. They all wore the uniform of the Yugoslav working man, a simple cotton sleeveless vest – ideal in the scorching, dust-laden atmosphere.

Nearing the Yugoslav border

Thirst was always stalking us, and having once asked a group of workmen for water, on seeing our fair skins and western dress they refused and just made fun of us. We turned away in despair, but were taken aback by their sudden change of mood. They pointed joyfully at the Union Jacks on the back of our kit, and throwing their arms around us, bade us return to their work-hut for refreshment. It was Malc who realised that they must have taken us for Germans, but on realising that we were British 'allies', were only too happy to come to our aid. The homemade lemonade flowed freely, and we said goodbye to our new friends amidst cheers, with our water bottles filled to the brim. We reckoned that these workmen must have suffered badly at the hands of the occupying forces, continuing to foster resentment, even eighteen years later. We'd just experienced how hatred can breed only yet more hatred.

Two Arabs driving brand new Mercedes Benz limousines took us to Belgrade and promised to pick us up again the next morning and take us on to Damascus where they intended to sell the cars at a handsome profit and then return for more. We therefore found two benches in the park and did our best to settle down for the night. Despite the aggressive police patrols, others had the same idea. It was only a year or so earlier that a dreadful earthquake had destroyed Skopje in nearby Macedonia, leaving those who survived homeless on the streets of the capital city. They were now refugees in their own country. Alas, the next morning the Arab cars never showed up, so we missed our opportunity to visit Syria and instead reverted to our old hill trick and climbed up into a lorry to wherever it might take us.

In Athens, we marched into one of the best hotels in town and begged the receptionist to let us sleep in a broom cupboard. This meant that for the next few mornings we emerged from our cupboard to take advantage of all the hotel facilities for which other guests had paid the earth. We caught the ferry from Piraeus across the Adriatic Sea to Italy, where we were picked up by a young American who kindly drove us to Bari. But there our fatigue and lingering dehydration eventually caught up with us, landing us both in an Italian charity hospital. I had become delirious through the night, but one morning as I came to my senses, a huge male nurse with a sparkling smile, thrust a tiny Coca Cola bottle under my pillow and explained that if I wanted to pee, this little bottle would have to serve. I soon realised, and with some concern, that a miracle was now demanded of me, for the bottle and its neck were miniscule and I had not passed water for at least twenty-four hours! Other patients were keen to make friends, one showing us his prize possession, his Roman Catholic prayer book with Mussolini's portrait bound into its pages alongside the Pope's insignia. We forget now what an extraordinary appeal the fascist dictators had, not only for these southern Italian peasants, but also for the British élite, urged on by the *Daily Mail*. This appeal spread to many aspiring intellectuals all across Europe, Ezra Pound, W B Yeats and Max Beerbohm even setting up home in Italy for a while, attracted by the promise of Mussolini's new Pax Romana. In the primitive hospital an injection of brown liquid was offered to all patients every morning using a shared syringe, the common needle being wiped down with a clean rag between jabs. At the sight of this Malc and I hurriedly clambered out of our hospital pyjamas and got back on the road to Rome, the Eternal City.

Malc was keen that we visit the open-air opera, staged in the vast Caracalla stadium which had been built by the Roman Emperor, Marcus Aurelius. With a cast of five hundred and an audience of seven thousand we basked in the wonders of *Aida*. As one act drew to its close, with the heroine singing 'O Patria Mia', a very moving and plaintive lament for her homeland, we were assailed by the screech of 'the lady with the tray' standing immediately behind us yelling so that all seven thousand could hear: 'Gelati icy cream!' The incongruity of this shrieking intrusion set us both laughing, but we soon shut up when the agitated faces of the locals around us told us they were thinking we were laughing at their beloved diva.

We continued north, overwhelmed by the beauty of the Italian landscape. On arrival in Florence, perhaps our favourite city, we booked a bed at the YMCA, only to find later that, because the hostel was full, we had been relegated to an open-air space under a huge tree in the grounds. It was nearing midnight when we were suddenly woken by a fearsome looking man shining a bright light into our faces and pointing the muzzle of his shotgun at us. Luckily, our tickets were pinned to our sleeping-bags, clearly on display. On realising we were legit, our assailant left us in peace, although I don't recall either of us getting happily back to sleep after that.

Summertime eventually ran out, along with our cash, so after our helter-skelter of adventures we made it home safely with many a tale to tell, and many more that are beyond the telling. My gap year had indeed turned out to consist of very hard work but certainly a deluge of fun into the bargain! But it was time now for me to embark on my academic studies at King's College London. As I'd hoped, Birmingham had taught me a great deal about myself, and surprisingly, since I had not been to church much, a great deal more about God.

CHAPTER 4

KING'S COLLEGE LONDON

As part of London University, King's College had won international accolades as a school of law, literature, engineering, peace studies and the arts – and, of course, theology. Its theology department accommodated some one hundred and eighty students in training for ordination who were joined by many others who were perhaps going on to become teachers of religion in schools and colleges. To mark us out as theologians we were obliged to wear black academic gowns and because most of the students were so very articulate and middle-class, I found it all very unnerving and worrying. However, as an inveterate chameleon, I soon learnt how to blend in with my new surroundings and it was not long before I began to enjoy the company of these extraordinary young people. It was not as if I was the only student from a working-class background to attend at King's, but I had been so sensitised to classism by my Marxist upbringing that I was particularly conscious of it and at times felt intensely alone and out of place. The daily train ride back and forth from college reminded me of how different it all was from my East End life, and acted as something of a cultural space-portal through which I journeyed home to my parallel universe.

Finding my bearings

I soon learnt that the Bachelor of Divinity undergraduates were divided into two groupings, the BD Pass contingent and the BD Honours students – the latter being required to learn Hebrew and Greek in the first year. Given that I had had immense difficulty even learning English, I made my excuses and sheepishly opted out. Dean Sydney Evans however, had other ideas and informed me that he would allow me to learn Greek during my first year and only then undertake Hebrew in my second year alongside next year's newcomers. I almost turned the offer down, fearing that it was all beyond me, but the Dean's faith in me deserved a grateful response so I set to, determined not to let him down. Within the year we were actually expected to be able to translate the whole of St Mark's gospel from the original Greek which was a tall order, but a fellow student who had studied the language at his private school helped me scrape a pass.

Other subjects included church history, biblical studies, ethics, doctrine, philosophy and so on, for which we would turn up in large numbers, clamber up to a seat in the ancient lecture amphitheatre, and there scribble down notes at hair-raising speed as the professor read his lecture to us. Some offered their lectures in a boring monotone, some were decidedly eccentric, whilst others did their best to brighten the mood by sharing the occasional amusing aside. During a lecture on the migration of the Hebrew people, Dr Joe Robinson remarked of their circumcision that whilst it had not been particularly noticeable within their own tribal culture, in the new situation, 'it stood out like a sore thumb!' The students collapsed with laughter and it took him a few moments to realise what he'd inadvertently suggested, at which he blushed with embarrassment. We understand however that he left the remark in his notes to brighten up his lectures for future students. Thus it was that we shared the great privilege of listening to such towering scholars as H D Lewis, Geoffrey Parrinder, Eric Mascall, Maurice Wiles, Christopher Evans, Dennis Nineham and Peter Ackroyd, who in later years were joined by female professors too.

One authoritative professor would habitually preface all his assertions about the Old Testament text with the phrase, 'it is not unreasonable to suppose that ...', and that was as far as he believed it was proper to go. While other students felt that this was pulling the rug from under their more literalist faith, I found this critical stance at King's very reassuring because it was this open-eyed honesty that had won me to the faith in the first place. It was a critical and thoroughly objective approach which transformed my understanding of what is meant by the word 'critique'. I had always assumed that to be critical was to dismiss something altogether, but these great scholars spoke of 'Biblical Criticism' because they held the biblical text in such high esteem that they knew it could withstand even the most rigorous interrogation. They believed that intense 'critique' would reveal much more of the profound wisdom which lay below its surface than would a naïve acceptance of its face-value meaning. The gospels carry many examples of Jesus himself critiquing the scriptures, for it was already an accepted method used in Judaism to dig out not just the superficial meaning of their holy texts, but also, to discover the holy wisdom that lay within them.

I have to admit, however, that while I warmed to the rigour of this academic approach to the faith, I was somewhat surprised that in all my years at King's, training for ministry, I was never once asked if I actually believed in God! No doubt it was assumed, but I still had the feeling that they were just too embarrassed to ask.

I was lapping up the wonderful treasure-store of new learning and managing so far to keep my head above water academically, even getting to grips with the complexities of the Greek language. But despite all that, I still didn't feel at ease. I was making new friendships with my fellow students, sitting and discussing personal concerns into the night in a way that I had never known before, and even getting a name for being on my feet and voicing my opinions at every opportunity. But what only I appreciated was that this was just a fresh way of doing what I had done at junior school: adopting a flamboyant, showy posture in order to be taken for a star when actually I was nothing of the sort. I'd often push my point beyond its own logic, or just mouth a headline I'd heard somewhere which sounded smart, but which I did not really understand. It was all a performance designed to hide my fears, whilst desperately seeking affirmation of the real me –

and that without being sure any longer whether 'the real me' was the East End lad or the middle-class academic. I'm struck now by just how self-absorbed and muddled I was, using others in my frantic bid to hide the fears within and yet, at the same time, genuinely loving the new friends around me.

I was burdened by two problems. First, I didn't really belong to the culture that now surrounded me at college, and second, that my new colleagues were able to absorb and retain names and facts that would just slip me by. Most of my new subjects demanded an exceptionally accurate memory, whereas philosophy not only fascinated me, but had no long lists of vocabulary, dates or data to remember. It offered instead the exciting prospect of tossing ideas up into the air and trying to get them to land in a coherent and creative pattern. The professor, H D Lewis, sported a lyrical Welsh accent and an academic's stoop brought on, I always suspected, by the weight of the philosophical tomes he always clasped under one arm. But it was when he introduced us to Plato's famous political treatise, *The Republic,* that I became really enthralled! In it, Plato argued that the world we see every day is really only a pale shadow of a much more real dimension that lay beyond it. Those who were especially gifted, he believed, were in touch with that real world, where the underlying idea of things resided, whereas most of us are restricted to concentrate on the unreal world of shadows around us. It meant that Plato would begin from a universal idea of catness and by deduction work down to find a flesh and blood cat in the world around us. Plato's student, Aristotle, greatly admired the thinking of his teacher, but felt sure that those things we see around us are indeed real and true in themselves because they already have within them Plato's other dimension of universal ideas. So Aristotle preferred the inductive method, where we see lots of cats about the place, and from that experience we infer the universal idea of catness. He denied Plato's notion of that separated real world, arguing that there was only one reality and it is here all around us where we see very real and particular things, but they are also examples of that depth which Plato called the world of ideas.

The thinking of these Greek masters was of course considerably more nuanced than this brief description portrays. But even then, my reading of Aristotle was helping me to see that to experience God we didn't have to look out into some Platonic nether region beyond or up in the sky, but that God was everywhere around us in the reality of here and now as the fundamental ground of all that is. What Plato was on to, I think, was that when we look at a thing, some just want to leave it at that and say, 'that's all there is to it.' But there are many of us – poets, artists, thoughtful scientists, or just ordinary folk – who look at the world and just know that there's a depth, a wonderful mystery, that sustains it, just as Being sustains Existence. But while Plato wanted to look outside the world into some supernatural realm for that, Aristotle could sense that the special mystery was right here with us in the things and people around us, but at a depth which takes some perceiving. And I was convinced that whenever I was grasped by that depth, what was hitting me was that whilst that depth could make a particular existence possible, it also brought everything together, sustaining and making everything cohere. And it was that essence of being that made everything, even being, possible – it was what I'd been learning to call 'The Ground of all Being'. It felt that these two Greek philosophers had pointed to a way to speak intellectually about the religious experience I had had. I did not believe, as Nan Upstairs had, in a Supreme Being – a being like all the other beings only a bigger and better being – but instead, God as the very ground of all being. There at King's College, and even now, this intellectual way of expressing these things makes my head spin. But it did help me to feel that my religious convictions, born of my personal experience, also had intellectual, philosophical bite. Each day, when I say morning and evening prayer from our modern Church of England book, it bids us pray, 'with one heart and mind', thus reminding me that my beliefs must always stand the test of reason, whilst my every thought should be inspired in turn by love. And this coherence is what can bring deeper integrity to our life and our prayer.

From the Angelic Host to the Hell's Angels

By the end of my first year at King's College I was aware that a great deal of change was occurring within me, but as the term ended, it was back to the raw realities of workaday life. During my year away in Birmingham I'd met David Collyer, a young clergyman who was now running a club for bikers and Hell's Angels in Birmingham's inner city. It was called the Double Zero club, in reference to the two wheels of a motorcycle. He invited me to come back to Birmingham and work at the club during the summer, and offered to pay me a basic salary for the privilege. The young bikers were rough and tough, but happily accepted me once they saw that I respected their unorthodox culture and hierarchy.

Late at night with
the Hell's Angels

Although their violent life revolved around their fast bikes and gang solidarity, I felt safe in their company, understanding perhaps from my own early experience in a gang, the importance of the gang's pecking order and their pride of belonging. No one who belonged to this club could feel alone whatever their background, their ability or the evident deprivations of their home life.

One night when the club seemed particularly full I had the clear impression that I had become the centre of their attention and that they had something special lined up for me by way of induction. At that time, quite near to the club's Digbeth HQ, ran a single lane flyover which took traffic from the city centre on to the main road out of town. I was told to jump on to the pillion of Tony's Royal Enfield and with a screech of tyres we accelerated off, surrounded by what felt like a hundred Angels. My fears mounted as we roared towards the flyover, gathered speed and then flipped across into the opposite lane to approach this narrow flyover from the wrong direction. I was terrified of any oncoming traffic, but pleased that we were travelling at such speed that at least my ordeal would be over in a matter of seconds – but each second felt like an hour! When we returned to the club, they sat me in the corner and let rip with a riotous party, although I could only look on, in something of a daze.

Among the responsibilities that David had given me was taking care of the clubhouse during the daytime and preparing it for the evening arrival of the gang members. The club was housed in the halls of the redundant St Basil's church in an old industrial quarter of the city and was plagued by a very unpleasant infestation of rats. I was on duty one Monday morning to welcome the city's vermin officer who turned out to be very different from anything I had expected. She was a rather wizened, rat-haired woman with pointed rodent-like features and a squeaky voice. She had long dirty fingernails and two protruding front teeth and had travelled all the way across town on the bus carrying two open-topped shopping bags full to the brim with rat poison. The rats had been appearing from a gap between two of our old buildings and she explained that she would insert poison into the gap using the twisted table spoon she had brought along for the purpose. Her difficulty soon became apparent however when the breadth of the spoon proved to be too wide for the gap between the buildings. She was despairing. 'I've never had this sort of problem before,' she complained as she walked off in sullen and sombre mood. The odd thing was, however, that despite having failed to dispense her poison, we never saw another rat on site! Had the rats followed her home to Hamelin, or had they simply downed tools in sympathy for the poor woman?

Whilst in the club, the members were very well behaved, each having their own locker for helmet and kit. If the juke box was kicked in precisely the right spot it would play 'Wild Thing' by the Troggs, and that without inserting a single coin. So the heavy throbbing rhythm of that song became our eternal accompaniment. David Collyer and his club attracted much attention in the *Birmingham Post* which one day headlined him as 'King of the Hell's Angels'. Little did the headline writer realise the calamitous mistake. The very next night we received a visit from an opposing Hell's Angels Chapter, demanding to know who had dared to call himself the king of the Angels. Before anyone got hurt David presented himself to their main man. Whether his dog-collar saved him or his hesitant explanation, we will never know, but we breathed again as the visiting gang withdrew. They did not leave, however, without signalling their superiority by indiscriminately discharging their weapons into the cubicles of our outdoor toilets. We thanked God on finding that no one had hidden in one of them during the terrifying intrusion. There was much talk that night about retaliation, but David managed to talk our members out of starting a gang war across the city.

It was odd, after the cocooned safety of student life, to experience again the exhilarating fear of gang conflict. I'd felt it years ago as a little cockney lad on the streets of East London, but these were huge, determined young men and tearaway young women, which turned the whole experience up to boiling point. And yet there were times, in their company, of serenity and calm camaraderie. It was strangely reminiscent of reading the biblical Psalms where one verse can indulge in lamentable hatred and blood-curdling violence and the next take us soaring to heaven. One day at the club would be spiked with vitriol and spite and the next, these same bikers, would be racing across the city carrying human organs and blood from hospital to hospital for the NHS transfusion service. Human beings are an enigmatic amalgam of hell and heaven. But what I was learning to appreciate among these bikers was that, when we probe deeply into someone's hell, we'll invariably find a human being longing to strive for heaven.

The swinging pendulum

Despite the volatile environment, I thoroughly enjoyed my time with the Angels and at the end of the summer returned to London regretting my need to revisit my cloistered and privileged life back at the university. It only took me a week or two, however, before I was at home once more with the academic vocabulary of which I had once been so in awe and enjoying the craziness of the student frivolity despite my inner insecurities. I was learning to belong somewhat awkwardly to two worlds, as different as they were one from the other. Today there are thousands of people in Britain who are distanced from their motherland and culture, no doubt creating in them similarly uncomfortable feelings of hybridity, only partly belonging to their new surroundings. But in 1966, I was still too young and insensitive to worry about others and too bound up in my own insecurities. But this nagging uncertainty about myself stayed with me and eventually surfaced in a most unpleasant and serious way.

By then my fiancée, Linda, had found a teaching post in London and so we saw one another more often. However, our relationship had been established in very different circumstances, well before King's had begun to challenge my understanding of myself so radically. Eventually I dared to share my uncertainty with her, but I handled it very badly. I suspect that I really did not know what was happening, but I did know that I needed to rethink myself and my relationships quite radically if I were to be honest with myself and her, rather than drift into a marriage founded on misunderstandings. I felt wretched because she had already made many sacrifices to keep our relationship on track and here was I trying unsuccessfully to explain that my side of the relationship was no longer working. Although I voiced my reluctance forthrightly, I was not yet mature or self-aware enough to be able to name my real reasons and offered instead a series of superficial and lame excuses. Eventually Linda decided to accept the inevitable, and in typically gracious manner, offered herself as a teacher in a poor part of Africa as I in turn went back to university, vowing never again to put another person through that sort of experience. I hadn't handled it at all well and had been quite selfish and brutal about the whole matter. I've lived with the shameful memory of the manner of that breakup ever since.

I had now exchanged life at my parents' house for a room at the ordinands' hostel in Vincent Square in central London. It was an arcadian hall in a leafy square surrounded by gorgeous trees and ornate cast iron railings. Scandinavian maids cleaned our rooms each day and we ate our meals in the oak-panelled refectory where Dean Sydney would preside at top table with his guests whilst students enjoyed wild table-talk and banter. No one had prepared me for anything like this, but self-indulgence is very alluring so I took to it like a duck to water. I enjoyed playing guitar in the student bar at the Chesham Club, drinking pint after pint into the early hours at the rowing club, always leading the singing and the crazy student games, and being the life and soul of every party. And yet, all the time it was slowly dawning upon me that, whilst I enjoyed the company of all these lovely friends, what energised me most of all was not the boisterous parties, but my more solitary moments of quiet thoughtfulness. It was here that I was most at home, seeking to be creative of mind, drilling down to the inner dynamics of being a human being, and especially of being human in the presence of the Ground of our Being. So whilst others, then and even now, see me as a typical extravert, in fact I score heavily in every analytic test as high on introversion. They fail to see where my real energy is coming from because, as I tell them, I like to keep my introversion to myself! I was admired by many for the performance I offered to the world, but inwardly I was still convinced that I could never be loved for who I really was, as the recent failure of my relationship seemed to confirm.

It was about this time that my folk-singing buddy Dave Ward came down from Birmingham to join me for a great adventure. We had submitted four of our own songs for a Christian Aid competition, words courtesy of David Collyer, and were delighted to be invited to sing one of them in Trafalgar Square to the assembled thousands. We produced all four songs as a vinyl record which sold well with all proceeds going to Christian Aid, and the Trafalgar Square day itself was an unforgettably glorious experience. I played guitar and sang harmonies while Dave sang the melody as usual so that together we succeeded in wowing the vast audience.

Dave & Laurie
with the crowds
at
Trafalgar Square

The smiling crowds were enjoying the sunshine, the pigeons were flying around us like doves of peace as Dave and I sang out: 'When you looked in the street just lately, did you really see people there? Or was it some half-human shadow for whom there was no need to care?' We could sing those same lyrics today and they'd still be challenging.

We sang too at the college freshers' concert which welcomed newly arrived first year students to King's during their orientation week. For that we were joined by our old buddy Roy Marshall. Roy was an accomplished gymnast and artist who was now teaching in London. When Dave had to return to his work in the Midlands, Roy and I would add to our meagre incomes by taking the cabaret spot at many of the lavish balls staged by the university's colleges across London. We became quite well-known on the circuit and on one such occasion joined another cabaret artist, Cardew Robinson, who was then very famous, but nowadays no one remembers him – and I hope no one remembers us either.

Although we were overloaded with essays every term, not one of them would count towards the degree qualification itself. Once the Greek and Hebrew exams were passed, it all depended on the dreaded 'finals' – four intensive weeks loaded back-to-back with examinations, staged at the main University Hall. For that purpose it had been necessary to select additional special subject areas in which we were to be examined. I, for all the reasons I've explained, plumped for a special in the Philosophy of Religion, a decision which had been reinforced at the end of my first year by being put forward for the Shelford Prize for Philosophy and being made a member of the Royal Institute of Philosophy by Professor Lewis. For the Shelford Prize, candidates had to appear before a formidable panel of philosophers for a grilling. The professors sat behind a large forbidding table in an oak-panelled room, which gave the impression of having been specially designed to intimidate interviewees. They pummelled me with questions including, I remember, one about the nature of what is called salvation history. I argued off the top of my head as usual, that history is as fluid as the time and space in which it is set and therefore probably not as linear as to allow for biblical salvation history as we've understood it. An examiner lent aggressively across the table and asked if I realised that the notions I'd just postulated were verging on heresy. I responded nonchalantly that I did not see why that should bother her since heresy certainly didn't bother me, at which point they ushered me quickly and quietly from the room. I could not believe it when they wrote to tell me I'd been awarded the Shelford Prize, in spite of my nonsense.

My special studies in philosophy allowed me to tangle with the revolutionary British empiricists like Berkeley, Hume and Locke, and with Professor Lewis we engaged the topic of the philosophy of mind. But all the time I was intent on seeing how all this could bear upon my deeply held socialist convictions that had stayed with me from my earliest days. Those convictions had been framed within Marx's belief in the foundational influence of economy, but I was now convinced that he had failed to understand human nature. Marx had assumed his astute analysis of capital and economy would enable the creation of equality in society. However, it was now obvious to me that the wealthy could just as easily use that deification of capital to let the market rule the roost and send the poor to the wall. As Amartia Sen, the Indian economist and philosopher is fond of saying: 'the market has a mind of its own but does not have a heart.' If the Marxists were right to say that the task of the human being is to bring justice and integrity to society, then that depended fundamentally upon the ability of the heart and the soul to manage the power of the economy – and the human heart was the very area which theology was giving me the opportunity to study.

In addition to majoring in philosophy of religion, King's also allowed me as an honours student to add in special studies of Hinduism and Islam, faiths which seemed to me to be of signal importance if we were to gain an understanding of where our global village of a world was heading. Wave after wave of global migration meant that Britain was not losing an empire so much as watching it move in next door. Therefore, to study the faiths of those incoming cultures seemed a helpful way into understanding our complex and questionable colonial history and better prepare myself for a life and ministry in a fast-changing religious world.

In addition to my degree studies those preparing for ordination took additional classes in pastoral counselling, liturgy, spirituality and even voice production – a necessity before the introduction of amplification into churches. To teach us to project our voices to the back of any church, we were placed into the practised hands of Miss Audrey Bullard, a consultant at the Royal Academy of Dramatic Arts. She was a woman of middle years and of ample dimensions with a personality and presence to match. She asked us all to prepare a particular Shakespearean soliloquy by writing 'ROT' in the side margin, which she then mischievously explained stood for 'Ribs Out Throughout!' She taught us how to mark the text in particular ways so as to bring out its full meaning as we read it aloud, and that helped me no end with my public reading. She pointed out the importance of using our diaphragm to good effect and on one occasion pounced upon a rather feeble-looking student and demanded that he place his hand upon her ample diaphragm while she demonstrated her wondrous breathing technique. 'Now tell me sir, what can you feel?' To which he was heard timidly to whisper, 'Corsets Ma'am?' The result of Miss Bullard's fun-laden, but very professional training was that each of us could thereafter be clearly heard in any church setting with the added bonus of a clear advantage when cheering on our faculty sports teams. She also taught me a salutary lesson about the use of the voice when she remarked, 'Gentlemen,' (alas ordinands were then all male) 'those attending a funeral will never remember what you said, but they will forever remember how you said it.'

My own family had experienced a funeral to remember only shortly before. My dad's mother, Nanny Green, continued in her cockney eccentricity to her dying day. Even on the last day of her life when she looked so pale and wan, she suddenly sat upright in her bed and demanded a bowl of eels. My mum sent her friend off with an enamel bowl to the shop for the steaming eels which Nan ate with relish. She then looked around the room, said 'that really hit the spot!', laid back down and died with a beaming smile spread across her face.

Into her coffin she'd determined that we'd place a very large crucifix she'd set aside for the occasion, suddenly claiming to be a committed Roman Catholic even though none of us recall her ever going anywhere near a church in her life. There was also some dispute about the name in which to register the death since we discovered that there was no record that any 'Ruby' had ever existed. Nanny Green kept us guessing to the last.

A friend for life

I have a very personal reason to be eternally grateful to Dean Sydney Evans for being allowed to study Hebrew in my second year at King's. This was despite the fact that whilst already hanging on grimly to Greek, this new linguistic challenge was leaving me feeling very stretched and discouraged. One day I was sitting at a quiet corner table in the student refectory with David Flatman bemoaning our troubles and sipping tepid coffee, as late-adolescent students are wont to do. Suddenly our heads were turned on noticing a young female student who was arriving for lunch surrounded by a group of noisy friends. She had joined her companions in the queue at the refectory counter and was having no trouble convincing everyone she met to drop a donation into the Oxfam box she was proffering. No one could resist her invitation, for in her bright lemon yellow dress she sparkled with such vivacity that she lit up the whole room – raven black hair and wide dark eyes set the place glowing. 'If only we had someone like that in our lives,' David remarked, 'we wouldn't be sitting here so depressed.' But life seemed to have turned against us, so we lowered our gaze and sunk back into our gloomy melancholy.

I was the only second year student in the Hebrew class amidst the brightest of the first-years, but I soon realised that amongst them was the girl we'd noticed in the refectory. And I spotted that she didn't have her own copy of the Hebrew grammar book we were using. Back in the East End we had always believed, as did Woody Allen, that Original Sin was buying anything at its retail price, so I leaned across and tried an opening line – 'I can show you where you could buy a copy of the Hebrew Grammar at a knock-down price.' Luckily Victoria turned out to be a farmer's daughter so perhaps that was why she was alive to the thought of saving a little cash. We hurried off to buy the book, decided we should meet again, and we've been meeting regularly ever since!

Our relationship was not, however, going to be without its challenges. Our backgrounds were as different one from another as anyone could imagine. I was immediately alarmed to discover that she was affectionately known as Tori, a name which grated on my political sensitivities. She obligingly explained, however, that many in her family called her Vicki and that she would be perfectly happy if I called her that. Later that year she invited me to visit her farming family on the South Downs, but there I felt completely at sea, intimidated by the wide open spaces and the rolling chalk hills. Vicki was naming all the wild flowers for me as we walked along the lanes, but I had to acknowledge that my own grasp of country matters went only as far as being able to distinguish between an oak tree and a telegraph pole. I keenly felt the need to learn the names of every tree, plant and beast, but Vicki told me that I should relax, let nature be itself and enjoy the scenery. However, it produced in me the fear that nature was beyond taming. It reminded me that the literary critic Walter Benjamin had drawn an intriguing parallel from the story of Adam who was invited by God to name all the animals. Benjamin then suggested that the problem with humanity however is that poor Adam could just not stop naming everything. For Adam is us, and we continue to have that desperate need to name and label, believing that that puts us in control and makes us dominant, even if it's only by 'capturing' everything around us on our smartphone cameras. And I was proving to be a good example of the old Adam, inwardly terrified that I could not name and control these wide open spaces where Vicki felt so much at home.

It wasn't plain sailing for Vicki either. When she first visited the East End with me I thought to introduce her to our local culinary speciality and so took her to my favourite eel and pie shop. I suggested she try the pie and mash and even asked for extra 'liquor' which I was sure would impress. Unfortunately the rest of the day did not go well, for although Vicki graciously managed to eat much of it, she felt nauseous all the afternoon. As the months went by we discovered that, despite the evident cultural clash, our interests and concerns were very compatible. The differences were not pulling us apart, but broadening our horizons and introducing us both to new wonders. We entered into student life together with new vigour and enthusiasm, learning from one another all the time, and I came to realise that with a person like Vicki in my life, I was clearly on to a winner, and all my friends agreed!

As I now look back on my life, I realise that in that meeting with Vicki I had become one of the lucky ones. For I was able now, perhaps for the first time, to love for the sake of the other and not simply for my own happiness. The old word 'concupiscence' has fallen out of fashion, and I think it's because it describes something we would prefer not to acknowledge, for it means to love someone for the benefit and pleasure it gives *us* – a perverse sort of self-love. But when there is true love, we find ourselves loving not primarily for our own pleasure, but because we feel wrapped in adoration of the other – we adore them for *their* pleasure and well-being. We speak of 'falling' in love, which rightly captures this experience of being overtaken by something not of our own making and being engulfed by a mystery which transcends us. It's an experience which can be a most delightful way to be drawn by God that little bit further into God's overwhelming love. And in falling for Vicki I was truly one of the very lucky ones, even though as the old song has it, 'love hurts'. For love, ultimately, all comes from God and God is all about giving self away, and that doesn't come easy.

Vicki and I were fortunate to meet just as our Bohemian student world was becoming newly influenced by the delights of Asian food and culture. Curry houses were just beginning to appear everywhere, always known as Indian restaurants, even though most were run by Bangladeshis. King's stood opposite India House so by creeping down the steps into the basement we happily found ourselves in their staff canteen where they were happy to serve us with the authentic flavours. The Asian culture was strongly promoted by the Beatles and others who were leading the British revolution in popular music and design. Vicki began making the most flamboyant multi-coloured 1960s dresses in the purples, pinks and yellows of psychedelia, a style which was flourishing in the London fashion outlets around Carnaby Street. She would always keep some material over so that I could sport a wide 'kipper' tie of the same glorious pattern as her dress and my lengthening hair, moustache and sandals were matched by her mini-skirts, large bright earrings and beads. As the new hippie music and fashion burgeoned, we even managed to obtain two much sought-after tickets to attend the all-night, mind-bending hippie festival housed in the vast Great Hall of Alexandra Palace. It turned out to be the defining event at the zenith of the hippie period and was aptly titled 'The 14 Hour Technicolour Dream', and if you weren't there you definitely were not 'in the zone'. John Lennon, Andy Warhol and a host of others mingled with the thronging crowds whilst the smell of sandalwood joss-sticks hung over the milling dancers and stoned-out poseurs who were all extravagantly dressed in the most wondrously creative garb. The striking costumes, the profusion of flowers and the atmosphere of love and generosity which pervaded the gathering will never be forgotten by those of us who were conscious enough to register that wondrous, 'out of sight' experience.

During term-time our regime at Vincent Square hostel was rigorous. Up early each morning and into chapel. There we soon developed what I liked to call the 'latrine crouch' which gave the impression of fervent prayer but in fact was a way of sleeping off the night before without the Dean realising that we were not locked in deep meditation. After half an hour of silence together the Dean would then disappear into the vestry and reappear to glide up the aisle to the altar, immaculately robed. He was the most meticulously dressed and disciplined man you could imagine, so much so that we joked that on some mornings he must gaze up at the altar muttering, 'God, you're late.' In reality, he cared very deeply for us all, despite the fact that he floated many feet above us. His humour was fittingly droll. On one occasion one of our colleagues arrived home after the lock had been turned on the front door and dared to use the only other way in, which was through the Dean's study window. He had clambered through into the Dean's rooms and was creeping silently across the study when he heard the Dean enter through his private door. The student darted behind the long curtains, remaining there as motionless as he could manage in his inebriated state while the Dean took a book from the shelf, snuggled down into his favourite armchair, and began to read. After at least an hour, he closed his book and casually remarked, 'Well, I'm going to bed now. I don't know about you,' and left the room.

With Ken Dodd
in King's
College
Ideal Idiot
competition

Vicki and I took on extra student responsibilities during my final year, Vicki in her Russell Square hall of residence and me for the Faculty of Theology. It therefore fell to me to organise our grand summer ball which had in the past always employed a few rather staid musicians to play waltzes, quicksteps and the Gay Gordons. But I knew I could do better than that! I brought in an East London thirty-piece orchestra with MC – and my goodness, could they play! I felt particularly proud of the superb musicianship, but towards the end of the evening when the MC called us all on to the dance floor for our final dance, I overheard one of the lecturers nearby aping the MC's accent and remarking, 'Where on earth does that MC come from – the local fruit market?' The jibe brought me up sharp, for although I had spent three years at King's delighting in the life, at heart there remained a distance between its culture and where I felt most at home. How on earth was I to gain the self-confidence to find myself, and be myself?

The issue raised its head in another way too. Whilst having a lovely day by the Thames for our college rowing regatta, the Dean invited me to stroll along the tow-path with him for what he referred to as, 'a little chat'. He had noticed that I had been 'walking out with young Victoria', and was therefore interested to know if that amounted to anything serious for me. On hearing that it did, he gently suggested that this relationship might be more challenging for both of us than would be helpful, for she came from land-owning farming stock whilst I hailed from the inner-city working classes. He meant well I'm sure, but this was in the days when his permission was required if ever we were to marry, so I played my cards close to my chest lest he scupper my chance of making what was likely to be the best decision of my life. I tried to shrug off his negative comments, but they once again brought to the surface my abiding anxiety. Perhaps it was true that I was just an imposter at college and others were seeing through my fabricated strategies to hide the truth from them and from myself. When I told her of the conversation with the Dean, Vicki was furious.

As the month of the final examinations drew close all students went into lock-down, apart from the privileged few with brains like planets who could sail through without losing a wink of relaxed sleep. The make or break examinations dragged on for weeks, each of us becoming more exhausted by the day so that when my last exam eventually arrived I felt like a wet rag. I decided that drastic action was required so I rose early that morning, bathed in luxuriously hot water, donned the suit I'd forgotten I had, bought a white carnation for my button hole, rolled my umbrella like a city gent and walked snappily to the examination hall as if I were a new creation. It was a ploy which bolstered my energy very well until the final whistle when I eventually put down my pen and slumped down like a drowned rat. I was so, so exhausted that to this day I don't know why, but I went in a trance to watch a game of cricket – a sport about which I still know little to nothing. It was bliss.

Lingering questions

During my long self-imposed confinement for revision, my task had been simply to get the stuff learnt. But now I was free to contemplate some of the nagging problems that had been piling up in the margins of my mind during all those years of study. I had in particular two lingering questions about the Hebrew Scriptures. The first was how to understand the many times that our present knowledge contradicts the biblical text. In the book of Joshua for example it says that Joshua captured the whole land of Palestine including all the major cities, but archaeologists have shown that that is far from possible and that the book of Judges probably offers a much more accurate description of a partial infiltration of the Israelites into Canaan with Jerusalem for example only being taken generations later in the time of the warlord King David. And similar and sometimes glaring discrepancies occur throughout the Hebrew

Scriptures, some stories historically accurate and others obvious fabrications. So what's going on?

The other problem I still had with the text was perhaps more impenetrable. It was exemplified in Deuteronomy 19: 21: 'Show no pity: life for life, eye for eye, tooth for tooth,'- it was the whole question of retributive justice, made even worse by the biblical picture of God himself as the dispenser of merciless violence. The biblical book of Numbers, chapters 16 & 17, record two hundred and fifty community leaders coming to Moses in the desert asking him to stop acting so dictatorially. Now, even supposing that he was right and his autocratic leadership was acceptable, what God did next, according to this story, is quite repugnant. He made the earth swallow up those who dared to voice their concern and even included the children they had with them, before setting fire to the leaders themselves. It was only the quick thinking of Moses and Aaron that then saved a further fourteen thousand, seven hundred from God's wrath. These Hebrew Scriptures certainly did not portray the God I believed in, nor it seemed to me the God Jesus believed in, despite his unquestionable Jewish origins. No wonder my dad, all those years before, had given up on the Bible after only a few chapters.

I was also concerned to read that when the Jewish exiles returned from Babylon to Jerusalem an intense racism became a central feature of their faith. Ezra, their priest, had exclaimed that marriages to foreign women had taken place, 'as a result of which the holy race has been contaminated.' It's not as if his only concern was to keep the religion pure, but he's referring to the purity of the Jewish bloodline. He tears his hair out and spews out a stream of racist abuse accusing not just some but all the local non-Hebrew people of vile practices, which he maintained had polluted the land and 'filled it with their filth from end to end' (Ezra 9: 2 & 11). It all makes for a very disturbing read.

And yet, despite all this, so much wisdom and penetrating insight was to be found within the pages of these scriptures that

I willingly committed myself to working these problems through. During my three years of intensive study of the Hebrew Scriptures, it was becoming clear that what is still sometimes called the Old Testament is a complex collection of texts originating from different contexts and periods across hundreds and hundreds of years – and not necessarily appearing in chronological order   What we then begin to discern is that the situation and culture in which each of those generations found themselves was a formative influence upon how they experienced the presence of God and how they then expressed it. Some of the earliest biblical passages and texts, for example, clearly derive from very extreme desert conditions, where cruel warlords and primitive tribal cultures were the daily experience of the people. Other sections portray the influence of high culture, philosophical trends and bejewelled palaces. And if we do not seek to interpret each text from an appreciation of its own context, and instead constantly superimpose upon the texts ideas, ethical principles and prejudices which derive from our own culture, then we will totally misunderstand the passage, and what it has to teach us. Sometimes our scholarly analysis of those ancient cultures and languages will allow us to see beyond their sometimes crude descriptions and it's then that we discern the nature of the actual experience of God which overwhelmed them so. We also begin to build up a picture of how one generation was sometimes able to learn from an earlier generation, helping them more adequately to interpret and describe their own experiences of the divine presence. Sometimes and often, those ancient people found it possible to experience and express greater truths than we are able to do. But to discern those truths we have to hack our way through their cultural baggage and our own, for they so often obscure the depth of that early wisdom from us. It's then that we realise that we will see further with their help than we could if left to our own devices.

But it's not only an understanding of the originating contexts that helps us in this endeavour, because Jesus himself is often recorded as looking back over that early Hebrew history and those early stories, and re-interpreting them. He sometimes set them aside, but more often than not, saw the truth within and brought that to the surface for us in a new way. He even made clear that that developmental journey of understanding would continue, by promising us that in future, 'the Spirit will guide you into all truth' (John 16:13), for God always has more to teach us – and we are such slow learners. And at King's, I realised that I for one still had a very long way to go if I were to glean even a little of the marvel and majesty of those Hebrew Scriptures.

It was Vicki who was instrumental in teaching me my next lesson whilst at King's when she suggested we both enrol as volunteers with the WRVS so that we could spend time away caring for young people who were seriously disabled. It was there that I met Peter, a young man who no longer had speech or the ability to do anything for himself, but who was nonetheless enjoying being away with us for a week's holiday. We were spending a day out by the sea when Peter was suddenly caught short, so I wheeled him into the nearby toilet and spent some time cleaning him up. Afterwards, he indicated that he wanted to spell out a message to me on his letter-board. His message was one of thanks for the intimate service I'd rendered him and it almost broke my heart, for he could never know how much I now owed him for teaching me a lifetime's lesson. For whilst King's taught us to talk the Jesus talk, and to do that very eloquently, there was nothing in the syllabus that taught us how to walk the walk. I was always quoting Marx's incisive observation in his thesis on Feuerbach, that 'Philosophers have hitherto only interpreted the world in various ways; the point is to change it!' but now it was being actively brought home to me that abstracted words of faith take us only so far, even when firmly believed. But Peter taught me that it's practical, engaged acts of love that take us more firmly to the heart of God. Vicki was forcefully reminding me that my studies were of nothing worth if they lacked that essential ingredient of loving service.

Little did I know then that the experience that would be formative in helping me find a way through all my muddled thinking was even then being conjured for me once again by Dean Sydney Evans. I had been impressed in a philosophy seminar by the presence of some visiting American post-graduates. They were forever relating the academic subject matter to the realities of life around us, their culture perhaps valuing the practical to a greater extent than we then did in Britain. So when Sydney once again ushered me into his study with a clear agenda in view, I was delighted to learn that he wanted to put my name forward for a scholarship to study theology in the United States for a year. What was on offer was a year studying Christian urban activism, group dynamics and pastoral counselling, all at Master's level and this I felt sure would give me the opportunity to couple the academic theology I'd been doing thus far with hands-on practical engagement. The alternative was for me to leave London for a final year of training at the college in Warminster whilst Vicki completed her degree studies at King's. We thought hard and long, eventually deciding to take up the Dean's offer. We were both equally pleased when I won the scholarship, even though, in order to get to New York in time I'd have to leave the UK before the great ceremonial gathering to receive our degree certificates from the hands of royalty. I had never been much enamoured of inherited monarchy in any case, so the decision was made, and I prepared to pack for my transatlantic adventure.

*   *   *

CHAPTER 5

AN ENGLISHMAN IN NEW YORK

It was in 1968, the year of student revolution across the western world, that I packed a hefty trunk, and sending that ahead, left England for New York City with 'suitcase and guitar in hand.' I'd never flown before – few had in those days – and the cheapest ticket took me on a very circuitous route. I flew first to Luxembourg where I presented my ticket for a Loftleidir flight to Iceland to take a connecting flight to New York. The young man at the check-in desk explained that although the ticket was valid, there was no aeroplane to go with it! So much for cheap tickets, I thought. He did, however, book me into the poshest hotel I'd ever occupied – mind you, that wasn't difficult since I'd never stayed in a hotel in my life. The next day I was in a slow, propeller-driven boneshaker which after some hours of cramped travel, skidded to a halt on an icy runway in Iceland. I had hoped to see something of that intriguing land, but after half an hour of being crowded into a small airport hut, we were all ushered back on to the now refuelled aircraft ready to take off again, this time bound for the eastern seaboard of the United States.

Good Morning America

New York's airport was named after the late president John F Kennedy who had won acclaim for averting a nuclear war with the Soviet Union by adopting a pugnacious refusal to allow their missiles to reach their base in Cuba. It's now known that peace was actually achieved by his acceding to Soviet demands for the removal of American bases in Eastern Europe, but it was the 'true grit' myth that appealed to the US voters. And so that aggressive style became a major characteristic of American foreign policy thereafter. Such revelations should have taught us not to believe political hype but alas, we seem addicted to it. I'd arrived a day late, so after fumbling with the unfamiliar American coinage, I eventually mastered the public dial-phone to make contact with the appropriately named Mr Buck. He had graciously offered to look after me for my first weeks in this foreign land, but was not fazed by my late arrival. He told me how to find the taxi to his home town upstate, for which he would be more than happy to pay the very considerable fare when I arrived. Having located the taxi stand for White Plains I found the driver arguing with a woman passenger who was escorting her disabled husband. There appeared to be ample space for his wheelchair in the stretch-limo' taxi, but the irate driver still yelled out: 'Why don't you leave him at home? We can't go driving these people around!' It was my introduction to the fact that the USA is a land of extremes. On the one hand I'd just experienced generous help from Mr Buck, but now encountered this aggressive insensitivity.

After a tortuous ride through the screaming streets of New York City I was out into the countryside on the thruway. Eventually I was being heartily welcomed into Mr and Mrs Buck's sumptuous home where I was to spend these weeks of induction into the American way of life before going back down to Manhattan where my college was situated. The next morning they took me off to a local restaurant for a breakfast of ten pancakes in a stack swamped in maple syrup, a fried egg, 'sunny side up', crispy bacon 'on the side', with croissants and jam to follow. I was beginning already to realise why so many Americans looked grossly overweight. The afternoon was spent touring the beautiful countryside around that part of their state and we arrived home in time for a large supper and my first taste of authentic Bourbon whiskey. I slept like a log.

After those weeks of being thoroughly spoilt by the Bucks and their friends, it was time for me to board the commuter train back to Grand Central Station, that temple-like reminder of the importance of the railways to the expansion of the nation. I then found myself stepping out on to 42nd Street, right in the heart of midtown Manhattan. I had now truly arrived. The numbering of the streets made it easy for me to find my way from 42nd to East 49th Street and along to the pleasant brick and stone façade of New York Theological Seminary, situated close by the East River and the soaring white stone towers and sweeping lines of the United Nations Building.

New York Theological Seminary

Built there in 1902, the seminary still continued its earliest traditions of combining a scholarly approach to theological study with hands-on engagement with the poor of the inner city. It had recently suffered from a dearth of student numbers and had therefore attracted the attention of a group of very radical academics and pastors from Union Seminary, who saw in this ailing college an opportunity to rekindle its original vision and experiment theologically in ways denied them at Union, the city's more established institution. The group was led by George W Webber, known to his friends as Bill, whose fame had already been established as co-founder of the East Harlem Protestant Parish, made famous by many books and documentaries. Bill's great boast was that 'New York

Theological Seminary lives on the hyphen between the Word and the World.'

The seminary was to be my home for the year, but first I needed to establish myself in the small functional room to which I had been assigned. Unfortunately, all my belongings were in the trunk that I'd shipped ahead, but which was still standing in a warehouse somewhere down by the Hudson River on the Waterfront made infamous by the Marlon Brando movie. I was warned that the dock area was a rough place to visit, but I was in the hands of an experienced New York taxi driver who drove across town through the slow-moving, horn-thumping traffic, chatting about the issues of the day as only New York taxi drivers can. We passed the pistol-toting guard at the dock gate and found our way into a huge warehouse surrounded by hauliers clutching their paperwork. We pushed through the heaving mass towards a desk clerk, but just as I was about to hand over my papers, another driver picked a quarrel with a guard and suddenly the whole hall was in uproar. Punches were being thrown and blood spattering in every direction. Then, without any signal or accountable reason, the riot quelled, and all became quiet, the hauliers brushing themselves down and chatting amiably once more. In the scuffle my papers had been ripped in two, but the clerk, showing no sign of being fazed by what had just happened, roughly Sellotaped the two halves together, and went off to locate the trunk. It was returned to us without fuss, but my heart stopped thumping only when we'd driven back across town, manhandled the trunk up in the college elevator and pulled it into my room. While the taxi driver sat swigging from his hipflask, I lay back on the bed and let my breathing return to normal, and in my musing realised just how much I was going to enjoy my year living in such an exciting city.

American classroom etiquette took me by surprise. Here there was no longer any requirement to wear a stuffy academic gown and instead, students turned up in their long shorts and newly-popular T shirts, clutching their notepads and the mandatory can of fizzy drink bought from the refectory automat. I soon became exceedingly grateful for this very different, laid-back culture for I'd arrived during one of the most extreme heatwaves Manhattan had experienced for years. For my first essay I thought I'd play to my strengths by choosing the title, 'Freud's understanding of religion as illusion'. The professor was himself a Freudian analyst and so I proudly offered him my script only to have it summarily rejected on the grounds that it was handwritten, and all essays had to be presented in double spaced, typed format. The other students, like wise virgins, had all brought modern typewriters from home, but in accordance with English tradition I'd brought only my trusty fountain pen. I eventually discovered that the college had two electric machines installed in a very cold basement room. They were for student use so, although typing up my essays became a necessary chore, at least I no longer had to wrestle with making carbon-paper copies, because the college also had a Xerox® machine which miraculously photocopied each page electronically and produced a legible, although rather fuzzy, replica. Such electronic technology was still in its infancy, but my new colleagues were well ahead of the wave, one even boasting that he had in his kitchen at home a small electrical oven that by means of electrical microwaves was able to boil water in the wink of an eye. I was reluctant to believe him.

Perhaps the greatest surprise of all came when I went to my first class which was to be about alcohol abuse. I prepared myself to scribble away at my pad as the professor gave his lecture, but instead he walked very casually up and down the rows of students giving out lists of addresses where we might meet alcoholics in Manhattan. He then declared that before we approached any academic study of the subject, he required that we make the acquaintance of an alcoholic person who was prepared to have a lengthy conversation. After this meeting, we were to write a verbatim report of the encounter describing the environment in which it took place together with a critique of our own emotions and some preliminary theological reflections upon the whole experience. 'Thanks guys and gals! Get those back to me as soon as you can and I'll see you at our next session. Goodbye.' Late that evening I went somewhat fearfully to my first Alcoholics Anonymous meeting in the back room of a church. There I was immediately befriended by a well-suited man who was more than happy to be interviewed in accordance with the strict rules of anonymity which our professor had stipulated. T.M. invited me back to his small apartment, sat me down at the kitchen table and proceeded to prepare himself a drink, which he did by carefully measuring out a shot of vodka into his barman's measure and then pouring it into his favourite glass. Throughout the interview he would turn to his bottle, measure out his next shot, transfer that very carefully into his glass and drink it down. He told me his story and explained how bitterly he resented alcohol and how it had overturned the happiness and cohesion of his family. And yet he felt fate had given him 'this cup to drink' and that being an alcoholic was now his established identity.

The experience of being with T.M. and having to reflect so carefully upon that meeting transformed the way in which I engaged with study and learning from then on. Why on earth had most of my education thus far not seen the sense of this experiential approach, always assuming that theory came before practice? The supreme irony was that at King's I had meticulously studied the philosophy of empiricism, which maintained that all knowledge was primarily based on sense experience, but the whole course had been based only on theory! I had read too of Aristotle's conviction that it is important first to look at the world around us if we are to access what is true. I also remembered the wisdom I'd gleaned from Dr Günzburg at Monyhull Hospital, who had insisted that whilst many doctors concentrated all their attention upon what they knew about the illness, he believed we should attend first to the experience of the patient. And now in New York I was being taken a step further, learning to recognise that a person should always be assumed to be the *subject* of their own life and never reduced by another to being the *object* of someone else's theory, clinical observation – or interference!

I was beginning to realise that deep within myself I had yet to undergo what would be for me a Copernican revolution. Copernicus is credited with the discovery that the sun does not move around our earth, but we revolve around it, and I had lived my life thus far very much as if the world revolved around me and what I thought. This perception had been subtly reinforced by a British educational system which had front-loaded me with information and theories and then sent me out to confront the world, assuming this to be the best way for me to serve society. I now had to face the fact that an approach of that kind only served to produce an élite cohort of leaders largely programmed to maintain the status quo. I now had to see myself, not as the axis around which my experience turned – a Cartesian assumption deep in the heart of European culture – but myself as just one part of a great dynamic interplay of equal beings within an ecology of interdependence. And the only force-field that could account for this interdependent coherence was not humanity, nor any theory, but that relational energy, the relativity we call love. Only that can hold everything together in the dance of existence and being in which we participate – the dance of life. In my 'dance' with my new alcoholic friend, I had nothing to offer him in his addiction, but a listening ear. He in turn said that he had nothing to give me but his story, and yet, for a brief couple of hours, we had both learnt, and been loved. Even when all the concentration seemed to be upon repeatedly filling the vodka glass, the true meaning was there in the midst and yet beyond us. The sun around which we all revolve is the centre of gravity we call transcendent love, and I believe on that evening we had both experienced it.

I was now determined to jettison my old assumptions, and value experience just as much as theory, realising that this had been the unacknowledged implication of the philosophy I had been studying in Britain all along. And it was not only to my own experience that I needed now to attend, but as I'd learnt at that Alcoholics Anonymous meeting and should have remembered from my cockney days, it was just as important to have an attentive ear to the experience of others. Many of my fellow seminarians were black pastors from the city, all passionately involved in the Civil Rights movement. Through the years, they had personally experienced more than enough of the hateful violence and the insipid prejudice that had reduced their societal status. The prevailing white majority culture had manacled their gifts and talents, enslaving them to the humdrum of daily manual labour. But their true giftedness was to be seen in their inspired leadership of their congregations. They were quick to pick me up on any expression of racism on my part and helped me to admit and address it, and yet readily forgave me because, being an uninformed foreigner, they felt I did not fully appreciate their history and heritage. I learnt from them that within the black activist community there raged a defining struggle between those who favoured Martin Luther King's pacifist confrontational methods which he brought from the South, and that being adopted in the northern cities by the newly-established Black Panthers. Their co-founder Hughey Newton wrote that the Panthers had, 'learned from Malcolm that with the gun, they can recapture their dreams and bring them into reality.' Malcolm, of course, was Malcolm X, who had adopted the X to stand for his original tribal name, now lost in the shadows of his family's oppressed history. We had a lecture from one of his Panthers, but his robust introduction to their founding principles reminded me of Lenin's methods which had made me appreciate how easy it is for humankind to mistake power for virtue.

Meanwhile, on the streets of New York, the student rebellions were raging, as they were across Europe. In Paris, students sought to throw off the stultifying prejudices of their right-wing press and politicians with their slogan, 'All Power to the Imagination', which really caught the mood of the times. The 60s had become conscious of itself. The American students' protests, however, were more overtly concerned with the escalation of the Vietnam War in which so many of their generation were dying to no purpose. I felt that I had no right as a foreigner to engage directly in the street protests. Instead I took instruction from a Vietnam veteran on how to give first aid support to those who might be injured by the truncheons, water cannon and rifles being used to disperse their gatherings. Our first-aid group stood ready to be called upon, but for some unknown reason we were never summoned and so I never saw action.

Interlaced with practical engagement, each college course involved critical reflection and academic research, but I found prolonged concentration exceedingly difficult during that debilitating summer heatwave. I would sit in the college library next to the ancient air-conditioning unit which would clunk away, its noise only eclipsed by the constant high-pitched screaming of the city police sirens or the incessant hooting of car horns. In New York the law only allowed motorists to drive extremely slowly, but they were allowed to make as much noise as their horns could muster. My dad had given me a few driving lessons, but I still needed to take my test. New York law stipulated that everyone undertake eight hours of intensive classroom tuition and pass a written examination, even before getting behind a wheel. I sat in the large hall with all the other applicants and read the first question: 'What do you do when driving along the pavement and ...?' The next question asked me about tailgating, and so the exam paper continued on, demanding translation skills as well as driving knowledge. I'd already learnt that 'I'm mad about my flat' translated as 'I'm furious about my puncture'. So despite the challenges of the exam's language I managed to pass the exam and the driving test that followed and was delighted when on that basis, many of my new friends were happy to toss their car keys to me, without my even having to ask. I therefore had the wonderful experience of driving a variety of huge American automobiles, so wide and bulky that they handled more like catamarans than motor cars.

By now the college president, Bill Webber, had become a firm friend and was intent on my joining a radically new theological programme. Metropolitan Urban Service Training, the MUST programme, embedded groups of graduates into challenging city environments where they learnt to engage with community projects and reflect theologically on what they experienced. Participants were drawn from far and wide whilst Bill and his staff brought in some of the top names in the field who were keen to be involved as mentors and observers of this new educational experiment. Our particular team of eight was composed of sociologists, a pastor, research graduates from both Union and General seminaries, a specialist in urban studies and myself. By now I was well into my study of group dynamics which was to prove especially helpful when, prior to our group's urban engagement, we were required to undergo what was termed a 'marathon encounter'. This was to be a non-stop twenty-four hour session during which we were locked together in one room accompanied only by a group dynamics expert whose task it was regularly to share with us his challenging reading of the power dynamics at play within the group. We all began in the usual pleasant manner, introducing ourselves around the group, but within the first twelve hours we were down to the bone, delving into our differing likes, dislikes, foibles, prejudices, sexualities, ethnicities and spiritualities – there were no holds barred. After another twelve hours of a roller coaster of tears, laughter, anger and bliss, we emerged thoroughly drained and exhausted, but as tightly knit and bonded a group of friends you could ever hope to meet. This enabled us to work and write together in the most creative ways. To describe this sort of relationship, the New Testament utilises the word *koinonia* which is usually translated as 'fellowship'. But the amazing power of this particular experience of team discipleship leads me to suspect that it would be better translated, 'solidarity'.

Each member of our MUST group was then inserted into an inner-city project. Mine was in East Harlem, working alongside a Puerto Rican gang calling itself the Real Great Society. All around their section of the Latino ghetto were posted enormous signs declaring that this district belonged to the RGS, warning other gangs to keep their distance. I was taken down to the gang's HQ by their 'gofer', a bulky and exuberant character, the fingers of whose right hand appeared to have been forcibly removed. He manifested such a personal presence that in his company you felt extremely safe, as long as you were on his side. I followed him up the steps of an old tenement block to the fifth floor and into a sparsely furnished room where he introduced me to Papa, the diminutive figure who sat behind a large desk surrounded by his attendants. Although he was small of stature, his slow and deliberate questioning made it clear that he was the Big Man and it was entirely in his gift to accept me or reject me from the gang's domain. His lilting Latino accent had a reassuring quality as he explained that some years ago their gang had been, like so many others, rampaging across the district, terrorising anyone standing in its way. But Papa had suddenly come to the conclusion that rather than fighting for no cause but to gain kudos, they could use their muscle to more creative ends. They cashed in all their ill-gotten gains and went along to a property auction where a number of the local walk-up tenement buildings were for sale. Papa had placed his men strategically around the room with instruction surreptitiously to intimidate any opposing bidders, thereby obtaining the lot for a ridiculously low price. The apartments were in a deplorable condition, so they persuaded a team of architects and builders to renovate the first floor with the help of local youngsters.

These trainees were then given the task of renovating apartments themselves, training others as they went. And so it snowballed to become the vast enterprise it now was. By the time I met them, they were a highly sophisticated outfit, although their methods of enforcement continued to be significantly less subtle. The police kept a respectful distance, grateful to see peace in such a challenging neighbourhood. Meanwhile, local families were lining up to take residency of the smart apartments, only too pleased to have their sons learning a trade and to see the district now a secure place to live, thanks to the presence of the Real Great Society.

Some of my
East Side friends

My month with the RGS made me appreciate that leadership did not always reside where those looking in from outside might expect to find it. The Real Great Society had worked from the bottom up, refusing to accept the dictates of outsiders, and had thus gained the respect of the neighbourhood, and by these means made their district a good place to live. Yet all this had to be weighed against the unconventional methods and hair-raising ethical code of those who had made it succeed. Could it ever be right to use questionable means to secure an end, even if the results were so astoundingly positive? It reminded me of Ezra and Nehemiah, those who had led the Jews to re-establish Jerusalem and the Temple after their long exile in Babylon. As I've already mentioned, they had racially brutalised the local people, but in the process achieved the wonderful result of rebuilding their own community. The Hebrew Scriptures even applaud them as heroes, and I felt the same way about the Real Great Society. The perplexing issue is whether the ends justify the means. It was a dilemma I would face many times in the future.

Our group reflections on these placements were overseen by our professor of Church and Society, Nile Harper. He constantly drew our attention to how the church majors on offering charity handouts rather than demanding the justice that would save people needing our charity in the first place. Perhaps, I thought, we prefer it this way because it allows those who give to feel pious, whereas to right the causes of injustice often requires us to give our power away to those who have been unjustly treated. Nile would ask his students, 'tell me who is really benefiting from the situations you are visiting?' and would then reframe the question by thumping the table shouting, 'Power! Power! Who's got the power?' When four friends take a paralysed man on his stretcher to Jesus, they go out of their way to lay him before Jesus for healing (Luke 5:17f), but it is noticeable that Jesus then tells the healed man that he himself must pick up his stretcher and carry it away. Jesus thus underscores that this healing has not simply been the removal of his physical paralysis, but the gift of freedom from dependency – no longer dependent upon the friends who helped him in the past, nor even dependent upon Jesus who had cured him. Jesus allowed everyone else to benefit – the paralysed man, the four who'd brought him and those of us who learn even now from this example of giving power away to the disempowered.

Nile Harper also taught us to guard against intruding into another's situation without taking their culture fully into account, and certainly never to criticise, nor seek to act upon a culture until we had more fully understood it. This was a formidable self-discipline, for it is rare that we even understand our own culture let alone that of others. It is often said, whoever first discovered water, it certainly was not a fish! I was in the middle of reading one of the course's set texts, *Christ and Culture* by Richard Niebuhr, when I was invited to attend a small party which was being given for Frank Oppenheimer, one of the famous Oppenheimer brothers of nuclear bomb Manhattan Project fame. He'd just returned from London, so drew me aside to chat, and in our brief but penetrating conversation he asked me what I thought I had learnt so far from my experience of American culture. I could only reply that being in the States was teaching me more about the British culture which had formed me than I would ever learn about America. I held my breath as he looked at the floor thoughtfully, but then he replied, 'yes, I guess that's all we can really hope for. But to understand our own culture would be a fine thing.' If we could understand our own culture it might help us see why we believe as we do, and why we are what we are.

A great deal of the 1960s American culture has now been incorporated into our British way of life, but it was all so foreign to me then, including their delight in reducing titles to acronyms. The seminary itself was always referred to as NYTS, my urban theology course as the MUST programme, and out in the city the Real Great Society was the RGS. Corporate America was leading the way with acronyms and soon the western world as a whole would follow suit. I met it later when it was extensively used during the regeneration boom of the 1980s, when specialist consultants used cryptic acronyms as a way of disempowering the people of the poor housing projects who were not conversant with their meanings. They certainly knew how to put the 'con' into consultation. For me, hampered by dyslexia, any acronym proved a nightmare. But I had a chance to score one point at least when I was asked to help write the student review that year. I produced a sketch introducing the fictional Christian Responsibility And Participation programme, remarking that those in the know always referred to it by its initial letters!

One afternoon, a participant in our psychology class, an elderly cleric named Walter Chater, asked if I might like to travel upstate at weekends to establish some youth work in his parish. From then on, very early each Sunday morning, I would go to Grand Central Station, and take the commuter train north up to his wealthy suburban parish of Harrison. We'd soon established a youth programme of crazy games, fun parties, buzzing discussions and walks for charity, and each Sunday the willing youngsters would turn up with their families to the parish church for the morning worship. I shared folk songs and the eccentricities, as they saw it, of the English. They introduced me to the rudiments of American football, baseball and even took me on Youth Weekends up to the snow-laden mountains of Vermont where they taught me to ski. Willing parents drove us up into that stunningly beautiful State, saw us settled into our log cabins and then left us to it. Just a few did stay to join in the skiing which gave me the opportunity for long evening chats. There I learnt that many of these outwardly self-secure parents were, at a much deeper level, struggling to keep themselves and their relationships together, whilst seeking desperately to understand their own children.

In my conversations with them I mentioned that the philosopher Herbert Marcuse had only recently published his classic, *One Dimensional Man*. In this work he argued that our competitive society pumps us all with ever-present media hype and advertising, promising that human fulfilment can be found in the acquisition of celebrity or status or in the purchase of ever more commodities, as if ownership was the royal road to fulfilment. Incessant pressure of this sort makes us concentrate our lives on striving for position, career advancement, public acclaim at any price, and above all, earning sufficient to afford this promised illusionary fulfilment. And this, said Marcuse, is an idea of such power that it dulls all sense that there could be another and more fulfilling dimension to our one-dimensional lives. We can exhaust all our resources on chasing the proffered illusions, but we're then hard put to imagine something altogether other, let alone endeavour to attain it. And that's where these young well-heeled parents seemed to be trapped. They were caught on the treadmill of a false promise that their children were yet to be convinced by. Marcuse's book challenged its readers to seek after an alternative political culture. But his ideas also prompted thoughts in me of how some Christians can also find their spiritual vitality dulled by institutional religious expectations and miss out on the liberating quest for deeper spiritual awareness, engagement and fulfilment.

But I'd heard of an altogether different approach to life from someone who'd been working in Africa. He'd been sitting at this desk working when he realised that he'd been silently joined by an African friend who continued to say nothing, but sat at the other side of the room quietly observing. Only after some time did he stand and address him by name, saying, 'I see you John Taylor,' and left as silently as he had entered. John says that it was a beautiful, affirming experience which felt as if there had been a meeting of souls, almost as if they'd been praying together, and what's more, a sense of fulfilment of what it meant to be real with one another. This profound attentiveness to another is so far removed from a one-dimensional existence that puts us in avid competition with others. It was akin in some ways to my early childhood experience of standing at the window and realising the depth of a presence all around me at that precious moment – sensing 'the eternal now' as Paul Tillich has it. I'd experienced another aspect of this when listening attentively to my alcoholic friend's story or when Peter spelt out on his message board his thanks when I'd offered him a little personal help. It was the sort of experience which makes chasing after status or striving to own things seem so limp and facile. It was the experience of being deep within the fundamental of being.

Christmas time in New York

As the winter came on, I was asked to sing with my guitar at a Christmas concert at Grace Church on Broadway. The spotlight in which I had to stand was of such intensity that I could not see the audience at all. I was therefore intrigued to know why the concert director had commended me afterwards for appearing so wonderfully relaxed in view of the occasion. He explained that the church had been full of New York's political and business élite, accompanied by their lavishly attired wives. I had chosen to sing one of the songs Charles Parker had given me in Birmingham all those years before, which included verses that specifically criticised politicians and businessmen for being insensitive to the real message of the baby born in a stable. To this day I thank God for that blinding spotlight.

Just before Christmas, Vicki wrote to tell me that as a special twenty-first birthday treat, her father had bought her a return ticket to New York and that we could therefore experience together the wonders of Christmas in a New York bedecked in shimmering lights, dazzling displays and gently glittering snowflakes. I hastily made arrangements for our time together and was generously offered the use of a small student apartment next to the seminary, all stocked up with Christmas fare and even a small plastic Christmas tree. The snow-laden streets of New York City at Christmas must be seen to be believed, and there was truly magic in the air as we took the subway down to Greenwich Village to buy two beautifully hand-crafted wedding rings. It was a singular joy to have Vicki with me in the city I'd learnt to love and to take her round to see all the tourist sites and many of the hidden treasures too.

The Reverend Chater had kindly offered the use of their holiday log cabin set deep in the magical forests of upstate New York. There we would have to melt snow to provide our drinking water and bring in extra firewood from the barn, as if we were early American homesteaders. When we arrived, a note was pinned to the door inviting us to visit the family who lived in the nearby cottage. And so we spent a very pleasant evening with them around a great roaring fire where the man of the house took especial pride in showing us his collection of hunting rifles whilst his wife prepared tasty home-made cookies. After our return to England, Mr Chater sent us pages from the local newspaper describing how this same gentle, hospitable host had set fire to shops in the local town, and whilst the emergency services were busy attending to the blaze, had robbed the town bank, shooting two bank clerks and making off with thousands of dollars. We were stunned. First impressions can certainly prove very unreliable!

A fist full of dollars

I finished my year of study at the seminary with my master's degree tucked under my belt, armfuls of friends and many new insights. But before I left for home, I had the opportunity to see something of the rest of that extraordinary continent. I'd been earning well, singing in the city night clubs where I could turn up on spec, knowing I'd be offered a spot as soon as they heard my English accent. In those happy days you could not put a foot wrong if you were an Englishman in New York, especially if you packed a guitar. I'd also been paid well for running the youth club so I'd saved sufficient to pay part share in the costs of a road trip across America with my student friend Richard in his Volkswagen estate.

We shared the driving and made our way north to Niagara Falls and then breezed through the windy city of Chicago, later picking up a hippie couple who paid for the ride by threading bead bracelets for us both. As we passed over the Mississippi River, the girl talked Richard into baptising her there and then. We stopped at the roadside, and as the two of them waddled precariously out across the slimy mud towards the water, both in a state of nature, it dawned on me just what an eccentric minister of religion Richard was. We ate our way across Dakota, heading up to view Mount Rushmore where sixty-foot-high faces of American presidents had been chiselled out of the granite rock face. In Yellowstone National Park in Wyoming, we struck up a conversation with one of the Park rangers who warned us that as we were camping in the wild we would need to look out for the black bears. He explained that the best way to escape them was to scale a tree because bears over three years old were simply too heavy to climb. Our problem was that of all the bears we did meet, not one of them was gracious enough to tell us its age. We realised just how vast and menacing bears can be when we sensed one night that a bear was prowling around our little tent. Rather than dare to look out, we sat up trembling all night long, praying that it would not lean on the tent and squash us. When dawn broke, we ventured out to find he had instead squashed all our cooking pots flat and chomped all the greasy heads off our wooden cooking spoons.

We journeyed on to Old Faithful, the natural geyser which regularly shoots gallons of boiling water into the air from deep in the heart of the earth. Although the hot springs stank to high heaven of putrid eggs, they offered a chance to get really clean after the long weeks of grubby hippie existence on the road, so we spent time luxuriating in their warm sulphur-rich waters holding our noses. In Salt Lake City we were shown around the Temple precincts by a Mormon bishop who walked us through a display of waxworks which illustrated the astonishing story of their 1,300 mile trek across the desert in 1846 in search of a safe haven. This had given the American people a religion to call their own, based on their belief that the angel Moroni had equipped their founder Joseph Smith with a pair of special spectacles so he could miraculously translate some ancient tablets into American English before returning them to heaven. The bishop was really friendly and encouraged me to write some comments in his visitors' book. So after thinking carefully I wrote, 'it's all gloriously American,' which, I'm glad to say, the bishop accepted as praise indeed! We stayed in the city campsite, and soon found that most of the citizens were registered as Mormon, but actually had no interest in religion whatsoever, just as, back then, Brits at home when asked their religion, would answer, 'Church of England', although they would never have imagined themselves inside a church.

As we drove towards the very heart of the 'Flower-Power' counterculture of the hippie movement, the car radio began to

127

play, as if by magic, 'If you're going to San Francisco, be sure to wear some flowers in your hair.' We screeched to a halt, jumped out and picked some wayside blooms, and decorating ourselves appropriately, drove on into the Golden Gate city. We stayed a few days in a hippie commune, living mainly on beans, garlic bread and fascinating conversation. The cool charm of the old town and the bay were so alluring we could have stayed for months, but instead we hit the coast road south to find a hippie beach encampment by the Pacific Ocean. There we stayed, enjoying the laidback calm of our fellow travellers, the stunning beauty of the cliffs and the majestic ocean. Each evening the community sat together to share a marijuana joint as we all stared lovingly into one another's eyes and feasted on love and peace for all. In good Jesuit fashion I accepted this cultural rite, but perhaps I never inhaled enough for the drug to have any impact on me at all. After the smoking we'd all dance around the fire into the night to the beat of drums played by a Sioux family of musicians. They told me how the faith of their ancestors brought them a profound sense of the oneness of all creation and the interdependence of all people. I remember those moments and those Beautiful People with great affection.

'California Dreaming'

We continued down the stunning coast road, then through the toxic fumes of Los Angeles, and headed off across Arizona, where we soon grew accustomed to wall-to-wall country and western music on the radio. After enjoying the miracle that is the Grand Canyon we headed south into New Mexico, but on the road towards New Orleans, suddenly both back tyres blew out at the same time. The car started to spin round and round, slewing across the road into the face of the oncoming mega-trucks. My adrenalin raced, time itself seemed to slow to a snail's pace, and with each rotation of the car I fought to steer into the direction of travel to halt the spin, eventually pulling to a halt, safe on the highway's central reservation having only fractionally missed a concrete bollard and an oncoming truck before coming to a standstill. The undercarriage of the car however was now much the worse for wear and so we drove gingerly into Albuquerque and found a VW garage which took it in overnight, allowing us the use of an elderly VW Beetle whilst they effected necessary repairs. Richard, who was not at all at home with the Beetle's manual gear shift, gave the lever such a yank that it sheared off entirely, leaving the car jammed in second gear. In the morning we trundled slowly back through the city, the car by now belching voluminous oily smoke, and drove it on to the forecourt of the VW garage. To my surprise the mechanic showed no sign of dismay, and nonchalantly threw the gear lever on to a heap of scrap and handed Richard the keys to our car. The result of this unforeseen episode however was that the repair bill was such as to deplete our funds. Consequently, we were forced to forego New Orleans jazz and head straight home to New York, eating as cheaply as we could all the way. We were both disappointed that our tour had been cut short, but by then I was itching to get back to the UK and to be with Vicki once again.

Astronauts teach us that re-entry is a very difficult manoeuvre, and dropping back into the English way of life proved a mighty challenge for me too. I was saying goodbye to 'carrots in jello on the side' and 'hello' again to safe streets and warm beer, with only a matter of weeks in which to reorientate myself before the wedding. Vicki let me keep my hippie moustache for the ceremony, although the long hair had to go. We were married in St Hubert's tiny Saxon chapel which stood in the middle of the cornfield next to Vicki's family farmhouse. On our special day the surrounding corn shimmered in the golden sunshine, the weather being so fine that Vicki was able to dispense with the white wellies she'd bought just in case. She was arrayed in a gorgeous white dress that she'd made herself, and whilst villagers pumped away at the church organ, our family and friends raised the roof of the tiny chapel with their singing.

So we began our life together oblivious of all the adventures that lay ahead of us. A pony and trap took us to the station after the village-hall reception and then all the guests crowded on to the tiny platform to see us off on our journey up to London. Our honeymoon consisted of one night in a friendly hotel in Richmond upon Thames, and the next morning we made our way to Canterbury where my final year of training was now to take place at St Augustine's College. In AD 597, St Augustine had arrived in Kent from Rome and founded his abbey, and within its precincts the college now stood. The ancient gatehouse looked across to the awe-inspiring Canterbury Cathedral, the mother church of the worldwide Anglican Communion. A few doors along Monastery Street from the gatehouse was number 4, a tiny terraced cottage in which Vicki and I would spend our first married year together. Given such a romantic setting it stood to reason that I should do the traditional thing, so I took my new bride in my arms, and carried her over the threshold. It was one small step for us, one giant leap into the rest of our life together.

CHAPTER 6

GETTING LAUNCHED

When I'd left for the States we had expected that on return I would study at St Boniface College in Warminster. But whilst I was away the decision had been made that graduates from King's London would henceforth spend their final year in St Augustine's College, Canterbury, at the very heart of the Anglican Communion. Vicki had now graduated from King's and so enrolled on a secretarial course at the adjacent Christ Church College, so we were all set up for a final year of study before my ordination.

St Augustine's College

We students numbered just over fifty in that first cohort, and we were joined by a very small staff headed by the newly appointed warden, the Rev'd Dr Anthony Harvey, the eminent young New Testament scholar and classicist. Anthony, who was to become a very close friend in later years, appreciated the scholarly rigour of British theology. But he saw this year as our opportunity to apply that learning to the world in which our ordained life was to be lived out. Although his intentions were admirable, and his heart well-placed, he was hampered by a career which thus far had consisted of only academic research at Oxford University and a mere four years of ordained ministry as curate in a posh Chelsea parish. He came with deep personal experience of the upper echelons of British society, but his lack of exposure to other sectors put him at a great disadvantage in his relationships with many of his new students. British popular culture was moving fast, creating what seemed to me an unfathomable distance now between where most Brits were heading and where the

Church of England was determined to remain. I perceived Anthony to be caught in the middle, not knowing in which direction to take his college.

St Augustine's College Canterbury

To teach us about the realities of modern parish life, student groups were assigned to neighbouring parishes. An excellent idea in theory, it fell down badly in practice. For many of the parishes were singularly inappropriate, and obviously chosen in ignorance. On one such visit George, one of our student group, was taken aside one Sunday morning by a young lass who was terrified that she had been made pregnant by a married man. George thought it appropriate to take this concern in confidence to the vicar, seeking advice on how to handle the situation. The vicar, however, shied away from the matter altogether, advising him never to become involved in such worldly matters, and to tell the young woman concerned to take it to the Lord in prayer. Disgruntled students therefore set about setting up more worthwhile opportunities themselves. In my case, a local minister was establishing a new Samaritan group in Canterbury, and he asked me to sit in and help with his seminars in listening skills, alcoholism and drug addiction. Since these were some of the areas I'd been working on in the States, I felt I might have something to contribute. Anthony on hearing of this, ushered me into his study to tell me to desist, and concentrate on what the college was providing. The pity of it was that although we shared the same passion for relevant theology, we were steadily drawing apart. I felt Anthony had been set up to fail by a system which, having provided us with bountiful theory, expected him to create ways for us to apply it in practice. However, I was now sure that theory did not come before experience, but that experience and scholarship should go simultaneously hand in hand.

Whilst in the States, I'd been hearing about the work of the Brazilian philosopher and educationalist, Paulo Freire. He had been experimenting with processes where the educator was more of a facilitator than an imparter of pre-formed answers, deepening the students' awareness of what their experience meant, and introducing information and ideas to help the class refine that awareness. In such a class all were learners and all were teachers in a constant dialogue. But this dialogical education, as Freire had termed it, had in no way been evident at King's, nor now at St Augustine's. Here it was only 'contextual' learning insofar as it hoped to help us understand a parochial context in order to inject our previously banked corpus of theological concepts in more digestible ways for that parish context. Paulo Freire's classic, *The Pedagogy of the Oppressed* was yet to be published in Britain, and even when it was, our colleges found it problematic. After all, for centuries our understanding and practice of education had been founded on a 'top-down' model.

Despite the problems, Anthony sometimes came up trumps, inviting eminent authorities on law, classical music, medicine and the arts to talk to us and share their wisdom. Some of the college placements were also exceedingly helpful in preparing us for the challenges, not least the morning some spent at the local hospital mortuary. My fellow student Duncan and I were greeted at the door by a gravelly voice: 'don't be afraid lads, come on in!' The mortuary attendant had once hoped to become a doctor, but had been smitten by a brain tumour resulting in his now macabre appearance: the vivid sunken scar across the front of his head being still very evident. He was bent over a white porcelain slab, washing down the blood ready for the next incumbent, and turning on us, screwed up his piercing eyes and asked: 'have you seen death before?' He beckoned us towards a wall of cabinets and, with his hand on a handle, began a long, blood-curdling description of what the morticians had done to the body we were about to view. We just wanted him to get it over with and open the blasted cabinet! In the event it wasn't so bad, until that is, he advised that whenever we were with a family looking on a dead relative it was important for us not to let them touch the corpse. He then demonstrated why, taking hold of the top of the scalp and yanking it from side to side so that we'd see that it was not actually attached to the rest of the skull as it slithered around inside the skin. Duncan and I thanked him for the demonstration and hastily withdrew to the other side of the room. We were then standing next to a line of plastic dustbins from which he pulled off the lid and hauled out a lung. 'This looks fine and healthy doesn't it lads, but now look at this smoker's lung,' and lifted out a foul-smelling lump of black jelly which was dripping red slime. As we made our hasty retreat to the door, we thanked him for giving us such a vivid and enlightening introduction to what was left of his clients and holding hands we dashed down the corridor to the loos. It was indeed a fine example of 'experiential learning', ensuring that we were now well prepared to face anything a parish could throw at us.

Vicki and I were in process of bringing our two lives together and it was not long before we were joined by a little puppy. We named her Gypsy because the local charity had found her wandering the city streets. We had cause to be a little anxious when we heard the news that the Dean of King's was to pay Canterbury a visit, fearful that our puppy would bounce all over the immaculate Sydney. As we welcomed him into our tiny living-room with all due deference, Gypsy came bounding up. The Dean, dressed as ever in a freshly pressed black suit, sat himself down, extended his index finger towards the puppy, commanding her to sit. Much to our astonishment she sat there mesmerised throughout the half hour while Sydney ate his piece of cake, drank his cup of tea, and shared his news with us. The moment he left, Gypsy jumped up and became hysterically uncontrollable, even leaving little teeth marks in our treasured armchair where the Dean had been sitting. Sydney had directed us to visit a parish in the south to see if it felt suitable as a training parish. However, when we suggested that it felt a little too well-to-do for us, he offered an alternative possibility – a sprawling housing estate parish in the north of Birmingham, the city of which I'd already grown so fond. On visiting the parish of St Mark, Kingstanding, we immediately fell in love with the place, and especially with the vicarage family, who would become very important mentors for both of us during our first years in our new rôles.

Our remaining months of student life continued to be a dazzling mixture of eccentric freedom, creative conversation and wild fun. As summer came in we gathered together an energetic team, threw open our college gates, and invited the community in for a Medieval Fayre. Some students dressed as motley jugglers, others attempted to toss a straw bale over the bar, whilst refreshments, games, handicraft and glorious decorations made for a wonderful fun-filled day. I'm now glad that Jimmy Savile turned down my invitation to open the event, but crowds of shoppers and townspeople turned up nevertheless, asking when the sky diving and the Pope's appearance were scheduled. I then remembered that the two students I'd asked to advertise the event around town were outlandish pranksters. The absence of His Holiness took a lot of explaining.

Yet despite these welcome interludes, my overall frustrations with the course did not make me an easy student for Anthony to deal with. I consoled myself by spending hours in the college's grand library reading the works of the latest theologians and cultural critics, and trying to discover for myself how a truly contextual theology might be practised in Britain. This meant not just importing previously learnt theology into any situation, but finding God *within* it and letting theology crystallise from that discovery. It seemed to me that one of the things that the incarnation of Jesus taught us was that the Divine is so thoroughly embedded in the midst of our reality that if we in turn embed ourselves in our communities, we will find God there within them. It was not, to quote Browning, that 'God's in his heaven, all's right with the world!', but things are *not* right with the world, but thank God that he's right here, in it with us. The way to learn about God would therefore be to seek God's presence in the midst of any needy community– and that demanded a theological method appropriate to the task. But what that was precisely, I could not yet fathom.

I confess that I was much more interested in this quest than in what was on offer from the college, and so I threw together my required essays at the last minute and complained about what I deemed to be the irrelevant forms of chapel worship. Just a few weeks before we were all due to be ordained Anthony Harvey asked me to see him in his study. By this time I had established an odd relationship with him. He was mostly very amiable and supportive, but at other times he quite took against my radical, argumentative ways. He explained that even after my five years of training and preparation, he now felt unable to sign the legal paper allowing my ordination. Vicki and I wondered what on earth we could do now. Within the week Dean Sydney Evans appeared at the college once again, and asked me in a very gentle and avuncular way, what I thought had caused the stand-off with Anthony. I stumbled through all that Vicki and I had concluded might be the nub of the problem. Was it that I had returned from the States and found re-entry into the ways of the established Church of England just too much to manage? I had not proved an easy student, that was for sure, and I had made my disappointment with the course very clear to Anthony. I admitted that whilst obediently jumping through the college hoops I had preferred to give myself to my own reading, thinking and local engagement. He listened attentively, and after a long silent pause, explained that he would talk this through with Anthony and felt sure that with care we would all find a way through the impasse. A few days later I received a letter saying, without further explanation, that the document had been signed, and that I should proceed as planned. With a sigh of relief, we loaded Gypsy and our few household possessions into our old banger of a car, thankfully bade our farewells to St Augustine's College, and struck north for Birmingham.

To be a Deacon

We arrived in the parish of St Mark, Kingstanding, to receive the warmest of welcomes from Father Geoffrey Harper, his wife Julie and their three little children. Geoffrey was a small Cornishman who was always accompanied by a lighted cigarette and an aura of attentiveness. He'd had the rooms of our new home fumigated for our arrival because, he explained, the previous owner had kept his racing pigeons indoors! Vicki and I set about making the place our own and then, for the final week before the great day, I joined my new colleagues for our pre-ordination retreat at the Diocesan retreat house in the countryside south of the city. Came the big day, it was into our freshly minted black shirts, dog-collars and cassocks, arriving at the church well ahead of the appointed hour in a reasonably relaxed frame of mind and heart, to make our final personal preparation for the moment we had been working towards for many, many years.

St Alphege Church in Solihull stood just across the old village green from the Mason's Arms where I'd sung and co-hosted the folk club years before. But today it was to the church that we came together from our various parishes to be ordained as deacons, and only after a full year of work in our own parishes, would we return for our second ordination which would then be as priests. Even whilst we waited in line, ready to process in for the service I found it hard to believe it was really happening. How could an awkward and rebellious lad from a cockney Marxist family, who still felt more at home in a street market than at a dinner party, be privileged with such an experience? The crucial moment of the service, as in any

137

ordination, was when each of us took our turn to move forward to kneel before the bishop as he laid his hands on our head to hear him pray that God should send his Holy Spirit upon us for the office and work of a deacon in his church. Those words made it clear that I wasn't being ordained merely into the Church of England, but into the worldwide community of Christian people – more than two billion of us, not counting those who were looking on from past ages. We were told we were offering our lives in service to God, but experience has since taught me that it's more to do with God offering life to *us*. Ordination is God's unfathomable gift, and like any vocation, we just have to accept it and allow it to love us into the person we are destined to become.

Geoffrey and I would meet together every Tuesday to discuss parish policy, to share out the visiting rota, and for Geoffrey to advise me on any areas of ministry that I was finding difficult. We would also discuss the latest theological publications, especially those we thought most challenging and relevant to the lives of the people we were there to serve. St Mark's congregation was certainly dynamic, providing 'meals on wheels', hosting clubs for the old as well as the young, the Sunday School buzzed under Sheila's leadership, the discussion groups were sizzling and the worship was uplifting and meaningful. The youth club, however, needed a pick-me-up, so that was assigned to me. My sermons weren't up to much because the couple of lessons we'd had on the subject at college never helped us to integrate our theological learning with the life of our people. So I stumbled along and learnt from Geoffrey, who was a master of connecting the Sunday bible readings with the felt experiences of our congregation.

I had to get used to people sharing with me the most intimate details of their lives, and never to show any sign of alarm or discomfort. In the event, it was not as difficult as it might sound, because at those times it was clear that they were sharing their deepest hurts and suffering, and I would find myself trying to hold back my tears rather than avoid showing signs of condemnation or surprise. Everything was changing for me, from romantic and theoretical notions about ministry to its raw reality. I was having to learn how to visit a family who were trying to deal with their son's suicide, and then go immediately to rejoice with another about the birth of a new child. And I had to find ways to make every visit count – not just to sup tea and make inconsequential conversation. It was an emotional roller-coaster and whilst it was quite exhausting, at the same time it brought great fulfilment and sense of purpose. It also made prayer essential, but I was still useless at it. Each morning at seven I was expected to walk up the hill to the church to join Geoffrey for our regular service of matins together, followed by a time of silent prayer. My difficulty was however, especially if I'd been with the youth club into the early hours, that I'd arrive late, tired and dishevelled, quite unable to concentrate on the prayers. Geoffrey despaired at my lack of prayer discipline and told me so, but given the circumstances, did not press it. He did, however, remind me of it from time to time, especially when he drove. This would be at great speed, and in a dispassionately carefree manner, holding his cigarette in one hand while emphasising his points by waving the other around in the smoke-filled cabin. With my eyes glued to the road ahead and repeatedly stamping my right foot down involuntarily as if to hit the brake, Geoffrey would jovially remark: 'that's how you should pray – with passion!'

Geoffrey and his wife had spent untold hours fund-raising for a new church to replace the nondescript hall which was all we had for worship. So many events took place there through the week that every Saturday evening, whatever we'd been doing, I'd have to join Geoffrey in packing away all the old trestle tables, putting out a hundred or so chairs, and setting up our make-shift sanctuary. When we were satisfied that all was ready, we would repair to the vicarage, where his wife Julie would have a cup of tea ready. There we would sink into the armchairs, and shoot the breeze, reflecting on how wonderful it would be when at last we had a proper church with a separate hall, and never again have to be night-time chair-shifters.

Sunday mornings saw the old hall filled with worshippers, and although we could only afford a small electric organ, we still sported a robed choir and a team of able servers who helped to adorn the worship with music, colour and movement. Although at that time it was not difficult to fill churches in more affluent areas of England, housing estates were a different matter. Geoffrey made it clear however, that our task as clergy was not to fill our church so much as to create signs of God's Kingdom in the community and homes of the parish, and this approach seemed to fill the church anyway. The national church remained at that time quite a rich institution, and therefore congregations were not expected, as they are today, to raise a large contribution each year for the maintenance of their diocesan and national church infrastructure. This left Geoffrey and me free to spend our time helping organise St Mark's exciting programmes, building community solidarity, encouraging its self-confidence, and deepening our spiritual awareness of God in the midst of every endeavour.

The parish's servant style of mission chimed in with the meaning of my new ministry as a deacon – a New Testament word for a 'servant'. No one is allowed to be ordained priest or bishop without having first spent some time as a deacon, and those later ordinations don't replace, but build upon, that diaconal, servant foundation. My dear friend, the author Susan Sayers, told me at her interview for priesthood: 'the diaconate is the heart-wood of priesthood,' and I've treasured that phrase ever since. A priest who forgets the servant nature of ordination, and starts pushing their weight around, is a real danger, as is any leader in politics or business who thinks their authority allows them to be anything other than a servant to those they lead. The reason for this stern emphasis by the church on servanthood in ministry is that Jesus said, time and again, that although his followers could see examples of leaders who lord it over their minions, 'it shall not be so among you!' (Mark 10: 43). Jesus had emptied himself 'taking the form of a servant' (Philippians 2:7), and that was the model for all who follow him. The story goes that Pope Gregory the Great fled to a monastery rather than have authority thrust upon him, but when they insisted, at his ordination, he took the title of Servant of the Servants of God to remind himself and those around him that the role of the ordained must always be that of servant. It has always seemed to me, therefore, that clericalism, which assumes that clergy have superior status, is a pernicious distortion of what ordination is all about. But, hey ho, I've sometimes fallen for it myself.

To handle holy things

The first year of ordained life fairly flew by, and during that time Vicki was adding to her secretarial skills by training as a primary school teacher and was soon eagerly snapped up by our local school. Clergy are allowed one day off a week, so from our Kingstanding parish, we were able to make little trips out to the surrounding areas, often driving through Sutton Coldfield, and out into Sutton Park, one of the largest Urban Parks in Europe. It certainly refreshed Vicki's rural soul, for the park was a vast expanse of heathland, woodlands and wetlands, supporting a rich variety of plants and wildlife, and on our walks we even came across the occasional cow or wild pony. Now that we also had Vicki's income to support us, at the end of each week we would splash out and purchase two cream buns. By managing our money carefully we even went occasionally for a pub meal. It all made for a very happy but busy first year in Kingstanding. But now I had to prepare for the next step along my journey when I would be ordained for the second time. This time I was to be made a priest when I would be given the responsibility and privilege of presiding at the Holy Communion service of the bread and wine, blessing the people and hearing confessions, whilst at the same time continuing to develop as a deacon.

Ordination Day
Made Priest 1971

The service this time was to be in the modern church of St Michael and All Angels, South Yardley. It was to be conducted by the same bishop who had been with us at our first ordination as deacons, the Bishop of Birmingham, Laurie Brown. But on this occasion, since I was being made priest, at the moment of ordination, all the priests who were present came forward to join him in laying their hands upon my head as he said the prayer which was to make me a priest forever. It was the moment I had been preparing for and studying for since Nop, so many years before, had asked me at my confirmation what I felt I should be doing with my life. That ordination made sense of all the years that had gone before, and I was to find, all the fifty and more years that lay ahead.

The party at home after the service was a fun affair. One neighbour had made some celebratory broad bean wine, and plied all the guests with it. It turned out to be exceedingly spirit-filled, and mum began to feel quite squiffy after only one glass. The very next day, however, it was back to challenging parish work for me. My first mass went smoothly, and I remembered not to make the mistake that Leslie, one of my colleagues, had made the year before. During his first year as deacon he had distributed only the wine with the words: 'the

Blood of Christ.' Now, as the priest responsible for offering the bread to the people as the 'Body of Christ', he went along the whole of the first row of communicants distributing the bread saying, 'the bloody of Christ.'

Another of the new priests was curate to the Rural Dean in a neighbouring parish, and a most eccentric couple they made. Vicki and I had been invited to dinner with them where we were introduced to their two cats, Bath and Wells. We were then invited to sit at the grand dining room table with the Rural Dean presiding, whilst his curate Simon processed in carrying a heavy silver salver, and offered to carve. He removed the ornate domed cover to reveal a cold Sainsburys pork pie which was served to us in silent solemnity. The thin slice of pie was accompanied on our plates by a small helping of rather over-stewed cabbage. Although the meal was spartan, I do remember the conversation being very entertaining, even though the Rural Dean took the opportunity to inform me that he had just put me on the deanery cemetery rota for the coming week. It meant that I'd be burying the dead every moment of the week ahead, and by the time Saturday arrived, I stood in front of a wedding couple with my coffin-shaped eyes, opened my book and began the marriage service with, 'Rest eternal grant unto them O Lord.' Luckily no one remarked on it afterwards, so I guess none had noticed that the words did not quite fit.

To the public gaze the thing that distinguishes the priest from others is that he or she presides at the Eucharist, also referred to as Holy Communion or the Mass. It's where the priest who, on behalf of all present, actually takes hold of bread and wine, and after asking God to bless it, then distributes it to the congregation as the sacrament of the presence of Jesus Christ with us. As we place the bread into the hands of each person we often say those traditional words 'the Body of Christ' – the English translation of the Latin *Corpus Christi* – and as it's digested and becomes integral to our own bodies, so it declares that Christ abides as intimately as that within us. That's the part of the priest's work that is seen each Sunday.

But every moment of the priest's life is similarly spent handling holy things, be it the intimate fears or joys of individual lives, or by working in the clubs and associations that God inspires in the community. For once we've seen the Presence of God in the simplicity of communion bread, we become even more alert to seeing God's sacred Presence in everything.

There are many of course who would dispute whether the presence of God has anything to do with it, arguing that the whole universe is as it is by fortunate accident. There are so many planets in the universe they say, that probability has determined that one of them would be able to support life like ours. But it seems to me that even scientific evidence is stacked against such a dubious claim. Stephen Hawking's famous book, *A Brief History of Time,* draws attention to how, even within the first hundredth of a second after the big bang, the ratio of neutrons, photons and electrons to nuclear particles was spot on for the emergence of some sort of life. And what's more, we can be thankful, to say the least that the particular orbit of the earth around the sun turned out, for some extraordinary reason, just as it did. If it had taken an elliptical path rather than a more circular one, it would have resulted in such variations of the earth's temperature that any life would have been quite impossible. And so the story of fortuitous coincidences goes on. The thought that this is just happenstance or possibility turning mysteriously into probability on such an immense scale takes a lot of believing – much more indeed than the belief that it was all in some way driven by a purpose. To this evidence, we can add, of course, our own experience of sensitivity to a depth in the things around us, and an awareness that our lives have some sort of meaning. When we take all that on board too it becomes a lot more than just likely that that bread upon the altar is indeed a way into perceiving the presence of the Ground of Being, of God, in everything around us.

From the first, Geoffrey had given over to me responsibility
for building up the small youth group. It was a small group of
really lovely local youngsters who met in the hall on Sunday
evenings to enjoy one another's company, and to play music,
table tennis and snooker. We started to include short
discussion sessions on topics of their choosing, and soon
realised that the concern which most disturbed them was the
dire lack of amenities in our area for our local street kids.
They wanted to find a way to offer to the next generation what
they themselves had gained by having a youth group of their
own. Gary Davis and Rob Sherwood, who shared a passion
for electrical gadgetry, built a discotheque record deck and
light show, whilst others rooted around for games equipment.
Just as the Bikers had been displaced by the Hippies, so now
the craze for young people was to shave their hair really short,
wear rolled-up jeans and braces, steel-capped boots, and adopt
a very aggressive and destructive lifestyle. This 'skinhead'
fashion was now at its peak, and it offered our local street kids
a vehicle with which to vent their inner angers and frustrations.
All Saints Hall, a little chapel situated in the southern half of
the parish, was hardly used by parishioners, and so Geoffrey
was happy for us to take it on for our new Youth Club project.
The youngsters named it the Powerhouse Club, and soon after
opening, we had more than a hundred and fifty regular
members. I'd cadged from the city repertory theatre a disused
stage backdrop with a menacing Aladdin's dragon painted on
its vast canvas. We hoisted it up so that it divided the hall into
a darkened disco area on one side, and a lighted space on the
other for games such as tabletop soccer, pool and table tennis.
The formidable Mrs Coal, a squat Brummie who seemed to
have lost her nose, very ably ran the canteen, and terrified any
skinhead who wanted to argue about the price of her Coca
Cola. She was genuinely committed to them, and deep down
they knew it. Carole, Rod, Margaret, Christine and other key
leaders undertook proper youth-work training, and I also

posted a flyer all around the parish asking for additional helpers resulting in three or four very able men coming forward to assist. I hadn't foreseen just how committed to the kids both they and our original youth club members would become, offering their time, their skills and their hearts into the bargain. What a gift they each were.

One summer the club was asked to take part in the Lord Mayor's Show when thousands of Brummies would line the streets of the city centre to cheer thirty or more decorated floats escorting the newly elected Mayor to Birmingham Town Hall. Our members were very keen to ride in a Viking ship so I talked a local firm into providing a long articulated lorry, and Fred, Richard and John, who'd volunteered from the community, designed and built a very substantial ship to mount on it. Authentic-looking costumes seemed to appear out of nowhere so that on that morning a very impressive Viking horde motored into the city. We were directed to take our place in the queue of floats preparing for the grand procession, and were lined up immediately behind the Methodist Church float, a huge lorry festooned with hundreds of enormous colourful balloons. After submitting the paper work for our entry I returned to find the street in uproar, the Methodist Superintendent striding up to me to complain bitterly. The problem was that, whilst getting into their role as Vikings, our skinhead youngsters had employed their wooden swords to burst every single balloon on the Methodist float until it was entirely bereft of any adornment whatsoever. That day did no good at all in fostering better Anglican–Methodist relations, but the kids had the time of their lives.

We did however have ecumenical success of a different kind when one evening into the club tripped a diminutive, and somewhat fragile-looking, Irish nun from the local convent who offered to help. She explained that her name was Éillis, but that the youngsters could call her Sister Eyelash. I was concerned that perhaps she hadn't reckoned on the dangers inherent in the skinhead culture, but in the event the youngsters took to her as their loving confidante. One evening, the girls totally demolished the ladies toilet, unhinging the pedestal from the floor, and ripping out the sink, flooding the whole room. They all came screaming out of the loo, and ran to Sister Eyelash who was sitting quietly in her usual place at the side of the hall. They snuggled up to her, and cried their eyes out, telling her of all their frustrations and disappointments with life. It was a costly but very productive night. When we grow up we quickly forget how traumatic being young can be, and many of our youngsters had no one to support them and so tended to get themselves into terrible trouble. Often all such youngsters really need is a Sister Eyelash who's prepared to listen and assure them of their love. Our Powerhouse members looked, and on occasion acted like hooligans, but most had the same inner loveliness that I'd found among the Hell's Angels years before. Nevertheless, at times they took some handling. One of our committed helpers, Micky Webb, introduced me to his works rugby club where I found out that playing works rugby against giants who had been operating huge steam presses all day was very different from school rugby! However, my new team mates offered me wonderful friendship, and even came down to help at the youth club after our midweek training sessions where their presence often calmed a potentially volatile situation.

New buildings & New beginnings

It soon became apparent that we needed to upgrade All Saints Hall so that it would be more appropriate to our club requirements, and for that we needed once again to raise funds. The youngsters led the campaigning, marathon dancing through the night, and Gary, Mac and Eric adding their names into the *Guinness Book of Records* for playing the most protracted game of Monopoly ever.

The eternal game of Monopoly

By then I'd made good friends at the local television studio, so we took over the local park for a charity football match against the 'TV All-Stars'. This raised such a substantial sum that our local Mecca Bingo theatre invited Hughie Green, then famous for his TV talent show *Opportunity Knocks*, to come and hand over the cheque. Having used the park for the football game, we returned to stage a fair which included throwing rotten eggs at volunteers in the stocks – I'd never realised before how eager the average punter would be to throw a rotten egg at a clergyman! A sizeable funfair was provided free of charge by Tankie Lane, a gypsy I'd met in the local pub. His crew turned up with all the fairground stalls you could wish for, and I went along to his home the next week to receive a large donation. I learnt much later that Tankie's lads were renowned for being able to stop their spinning dials on a pinhead and rig every stall for a guaranteed profit, and I never knew – honest!

Not long after the opening of our new Youth Centre, the parish had even greater cause for rejoicing. The great day arrived for the consecration of our new St Mark's church, with its inspiring new sanctuary, full of light and wonder. Julie had adorned it with superb tapestry hangings, and designed glorious robes for the ministers to wear. Geoffrey had given years of prayerful thought to how everything should be laid out to signify both the transcendent presence of God whilst, at the same time, the closeness of God to each and every one of us. The power and love generated within that new church building thrust us outward from the wonderfully refreshed worship into loving action in the parish. So we now seemed to be involved in every aspect of the life of the community, from the shops and Bingo theatre to the workplaces of the industrial estate, the schools, the technical college and the homes of the parishioners, whilst all the time Gwen Lee and her team continued to prepare tasty meals for the housebound, and our day centre. Vicki, as well as being deeply involved in the Powerhouse club, helped the congregation run the children's holiday Playsafe scheme for local children, and when Christmas arrived, our youth club members visited the British Legion Club to sing Christmas carols. Although our skinhead choir didn't sound very professional, we managed it through without too many mishaps. For hot chocolate afterwards we repaired to the vicarage, and were met by Julie, the vicar's wife, who was surprised it went so well. She explained that choirs in the past had been hounded off stage with a hail of glasses and empty beer bottles. I can only surmise that the Christmas angels had been on our side that evening!

The youngsters were keen to explore the new St Mark's too. They discovered that by setting up a long ladder, they could access a large hidden space in the roof from which their equipment could project images onto the plain white wall at the rear of the sanctuary. The lights dimmed as a hush fell upon the congregation who had turned up from all across the community, and were now taken on a multimedia experience of the Good Friday Stations of the Cross by our youngsters, with our young people all dressed in their tableau costumes. It was one of the most moving and inspiring experiences of worship I'd ever taken part in. With the congregation agog, I shared a deep sense of pride in what their young people had achieved. They'd given us all new glimpses of God's creative love in the midst of the challenges and sorrows of our world.

Ministry in Kingstanding, as gloriously enjoyable and fulfilling as it was, was nothing less than exhausting. Vicki and I therefore went on a camping holiday across Europe. To save on cost, Mel, a fellow student at King's joined us with his fiancée and the four of us crammed into our little car, tying all our camping equipment on to the roof. Our adventure included our first visit to communist Bulgaria, where the inquisitive peasants could not understand why our steering wheel had been installed on the wrong side of the car. We were in awe of the mysterious beauty of the dark candlelit Orthodox churches and the sonorous bass voices of their sung liturgies, and we gloried in the wonder of Istanbul's magnificent St Sophia cathedral. We travelled far and wide, and were often so tired that on occasions we would not bother to find a proper campsite, and would pull off the road and erect our two little tents in any available lay-by. In just such a spot by the Greek–Turkish border, we'd slept well only to be woken the next morning by the rumble of heavy vehicles pulling up alongside us. On peering out from our tents we realised that we were now surrounded by enormous Greek tanks and military hardware! We hastily bundled our gear into the car, and drove off in our nightclothes for fear of being arrested, realising that we were perhaps the first to hear the news of the new tensions on the Greek–Turkish border. It was soon after our European escapade that I was invited to preside at Mel's wedding, and at the reception afterwards, somewhat startled the guests by telling them how much I'd enjoyed the couple's honeymoon!

Vicki and I returned from our holiday much refreshed, and ready once more for the daily challenges of parish ministry, but after more than ten years at the front line of urban parish life, Geoffrey was laid low with pneumonia after a fundraising hike in the pouring rain. His service to Kingstanding had been tremendous, almost saintly, but he was grateful to be offered a less taxing post back in the sunshine of his native Cornwall. This now left me in charge of the whole parish. The youth club was now well established with Alan its own salaried youthworker, so I was able to tear myself away from my focus on youthwork, and attend to other parish responsibilities, which I relished. I did not have to wait long however before a new vicar was appointed, and the bishop asked me to think about moving to a parish of my own. It was just as well because the new incumbent was very keen to wipe the slate clean of the past, and make his own mark on the parish. Unfortunately, in so doing, he alienated quite a large proportion of the congregation, sacking the organist, the choir and some of the leading laity. I was sad to learn later that once I'd left for pastures new, he sent the youth-worker packing without replacing him, and closed down the Powerhouse youth centre, leaving the building deserted.

This taught me the very important lesson that the church is its committed congregation, and not its clergy. The clergy may come and go and do their thing, but in so doing can easily make or break a parish if they do not tread gently upon the earth, paying sensitive attention to the talents and gifts of those they serve. But the passage of time has taught me another lesson. On the fiftieth anniversary of the consecration of the new St Mark's building, I was invited to return to Kingstanding to help celebrate, and whilst just a few of my old friends were still there, I was also greeted by a now thriving congregation, and their recently appointed priest who had clearly won their hearts. Christian congregations, like nature herself, can be very resilient and forgiving.

* * *

CHAPTER 7

UNDER SPAGHETTI JUNCTION

I had learnt so much as curate at St Mark's church in Kingstanding, but above all I had experienced love as a verb. Jesus gave us just two simple commandments: to love God and to love our neighbour, and I'd found out that being deeply involved in a Christian community is a great way to do both. But now it was my turn to become a fully-fledged vicar with a church of my own where I could help build a loving Christian community as it witnessed to God's practical love across its neighbourhood.

One of the many things I'd learnt from Geoffrey Harper, my training vicar, was that if you're going to understand your parish and its people and if together you are going to accomplish anything of really lasting value, then it is important to stay for quite a long while. Benedictine monks and nuns, when they take their life vows, promise obedience, conversion of their life and stability. Stability means that you stay put and don't go wandering from place to place or from thing to thing, but engage deeply with where you are and with those with whom you share in community there. So my next parish had to be somewhere where the people felt that I was the right person for them, and I had to know that I could love that place and its people enough to stay put for a good ten years. The bishop suggested a prestigious parish with a massive church, but I had my eyes on something rather different and he eventually relented. For hidden away in a neglected corner of the Erdington district of Birmingham was to be found the less than impressive parish church of St Chad.

The building itself was a sorry affair, just a shabby, flat-roofed temporary construction attached to a church hall where the floor had rotted away exposing deep holes. There, however, two struggling Methodist congregations in the parish and the three congregations had already spoken with enthusiasm about combining and moving together on to one site. The vicarage was a simple semi-detached house with a very tiny garden, but to which had been added a room which could easily serve as a study. We both felt sure that this was precisely the sort of forgotten, back-street church which probably had a lot more going for it than outsiders might realise. Once we'd had a chance to meet some of the local families, we became totally convinced that we wanted to become one with them.

I had recently been reading new, fascinating studies which were using the latest techniques of archaeology and documentary research to piece together a more authentic picture of first century Galilee, the context in which Jesus himself had operated. It was clearly evident that he had chosen to minister not among the well-heeled or well-educated of the day, but primarily alongside ordinary artisans and labourers in the forgotten backwaters of the Roman Empire. The villages which were home to him were often considered by society to be of little consequence, the Bible telling us that Nathaniel, on hearing about Jesus, exclaimed, 'Can anything good come from Nazareth?' (Jn 1:46). The south of the country, with its heart at Jerusalem, had been battling with the north for hundreds of years, and so Galilee, where Jesus was born and bred, was now looked upon by zealous southerners as still untrustworthy and irreligious. St Chad's Erdington seemed to be just like Nazareth, forgotten and falsely assumed to be of no account, so for me this was truly Jesus-shaped territory, and that's where I wanted to be.

St Chad's church was in a small side road close to the massive new 'Spaghetti Junction' interchange which linked us to Birmingham's city centre not far distant, as the connecting M6 motorway ploughed its path through the industrial landscape of the West Midlands. Through the heart of the parish ran the Tyburn Road, originally created to ferry workers by tram to Fort Dunlop, then the world's largest factory. The workers for this great enterprise had been housed in a purpose-built estate of terraced brick houses at the centre of which now stood our little St Chad's church. On the other side of this Tyburn Road were situated a vast steel works and other heavy industry. A few pubs, small shops and a primary school served the community which included other larger homes, many multi-occupied, and an estate of semi-detached properties.

Being the new vicar

Vicki and I were arriving just as the country ventured upon one of the greatest upheavals of its recent history. It was in that very year, 1973, that the Yom Kippur War erupted in Israel, leaving the Egyptian army in tatters and quadrupling the price of oil overnight. British commerce tried to find savings by reducing our workforce to a three-day week but inflation soared to twenty-three percent. Shakespeare's phrase, the 'Winter of Discontent', was appropriately used to describe this time of strikes, untreated sewage, uncollected garbage, bodies not being buried and excessive electricity cuts – so bad that friends from abroad sent us a box of candles! Racist organisations were burgeoning once more and the IRA was now bombing English cities. All this prompted us to look desperately for something to brighten the horizon.

But whilst Britain was being shaken to its foundations, the little church of St Chad's was being spruced up in readiness for the arrival of its new vicar. Its now thirty-year-old 'temporary' worship area scrubbed up well, which spoke highly of Terrapin, the company that had designed it. The bishop who had first opened it had, however, remained sceptical and, on taking his first look, whispered to his archdeacon, 'Terrapin and Seraphim falling down before thee!' The service saw a packed church. However, the next morning, when all the visitors had left, I walked into the church for my first Sunday with my new congregation, only to realise just how sparse the home team was. That same evening I'd invited them to join us in our new home, where they noticed we'd carpeted the study

155

with claret and blue carpet tiles. They were immediately impressed, assuming that I therefore supported Birmingham's Aston Villa, and at this early stage of our friendship I thought it expedient not to mention that these were also the West Ham United colours of my childhood.

In view of the ecumenical intentions, the very next Sunday evening I began going along to worship at our local Methodist churches and realised at once that I had a lot to learn. I was disappointed to find that the minister did everything with little to no participation by the laity, but I was overjoyed to hear of the tradition in Methodism of the class meeting, where small groups would meet regularly to discuss the faith together. I too was keen to emphasise Christian lay education and I saw that as essentially a group exercise. For one of the first things Jesus did in ministry was to call together a group of learners, his disciples. It was a togetherness which reflected the very nature of God as a relationship – Father, Son and Holy Spirit – reaching out constantly in love. We might even dare to say that God the Holy Trinity is a united group! So meeting together in unity was the obvious way forward for our Christian learning and for our worship.

I was delighted to see how, despite our different denominational traditions, everyone was getting on so well one with another. But the decision had finally to be made as to which of our three church sites was to become the final home for our united congregation. Although the St Chad's building was somewhat dilapidated, it did have a large area of ground around it, ready for development, so we were overjoyed when quite independently, all three congregations determined upon the site at St Chad's. We were keen to implement the decision as soon as possible, and the day was soon upon us when we processed through the streets from our former buildings to converge upon St Chad's in Stoneyhurst Road. There we took part in a memorable service of thanksgiving where we signed what we called our Intention to Commit document. To stay true to our roots, we alternated our services. So together we followed the Methodist service one Sunday and the Church of

England service the next, whilst our evening services took on a new flavour by centring upon a particular social or faith issue each week.

Signing for
Church
Unity

For one of our Methodist members, our sharing of services presented a huge personal challenge. Milkman Jack Hall was a squat, jovial Brummie of deep conviction who was always ready with a smile and an offer to help. He had been a socialist all his life, and during the war his faith had led him to become a conscientious objector. He had also espoused a life-long commitment to abstinence from alcohol. Jack told me that he'd been praying hard about this for a long time, and that he'd been led to look carefully in John's gospel where Jesus had prayed passionately that all his followers would become one, just as he knew himself to be one with God (John 17). Jack explained that it had therefore become obvious to him that our unity was even more important than his personal conviction about alcohol, and therefore he was not only willing, but fervently wanted to receive the fermented wine used at Anglican services, in unity with everyone else. I felt privileged to be a friend of this man, for Jack was teaching me a profound truth about the meaning of Christian faith in practice. Then, with a twinkle in his eye he added, 'so you'll only give me a little sip won't you, so I don't get too fond of it.'

We now had a combined congregation of a workable size with plenty of leadership experience from the three churches, and lots of kiddies with good Sunday School teachers and young families. With so many black youngsters in the church's Boys' Brigade, I knew there must be many committed Caribbean families around even though they were not themselves attending our services. I was also aware that in the early days they had been greeted by foul white racism on arriving at the doorsteps of the English churches, so were now understandably reluctant to turn up alone to a predominantly white church with no guarantee of a better welcome. I had the suspicion that if I encouraged the women from a number of black families to come along together, their combined numbers would bolster their self-confidence and they'd experience a lovely welcome at St Chad's. After that, we never looked back, and soon became a well-integrated congregation.

The little church became quite popular in the community. It even attracted Baptists, URC and Roman Catholic members. A Polish family began attending and so I popped round to visit them at home. The door was opened by a woman who unfortunately spoke no English, but she readily invited me in and gestured that the family were all out at work. She offered me a seat, gave me a glass of Polish vodka and as I sipped away she vanished into the kitchen. She returned holding an enormous red plastic mixing bowl containing sparkling silver globes. It was clear that I was expected to accept one of the globes as a gift, but having done so I was not at all sure what to do with it. There was a chance it was a Polish Christmas tree decoration, but she continued to stand silently before me smiling and expectant. The time had come to make up my mind. Since she'd given me a drink and the bowl had come from the kitchen, I came to the conclusion that it must be edible and so took a tentative bite. My teeth easily cracked open the ball's outer shell and so I continued to take manageable bites to accompany my vodka. She smiled, and I smiled, but I never did learn what the silver sphere really was. Even now, I imagine her sitting with her Polish family giving them her account of my visit and finishing with, 'and you'll never guess what he did with it!'

Soon after my arrival I made a serious error after agreeing to be authorised to preach in Methodist churches. A month later I was telephoned by the Methodist Superintendent asking why I hadn't turned up to a preaching engagement, thus leaving the expectant congregation in the lurch. I explained that I had not received an invitation and listened apologetically as he berated me for not following the Plan. I had to ask what on earth a Plan was, but he would not take that as a valid excuse. He assumed that every Christian must surely know that the Methodist Plan was a preaching rota which clearly named me as the preacher for that evening. It made me realise how bizarrely all our churches assume that any newcomer knows how we do things, and what our strange terminology means. Our churches must become alert to what an eccentric sub-culture we've become, even if our particular church considers itself really welcoming.

Confronting the cultural differences between the Church of England and the Methodist Church was bound to be challenging because of our differences of theological emphasis, our conflicting regulations and systems of accountability, and our very divergent history. At St Chad's we were also seeking to bring together White British and Black Caribbean cultures. These challenges introduced us to the joys and complexities of what it is to belong to a culture – what it does to us and how we then see ourselves. A culture is that which we learn or acquire as a member of a society or organisation when we are socialised and learn to belong. It comprises a great deal of inherited behaviour and thinking drawn from agreed customs and values and the distinctive ways of living and learning which come together to constitute a specific discernible human group or society. My experience of being born into a cockney culture, moving to Birmingham's Brummie culture, to central London and then New York, had already alerted me to the wonders and expectations of humanity's different cultures. But it had also taught me that when cultures meet one another there is always lurking the pernicious danger of assuming that our own culture is better than the other; of thinking we are the best or even the most godly! The early missionaries of the British Empire sometimes believed that their task was to 'civilise the natives', which they took to mean imposing their own British culture upon them. This happened simply because their culture had already convinced them that theirs alone was an authentically Christian culture. Even missionaries today, both at home and abroad, can unconsciously impose their own religious and social culture upon another and forget that sharing the good news of the Christian gospel should be a truly liberating experience.

The philosopher, Jacques Derrida, observed: 'no context permits saturation', by which he meant that if we only allow ourselves to operate or observe from our one perspective or culture, we'll never see the whole picture and will be left with false notions of the truth, just like some of those missionaries. But, Derrida went on to say, 'no meaning can be determined out of context'. So as well as seeing things from other perspectives, we also have to learn the truth about our own culture if we are to arrive at any semblance of a mature perspective. In today's world many people grow up inside a culture which is not of their own heritage, and they have to wrestle with the question of where they now truly belong and to which cultural heritage. Indeed, in today's global village of a world, many cultures have themselves broken out of their old silos and increasingly a new cultural 'hybridity' is becoming the norm. For some that can make for adventurous living but, for others, an ongoing crisis of personal identity. Coming to terms with human hybridity can also give us some insight into the old theological question of how on earth Jesus could possibly be both human and divine: the ultimate hybridity.

Home and away

I had learnt from my early experiences just how important it is not to become so enamoured of one's own culture that we are blinded to the bigger picture. So when Vicki and I had an opportunity to visit a culture entirely different from our own, we jumped at the chance. My continuing commitment to socialism led to an opportunity to visit the Soviet Union which, at that time, was beginning to accept western visitors, albeit only under the strictest supervision. Our travels were to take us across Russia, Ukraine and Belarus – the three countries of the united medieval *Ancient Rus* – and it was in Moscow itself that I had my first experience of how nationalism is often underpinned by blatant lies. We were visiting the national war museum, and were shown a huge map of Europe as it had appeared in 1941. It clearly displayed the whole of Europe, including the UK, under Nazi occupation, implying that the Soviets had liberated us all. That falsehood made me wonder to what extent I, in similar manner, had been swallowing a fabricated history of the British Empire all my life.

Our journey to the Soviet Union also marked the beginning of a lifelong friendship with Michael, who had been another member of our touring group. This remarkable young man had been brought up in a children's home, and although our vicarage had only a very small spare bedroom, it was certainly better than his unpleasant digs. So he was pleased to accept our invitation to come and live with us, and soon became one of the family. Some years later he met and fell in love with Regina, a young Brazilian woman, and after their marriage, they made the brave decision to move to Brazil. There Michael had to learn the language the hard way, by looking at hours and hours of Brazilian television. He found a job in their city hospital, and they settled down to raise their very own family. It was a wrench to see them leave, but I promised that one day I'd visit them in their new home, a promise which I was able to keep only many years later.

It was just two years after our arrival in our parish at Spaghetti Junction that we welcomed another new member into our family, Rebecca Jayne Green, weighing in at 8 pounds 4 ounces. It was at the local Good Hope Hospital that she came tumbling into the world and has carried on being full of bubble and squeak ever since, filling our lives with a new kind of joy and challenge – parenthood. I'd never been present at the miracle of birth before, and although I'd baptised many an infant by then, I'd not had that glorious opportunity that new dads get of sitting for hours by the cot just staring in overwhelmed wonder at the little ears and fingers of their new-born. Seeing the birth itself startled me. How could such a tiny and vulnerable being come through nothing less than a very bloody rugby scrum, only to be held up by its feet for a time whilst being slapped about on its rear end until it cried, but then immediately snuggle comfortably down in the cot as if nothing untoward had ever happened? The birth of Hannah Claire two years later was no less wondrous, although she certainly caught us napping. We were still at home when the midwife suggested it was probably time for me to call an ambulance and to make everyone a cup of tea whilst we waited. I told myself not to become too excited because I knew, from what I took to be my wide experience of these things, that it would still be some time before the birth itself was properly underway. Suddenly I was woken from my reverie by the midwife shouting to me from upstairs, 'Mr Green, I think you'd better come up, your baby's coming!' And so she did.

I was then, and still am, thrilled to have two daughters – one for each knee. Like all new parents we had to learn on the job, but we did have a copy of Dr Spock's paperback, *Baby and Child Care*. Luckily this Spock was not the one who later would 'dare to boldly go', but a well-respected, wise paediatrician, whose book appeared on the shelf of almost every young parent at that time. The joy of boiling, sterilising, folding and pinning old-fashioned nappies is, perhaps thankfully, not today's way, but the sheer, exhilarating physicality of it all still brings home to us the intense reality of our human creatureliness. Western society leaves us with a fantasy notion of the human body, extolling its perfection whilst hiding its naturalness behind exotic cosmetics, picture filters and airbrushing. As young boy scouts around the campfire we would sing, 'O, you'll never get to heaven with your powder and paint, cos the Lord don't like you as you ain't!' Our modern bubble-wrapped existence allows us to live an 'out of the body' existence most of the time. I wonder if that's why endurance sports and physical adventure can today be such a turn-on, because it remains one of the few ways open to us to experience what we really are: part and parcel of the natural world all around us.

Seeing both of our amazing daughters born reminded me of the elderly Nurse Batey who, after seeing many births and many deaths, had shared with me her conviction that both were part of one and the same mysterious miracle. Mary Queen of Scots, awaiting her execution, embroidered on her Cloth of Estate, 'in my end is my beginning', and T S Eliot had famously ended his poetic masterpiece with those same words. But he had insightfully also begun the poem, 'in my beginning is my end'. Nurse Batey believed that our beginning and our end were not only related to one another, but were sewn into the dynamic of something even greater. And now here were two new little souls shining yet more light on the mystery and offering to share the miracle of life with us through the years to come.

Rebecca &
Hannah
'One for each
knee'

All this time our Methodist–Anglican partnership was progressing extraordinarily well. Our congregation at St Chad's was committed to reaching out in service to the community, and working together with that aim had welded such firm friendships that we found our differences over doctrine or styles of worship a matter of fascination rather than a cause for argument. Our evident unity brought us into contact with

Birmingham's Council of Churches, and through them we were asked to join Birmingham's delegation to Frankfurt, our twinned city in Germany, where that year's Kirchentag, a gigantic church conference and festival, was to take place. I was joined by our Anglican churchwarden Fred Doughty and our Methodist church steward Ray Young, and that very enjoyable visit spawned the idea that we as a congregation could form a link with a Frankfurt parish. I set about brushing up my meagre German and made a fruitful connection with Rolf Weber, the pastor of the parish of St Peter's Frankfurt, and the next summer they happily received a full coachload of St Chad's folk for a week's holiday, staying in the homes of the German parishioners. I noticed, as we alighted from the coach after our long and exhausting journey, that our hosts looked rather apprehensive on suddenly realising that a large proportion of their British visitors were black. However, after only a few hours, we were striking up friendships, some of which were to last many years. There was therefore a clamour to play host when, the next year, our new German friends came to stay with us in St Chad's parish. Vicki and I still enjoy a very close friendship with Hermann and Sigrid Dueringer, Hermann then being a curate at St Peter's, although he went on to become the academic director of one of Germany's most progressive theological academies.

At the Frankfurt Kirchentag I had also made friendships with Christians in West Berlin. At the time this was a city marooned by the surrounding communist East Germany, the DDR, and which had therefore assumed a highly charged political significance during the long Cold War. The communist government had confiscated most churches and left them as ruins, and their Christian pastors were harassed and frightfully restricted. I did however love roaming the back streets of East Berlin where the dowdy old tenement blocks were still riddled with bullet holes from the war and the occasional shabby shop sold very basic stuff to the locals. My German was now good enough to strike up conversations with the men who liked to sit together outside their front doors, and I was much taken by the intensity of their sense of belonging and solidarity amidst the hardship. Although they resented not being allowed to visit their families outside the Eastern Bloc, they shared a vibrant camaraderie which was of course highly valued in a communist state. To this day a few of those old East Berliners still have a nostalgic longing for that simple togetherness, which was lost after the fall of the Berlin Wall.

Addressing issues

Church life at Spaghetti Junction was both absorbing and fulfilling. Vicki helped develop a thriving pre-school club, the Sunday School was bursting with life with Madeleine, my secretary, at the helm, and the lively youth group St Chad's Action Now (SCAN), spent Saturdays decorating and gardening for the housebound. The Boys' Brigade won all the marching band prizes, with Chris and Colin, its leaders, organising a massive camping holiday for them each year. On special Sunday mornings the congregation would walk around the parish behind their band, with runners flying ahead dropping leaflets through letterboxes and into the hands of those who came out of their houses to wave and cheer. What with that and all our social activities, if you lived in our community there was no getting away from knowing about St Chad's. The church building was not pretty enough to attract weddings, but we baptised all comers whilst also inviting parents to join our classes and think carefully about their own faith. Quite a number responded to the challenge, one such mum even in time becoming our dynamic churchwarden.

Indeed, there was so much going on inside and around the church that the dear old building was now unable to cope, and it became imperative to attend to the problem. Selling our two Methodist buildings provided the wherewithal to replace our dilapidated wooden shack with a new brick hall, spacious and light enough for all our needs, offering us another channel by which to meet and to serve the community. We even had sufficient funds left over for the old sanctuary to be reordered and spruced up, allowing our worship to flourish with evermore creative liturgies, always with an eye on its relevance to our community.

I loved being in the thick of all the action, but as I look back I regret now that despite my absolute belief that loving relationship was at the heart of everything that was good, my prayer relationship with God was still lacklustre. The psalm says, 'unless the Lord build the house, those that labour, labour in vain'. And there was I, working my socks off, spending every hour out in the parish or working with the congregation in building up our shared life, but with my own personal journey with God not receiving anything like as much attention. I feared that I was guilty of the fault with which T S Eliot charged Thomas Becket that, 'the last temptation is the greatest treason, to do the right deed for the wrong reason.' Was all my parochial activity motivated by a need to hide my own sense of inadequacy from myself? Was it to prove to myself that even this lad from the East End could after all hold his own in the face of the church's institutional expectations? I continued to struggle for words and my memory was still letting me down, so I worked like mad to make up for it. It would not be right however to give the impression that I was only energised by my lack of self-worth, for I always retained a very real delight in the people around me – a genuine love for others that lit up my life, and made it all so lovely and worthwhile. It's just that on the inside I could still not believe that anyone could love me in return, and that brought on occasional days of deep depression.

Nor do I want the reader to imagine that my problems were indicative of any lack of belief in God for that remained rock-solid. When I remember those days, I'm surprised that even when feeling very sorry for myself and looking in every direction for affirmation, I never once lost my sense of the reality of God, that mystery which made every possibility possible. I was constantly amazed at life, and felt the truth of

Einstein's remark, 'the most incomprehensible thing about the world is that it is comprehensible'. Some experience a deep sense of wonder at seeing the glories of nature, but for me, urban to my core, I would roam the city streets and marvel at all the life and bustle, the architecture and infrastructure, and know I was glimpsing something spiritually significant. I could even look across the room at a chair and have a deep sense of the miracle of its existence. This sense of wonder is the experience of many people, although each of us find it in different ways and in different places – in music and the arts, in the wonders of scientific discovery, in sex or in relationships. The philosopher, Rudolf Otto, called this profound encounter an experience of the numinous. He described it as an encounter with the 'other' which is outside the self, transcending us and yet having a fascination which draws us towards its mystery. It's very telling that he entitled his famous book about all this, *The Idea of the Holy,* describing it using a Latin phrase, the *mysterium tremendum et fascinans* – for he recognised it as *mysterious, fearful and yet fascinating.* This was an experience I certainly shared, and so really was at a loss to know just why my prayer was so lacking.

I was also among those who experience that overwhelming mystery as imparting a moral imperative, the conviction that this mystery, this truth which surpasses all our human understanding, demands that we do something to put bad situations right: to bring rightness, or 'righteousness'. No doubt this is why the Hebrew Scriptures, the Qur'an, and our New Testament, all stress how much God is the Lord of justice and right action. It was this divine imperative which prompted me and others to be so involved in such initiatives as the 1981 People's March for Jobs. The marchers arrived in Birmingham from Liverpool on their way to London to protest at the way in which dire unemployment was then shredding the lives of working people. From 1979 to 1984 a third of our industrial base had been deliberately closed down by Margaret Thatcher's government in favour of a service industry economy. This allowed France and Germany to forge ahead with production whilst thousands of our skilled workers went to the wall. Having hosted some of the protesting marchers at the vicarage, I joined them the next morning for their procession through the city centre. During the march a BBC news cameraman caught me on film dressed in my cassock and holding my fist aloft in a socialist salute. I think I was quite lucky to receive no reprimand from the church hierarchy, but it did lead to my being selected to become chaplain to Birmingham's socialist Lord Mayor for a while. This allowed me to offer a Christian voice within the political fray of the times. Some like to say that politics and religion don't mix, which makes me realise they've never thought about the words of the Lord's Prayer which prompts the millions of Christians who say it each day to ask that God's 'will be done on earth as it is in heaven.'

Just as our newly refurbished buildings were opening for use we heard the news that the council had decided that since the through-traffic coming from Spaghetti Junction should have priority our local roads were to be closed off with the result that St Chad's would become isolated from its community. I spent many weeks canvassing and drafting a document which we sent to all the members of the appropriate council committee with copies for the local press. We then gathered some willing mums together and had them crossing back and forth across the Tyburn Road with their baby-buggies all afternoon which brought the commuter traffic and the motorway itself grinding to a halt. As a result the planning committee reduced the speed limit back to its original thirty miles per hour and rescinded the disruptive local road closures. Just before we set our campaign in motion, I'd had a call from a local church minister warning me that it was not right for a minister of religion to engage in what he took to be a political battle, especially one that was bound to fail. His intervention taught me never to let a local community be unnerved by those who tell us the 'powers that be' can never be defeated, nor even contradicted.

Our more public profile resulted in the screening of a TV programme about the life of the parish, which was another wonderful opportunity to challenge viewers with the thought that Jesus was a revolutionary character, not just the pious irrelevance many took him to be. BBC Radio also involved me in developing a children's series called *The Green Machine*, in which an imaginary and very noisy machine would whisk us off to extraordinary locations where, by means of riddles, songs and stories, the life issues that the children were raising could be addressed. During one late night recording session, in the middle of all the fun of making the programme, the producer noticed me sitting at the control panel nonchalantly flicking an odd-looking nob on and off. He casually remarked that it would be best not to do that because I'd just switched the national broadcast of Radio 3 off for a second or two. It hadn't dawned on me that a nationwide programme was being channelled through our little tatty BBC studio.

Life in a diverse parish

I especially enjoyed visiting parishioners. Old Mrs Wilson asked me to sort out the noises in her home, repeating all the while: 'that husband of mine is just not dead enough!' A short prayer did the trick for her, but another visit left me in tears. Once on my hospital rounds, I'd promised to visit a local young woman when she got home with her new baby. I turned up on the day appointed for her homecoming, but found her sitting alone with her baby sobbing her heart out in a house that had not one stick of furniture left in it. Her husband – who had visited regularly every day whilst she was still in hospital – had absconded with all their belongings and was never seen again. We mobilised the community and soon had her home filled once more with pieces of second-hand furniture, but it never made up for her loss of trust in others and her heightened sense of vulnerability – for herself and her child.

On more than one occasion I was called upon to help where strange things had been going on in the home of a parishioner. It was usually just a matter of a supportive visit, a listening ear and a prayer for peace. But on other occasions, it was not easy to know what to do. Frank came home from work one day, to find his very able and sensible wife Claire huddled up on the floor in a very nervous state. All their furniture had been mysteriously moved out of the house and piled up in the back yard. What befuddled Frank was that he doubted whether he himself would have managed to get some of the larger pieces through the back door. However, Claire maintained that she had been surrounded by a terrifying whirlwind which had just picked the furniture up and whisked it away. There seemed to be no rational explanation whatsoever to account for the evidence before us. We therefore went round the house together sprinkling holy water everywhere and praying for peace and a settling of the disturbance. After that Claire and Frank slowly got back to normal with nothing out of the ordinary ever occurring again.

To the south of the Tyburn Road stood the British Steel factory which produced gigantic steel tubes to very high specification. I would visit each week to walk the factory floor and get to know the workers, picking up on personal concerns or shop-floor issues, but also taking sessions with the apprentices alongside the union rep and the factory's personnel officer. Although I was able to be of service to a number of the employees on a personal basis, my problem with chaplaincy was that however I played it I was always assumed to be on the side of the management. Since they were the ones who were allowing me on to the site as chaplain, they probably expected me to bless rather than question how things were done, and the fact that God might be interested in the quality of industrial life and working conditions was on no one's radar. I'd certainly never heard a sermon about the issues of industrial work. I did manage to engineer a visit to the factory for our new bishop, Hugh Montefiore, and he did his very best. But it only issued in a photo opportunity for the company and not much more. Bishop Hugh had been paying a welcome visit to the parish, and so I also took him along to the Raymond Priestly nursing home where I also acted as chaplain. He presided at a short service with all the residents sitting around the room, some taking an interest, but most only vaguely aware that we were there. Hugh then took pains to walk around, being friendly to the assembled staff and the nodding patients. He returned to where I was waiting with his eyes open in astonishment. 'That dear old lady in the far corner is very muddled, poor dear. She had a glossy magazine open, so I asked her what the nice pictures were, but they turned out to be soft porn!'

The Church of England was at that time still not accepting women as priests. I therefore wrote a letter to Bishop Hugh informing him that my friend Renate, an ordained pastor in the Lutheran church, would be presiding at our united Holy Communion service at the invitation of the Methodists. As was allowed in Methodism, we were going to use the Church of England service book. This meant that, quite legally, we Anglicans would, for the first time in England, be attending an Anglican Prayer Book communion taken by an ordained woman! Immediately after the heart-warming service, we travelled to where the ordination of men only was taking place and standing outside, we handed out leaflets promoting women's ordination. One priest snatched one from my hand, tore it up and threw it in my face. But we persevered in our attempt to draw attention to the issue, and were very happy to have grabbed a front-page mention in the *Birmingham Post* the next morning.

Another major presence in the parish was the Rover Cars management training centre. Because of my own interest in adult learning, I was pleased to be regularly invited to participate in training seminars, completely free of charge. I learnt there of a much contested new approach which was called Servant Management, and at the seminar I was delighted to draw their attention to the servant ministry of Jesus – maybe the concept wasn't so new after all! The training I received at Rover Cars was very helpful when I became involved with the setting up of a Community Centre in a disused local authority building. For many years the vast edifice in the north of our parish had only housed Roy, the caretaker, and his wife, Sylvia. After some years of tough bargaining with the council we eventually saw the refurbished Kingsbury Road Community Centre open its doors to the local folk, with a grand multicultural festival. Once we had it well established with Peter as the new director, I was able to relinquish the chair, step back and let it develop in its own way.

In today's church, a parish priest and congregation might be hard pressed to spend so much time building up non-Christian organisations in their parish because pressure is now on to see mission as primarily concerned to increase the size of the congregation. This interpretation of Christian mission has become a primary thrust of Church of England policy and, some would say, for a good reason. But it would have precluded many aspects of how St Chad's went about its mission. We saw ourselves as seeking to be the Body of Christ in the world, and because Jesus was never concerned to build up his body so much as to sacrifice it, we too gave ourselves away as much as possible to the community. Since then the Church Urban Fund and others have undertaken research proving that offering service to the community and addressing ethical social concerns in this way actually attracts new Christians anyway. That certainly was the case at St Chad's where the congregation grew and deepened, not because we touted for custom, but precisely because of its commitment to the Kingdom of God in the community.

St Chad's
with its
new hall

Until it was actually being constructed, none of us were told that the government was building a youth prison in our parish on our one remaining green space. We protested, but to no avail. I was invited to become the chaplain so that I could visit the youngsters and I was appalled by the way they were treated. One day the 'great and the good' from the city were invited to view the new building. A special buffet lunch was offered, and two of the youngsters were asked to attend to show the visitors how successful the regime was in reforming its inmates. The chefs stood behind the buffet table in their white uniforms as all the visitors were served. But then one of the youngsters saw his opportunity, picked up an enormous bowl of beetroot and threw it into the air, smothering all the visitors in red vinegar! I rejoiced to think that he had found such a powerful way to rebel against being exhibited like a zoo animal, although I may not have felt so positive had I been more directly under the descending beetroot.

On Saturdays I still managed to get away to play works rugby against strapping great lads, so I'd often be harbouring injuries and limping up the aisle on Sunday mornings. When my beloved rugby eventually had the better of me, I took to running marathons instead, often accompanied by Rodney, my next door neighbour, who found very strenuous exercise a good way to keep his alcoholism at bay. We ran the Wolverhampton marathon together although I let him steam ahead after the first ten miles. I ran my last marathon in Berlin where I found it amusing to see that, unlike the Brits, the runners took the whole thing very seriously indeed. But eventually I also had to give up marathoning too, so no more was I witness to the race's patent miracle cure. In the dressing rooms beforehand, all my fellow runners would be telling me of their injuries and health problems, but as soon as the starter's hooter sounded, the miracle healing took place and they would all speed off leaving the likes of me to plod my way more slowly round the course.

We'd now been at St Chad's for seven years, our little family was well settled, and I felt thoroughly fulfilled being the vicar of such a diverse parish with its exciting and vibrant little church right at its heart. The congregation was proud to feel that in many ways we were blazing a trail, demonstrating how the togetherness of two Christian denominations could bring new life to a church and its community. The church at large designated our united parish an 'Area of Ecumenical Experiment'. But I declared that whilst we were united just as Jesus intended his followers to be, their alternative 'experiment' of a church divided into separated denominations, had spectacularly failed! We enjoyed our unity even given the diversity of our worship and different understandings because it allowed us to look beyond the superficiality of religious niceties. We were deeply engaged in the neighbourhood of which we were a part, our adult Christian education groups were buzzing, and our people were playing their full part in decision-making and the running of the many programmes on offer. Knowing there was still much to do, I was looking forward to another seven years in my Spaghetti Junction parish with eager anticipation. But they do say that if you want to make God laugh, tell him your plans

CHAPTER 8

THE PRINCIPAL OF THE THING

I counted myself extraordinarily fortunate that ever since my return from the States I had had a close mentor in the person of the Revd Dr John J Vincent who made sure that whilst at St Chad's I still kept up to date with the most radical theological thinking. I'd met John just as he was establishing a Christian community in inner-city Sheffield which was devoted to social action, thoroughly underpinned by theological reflection and analysis. I'd become a very committed member of what he was calling UTU, the Urban Theology Unit, which entailed meeting with John regularly. This meant I was learning from him, and eventually helping to teach the UTU courses all across the West Midlands where we assisted Christians in reflecting theologically upon their own urban communities so they could engage more purposefully. Although John could easily have become a university professor, he chose instead to devote his life to Christian action alongside the poor, and this was resulting in new liberating approaches to theology. In UTU we were intent on making this new style of theology accessible, not just to academic types, but to the poor and marginalised themselves, and it was certainly having an impact at St Chad's.

Theological research with a twist

Just when I was feeling the need to take my own thinking to a new level, John contacted me with an enthralling challenge. My former seminary in the States was now offering a course which would lead to the award of a doctorate from New York State University. It would entail the same academic rigour as any other doctorate, but its research element would not take place in the library, but back in our own communities. This would mean that my congregation would play a full part, not only in the research, but also in the process of learning itself. It seemed such a brilliant opportunity for them that the parishioners gave me their full backing and looked forward to being involved. This approach also confirmed my conviction that truth was not founded on pre-conceived theories, but on paying attention to our life experience. For when Jesus said, 'I am the truth' (John 14: 6) he was underscoring the fact that truth is not so much a predetermined statement as a relationship.

I therefore set to with a will, spending holidays reading and re-reading piles of books about culture, political theory, theology and philosophy, whilst the children played on the massive climbing frame that I'd built for them. Visits were also made to New York once more, where our studies were supervised by Professor Richard Snyder and John Vincent.

Back at
NYTS
once more

As I mused upon what I'd learnt from my own past experiences, it was as if I was peering into a box of jumbled jigsaw pieces, my task now being to try to bring them together into a coherent picture. Having grown up in a committed socialist family, it was important for me to go back and look first at what Karl Marx and other socialists had to offer Christianity. I was particularly taken by the work of a Marxist group from Frankfurt, known as the Institute for Social Research. It was led by Max Horkheimer and included such towering figures as the arts and literature critics Leo Lowenthal and Walter Benjamin, Erich Fromm, the psychoanalyst and Jurgen Habermas who teamed up with Theodor Adorno to remodel Marx's theories of economy and culture. In their own pre-war Germany, they'd experienced how Hitler had bamboozled the German people with his manipulative media and hype, and compared that with what they were now finding in America where they'd fled to escape the Nazis. Life there was full of 'must have' goodies, ever faster food, dreams of celebrity and screens promising the fantasy of personal fulfilment through buying ever more stuff. They looked at all this, and asked the question I was taught to ask in the States: 'who is really benefiting?' They could see that these plentiful commodities were as little able to deliver on their promise as were the Nazis, with their delusional dreams. The Institute's thorough analysis of societal forces they called Critical Theory, and reading their books about economics, culture and personality reminded me of those American parents I'd met years before. They, who had so much economically and career-wise, nevertheless had told me they still felt they were missing out on something more fundamental to human fulfilment and wellbeing. They too felt bamboozled and alienated from their better selves.

Adorno had been especially influenced by another socialist hero of my youth, the Italian Antonio Gramsci, who pointed out ways in which this stultifying situation might be countered. For just as Edvard Munch's famous painting *the Scream*, and the devastating novels of Franz Kafka, had expressed so poignantly our despairing agony of impotence in the face of these pressures, so our very best artists, educationalists and promoters of cultural change can in like manner, said Gramsci, offer visions of a life more fulfilling than that offered by the empty promises of the glossy advertisements and the dulling onslaught of our bloated celebrity culture. Gramsci believed that visions like this can alert people to how and why they are being manipulated by our culture's pressures. This, he thought, could give them the courage and determination to free themselves, and change themselves and their society for the better. Poor Gramsci paid dearly for encouraging us to think outside the box. Some of his most penetrating analyses were written in one of Mussolini's prisons where his teeth literally fell out on to the page as he wrote. But he knew that in order to help ordinary people confront the forces that enslave them, we must begin by bringing them to a consciousness of how they are being manipulated by inhuman forces. He called it 'conscientisation' – bringing people to an unblinkered consciousness of their predicament.

All these ideas were in my mind as I gathered a group of St Chad's people together to help me with my course of study. They agreed that there were astonishing parallels in the Bible with what I'd been reading. They recognised that Jesus had also been 'painting pictures' of an alternative society – a way of living together he called the Kingdom of God. It was where people would no longer be at the mercy of harsh new entrepreneurial employers, and forced to queue up in the market place waiting for a chance of a little employment in the vineyard. Neither would they be subjugated to the Jerusalem Temple authorities who made religion into an oppressive, power-seeking institution at the expense of the common people. Predating Gramsci by nineteen hundred years, Jesus brought to such situations a barrage of challenging parables, healing signs, teachings and prophetic actions. Each made those around him more conscious of the causes of their oppression, pointing them to the alternative Godly society. He shone light into the fissures and crevices of the oppressive manipulative system, and those who had been benefiting from it crucified him for doing something so threatening to their controlling regime. But Jesus had graphically described how the Kingdom of God society looked, and by giving his people these glimpses of the best possible alternative, made them conscious of their present cultural confinement. The parish group saw that this was truly the 'conscientisation' about which those modern theorists had written.

But Jesus went much further, by empowering his followers to begin actually living that new Kingdom society then and there, even in the face of the prevailing culture. And this allowed them to share his joy, and experience an inner freedom from the alienation which had constrained them. Just as God had rescued the Hebrew slaves in Egypt and brought them to the Promised Land, so now Jesus was intent on rescuing us from the slavery of our 'One Dimensional' existence and bringing in the Kingdom of Heaven. Jesus was living up to his name, for in Hebrew, his name means 'rescuer'.

As the St Chad's group looked at all this, they came alive with enthusiasm and decided to study the parables of Jesus to see how he used these stories to bring this new consciousness to his people. They soon realised that what the parable stories all had in common was that they would begin by describing a common scene from Jesus' surroundings, but then, just when he'd got his audience settled into the story, it would swing around and present them with a challenging alternative ending – a Kingdom of God ending as opposed to that expected by their oppressive society. Jesus' listeners were being introduced to the fact that perhaps Samaritans were human beings after all, that perhaps employers in the vineyard should be generous rather than keep day labourers in their place, and that perhaps it was worth the uphill battle of trying to live the Kingdom of God life if at the end of the day the seed you sow yields a hundredfold! His miracles too were awakening his followers to the scandal of their confinement and showing them they could be healed: they could take up their bed, stand up for themselves, and walk tall (Mark 2). All his teaching, his stories, his actions, were geared to liberating his followers from life as it was, so that they could reach out to life as it could be. And he called that the Kingdom of God where the love, justice and mercy of God beckons us and empowers us to act responsively.

After discovering this, our St Chad's group decided that their response would be to create an acted parable of their own and renamed themselves the 'Parables in Action Group'. They had already bonded wonderfully well, especially after spending a weekend away together where Thien, our Vietnamese member, cooked us a very challenging dish of chicken feet! Realising that the vividness of the parables was due to Jesus' careful observation of the world around him in Galilee, the group followed suit, and began a very thorough look at their own locality, its history, health, education and employment problems. They investigated the plight of local poor people, the marginalisation of their black or disabled members, the relativisation of women in their society and so on. They produced real-life case studies and set up role-plays. Ron was out and about taking photos, and others drew big maps and charts to describe the area and portray its development. But all this work did not result in a very rosy picture of our locality, and so they needed now to find a way to represent the alternative Kingdom of God picture of how things ought to be. They decided that this might best be done by creating a place where anyone could come together to get help, redress wrongs, and find support in times of isolation or need.

They were people who had never done anything like this before, but I encouraged them to take charge of all aspects of their new project and not allow outsiders to take control of their Acted Parable. They raised the cash, underwent intensive training with the Citizens' Advice Bureau, and set up their centre at the church where locals could congregate. And in addition to all this, they continued to meet as a group to reflect on what was happening, take forward their critique of it all, and look constantly for imaginative connections between Jesus' teaching and each step of the project's journey, so as to keep it as faithful as possible. During two more years of action and reflection, they empowered many in the community and developed for themselves a fascinating and novel theology of power and powerlessness. I wrote it all into my doctoral dissertation, nobly typed up by my secretary, Madeleine, but also published their story in my first paperback, *Power to the Powerless*, which was acclaimed by the *Church Times* as a Book of the Year for being 'a rare insight into what Liberation Theology could look like in a British context.' The congregation too were soon all playing their part in the work of the project, learning together as we went and experiencing the very obvious presence of God in it all. It helped St Chad's come alive in new ways, with our worship becoming much more related to the realities of our day-to-day lives and using our 'acted parables' methodology in many areas of our congregational life. The whole process had been a heroic undertaking. Sue Draper, a group member, summed up her experience of the project wonderfully well when, with a beaming smile, she declared, 'before we did all this, I thought incarnation was something you got out of a tin!'

Surely not me?

I had an idea that the parish could open its doors as a backstreet Mission Training Centre, where interested folk could come from across the West Midlands for seminars in urban theology, social engagement, lay formation and community living. But Bishop Hugh phoned, asking me to consider an advertisement in the church press. He explained that applications closed in just two days' time so if I put my name in immediately, that would give me time to consider whether it suited me. I could always withdraw if it didn't. The advertisement was for the national post of Principal of the Aston Training Scheme, a two-year course of education and formation for young men and women, prior to their going on to a residential college before their ordination. I was immediately attracted to it, because it was open to the transformative educational methods I'd been working on, it had strong academic backing from the Open University, and, most of all, its purpose was to introduce theology and open up a chance of leadership to people who would normally be denied both. It was a place where my hopes for the democratising and contextualising of British theology might have a chance to flourish. Bishop Hugh had said the job had my name on it, and I could not but agree that it suited me well, and would offer me a broader canvas to engage with those things which were now concerning me most.

I returned from a very full day of intensive interviews in London to be phoned that very evening to be informed that the national church had decided to offer me the post. I had been so blatantly honest about my radicalism, and so candid about my strengths and failings that I could only mutter, 'You do know it's Laurie Green you're phoning?' To my utter astonishment, they were indeed sure, and it was this appointment that was to start me on a new and very significant chapter of my life's journey.

I was anxious about breaking the news to the people of St Chad's. But I need not have worried, for having expressed how sorry they were that I was leaving, they seemed to see it as a feather in their own cap that I was going to what they saw as such an important post. With the new job, however, there was no house provided as there had always been in parish work so Vicki and I decided that this was our chance to live in a thoroughly multicultural area of the city. Seeing that there was in Handsworth a large Edwardian house going for a song, we decided that was to become our new home. The area was considered disreputable, but it was within our budget. We were looking forward to being surrounded by the Rasta culture, its music and annual Carnival, although our black parishioners were appalled and gasped: 'you can't go there. It's full of black people!' It was true that it had a very 'bad' name, so not long after we'd moved in, our old Biker friend, Eric, when he came to visit, was offered more than he bargained for. He'd located our road successfully, but when he slowed his car to look for our particular house, a rather unkempt and drug-ridden woman had jumped in alongside him and reeled off her menu of sexual favours. We nevertheless decided to go to Handsworth, feeling sure that as we got to know some of these marginalised people, and became accustomed to its great range of cultures, both we and our children would learn incalculable lessons from our encounter with human life in all its fullness.

However, the house itself required a complete overhaul so our dear friends from St Chad's came over at weekends to hold decorating parties. Whilst church steward Ray stripped out the old plumbing to create a proper bathroom for us, a dear man I'd first met on the shop floor at British Steel, gave up his holidays to strip the kitchen of wet rot. We loved the house once it was renovated and loved the neighbourhood too, settling down to worship at the local black Anglican church which stood opposite the Saddam Hussein Mosque just along the road. I was invited to become the one white face in the church choir, whilst Vicki worked in a predominantly Pakistani school as a pre-school worker, helping prepare children and families for the British schooling system. Our whole family benefited from her group's outings because Vicki would afterwards bring home gloriously spicy morsels they'd shared for their picnics. Our Vietnamese neighbours had tiny, adorable twins called Kung and Fu, whom our girls loved to mother. But Vicki and I were somewhat alarmed when, one afternoon, they reported that Kung and Fu had eaten all the heads off the flowers in the front garden. Their parents explained that in their country, flowers were grown for food, but we still secretly wished they hadn't denuded the garden of its little bit of colour.

Each day I would travel across the city to my new office which was situated next to the university on the Selly Oak Colleges campus. Alec Knight, the vice-principal, was helping me into my new role, and we soon found we held very similar views about adult education and clergy training. The most formidable presence around was undoubtedly Bridget Edger, the gloriously ebullient secretary, beloved of every student and an uncompromising champion of the course. I set about bringing in a very exciting array of voluntary part-time staff, among them Barry Thorley, who brought a charismatic personality and his black experience, Renate Wilkinson, my Lutheran friend, Peter Sedgwick, with his academic acumen, Philip Cliff, a New Testament specialist, and Robin Morrison to help encourage self-awareness. Geoff Milson already ran fabulous courses for those approaching study for the first time, whilst the feminist, Bridget Rees and Derrick Rowland helped as group consultants. I asked Geoffrey Harper, who had trained me in Kingstanding, to become our chaplain and he delighted in telling friends, 'Laurie phoned me knowing that I always had trouble getting him to attend Morning Prayer on time, and here he was asking me to become chaplain to the students on the grounds that, "I can't get the blighters to pray," Oh, the irony!'

Geoffrey's challenge struck home and prompted me to bite the bullet and get myself a spiritual director cum confessor – someone to talk with regularly and confidentially about my prayer life, or lack of it. The Franciscan friar, Brother Bernard, nobly took me on and encouraged me to visit the Benedictine community at Burford Priory. There I learnt from seeing the nuns and monks putting themselves in God's presence and just letting it happen. But could I ever allow myself to be so vulnerable? I had known the mysterious presence of God since I was a child, but I was fearful of prayer and wanted the territory mapped out for me before I ventured forth. Brother Bernard helped me to realise that my worries were also related to the presence of yet more fears which were lurking in my subconscious. As a young lad, some youngsters had once tried to drown me for fun, which left me terrified of water. The streets where I'd grown up were certainly never to be trusted, and my word-blindness left me tongue-tied whenever asked to read or speak off the cuff. So now I preferred to remain in the shallow end of prayer, rehearsing my long list of intercessions and saying the well-worn and familiar prayers. Brother Bernard suggested I cut out the words and just trust myself to God – but I feared drowning in the abyss of the mystery!

The unusual enterprise

In order to be accepted for ordination into the Church of England at that time, a candidate had to be sponsored by their parish and their bishop who would send them along to a weekend of intensive interviews covering such areas as academic competence, personal maturity and the development of their vocation. Those interviewers would then meet in camera to decide which of the candidates they could recommend to their bishop for training and ordination. It was soon realised that many who seemed otherwise acceptable were lacking basic study skills which our two-year non-residential course had originally been established to rectify. It had been called the Aston Training Scheme after its founder, Mark Green, the Bishop of Aston. The course proved so successful, that by the time I arrived as its principal, the selectors were sending not only those who needed help to study, but others who were lacking an appreciation of the breadth of our denomination. Some students had only experienced a high catholic style of Anglicanism – what we call in the trade 'up the candle' – and at the other extreme, there were those who were naughtily referred to as 'happy clappy'.

Others came, either because their experience of life thus far was somewhat limited, or because they were very new Christians who obviously had a calling, but were not yet able to know for sure where it should lead. Roger, for example, was a young man who had not been near a church, but was walking home from work one evening when he felt obliged to stop and listen. He could take you to the very tree where it happened. He heard a voice, as if from the Almighty, telling him that he was wanted as a priest. He was so embarrassed that he tried to hide it from his wife, who eventually demanded to know what, for the last few weeks, had been worrying him. When he outed with it, she wisely told him to go to the local vicar and see what he made of it. A couple of years later he found himself as one of our students, but thus far, with not much experience of the faith. I've never seen anyone so receptive and eager for knowledge.

I also soon came to realise that a high proportion of our students were arriving because the selectors felt they would not be appropriate leaders for the very conservative style of church they themselves preferred. Their prejudices seemed to cluster around the three issues of class, sexuality and gender – precisely the prejudices I was concerned to see eradicated from the Christian church. I had heard that one selector had decreed that one of her candidates could never become a Christian leader because, she said, 'he's only a carpenter!' Did she not realise the irony of her remark?

Our student body had therefore, over the years, become an extremely broad-ranging section of the population and not at all the 'also-rans' that those outside the process were assuming them to be. The consequence of this was that if, for example, a candidate with a doctorate were recommended with the condition that they first come to us, their vicar and the poor candidate could feel angry and write damning letters about the recommendation to their bishop, who sometimes caved in and reversed the decision. Some students therefore arrived with quite a chip on their shoulder whilst others knew from the start that our course was exactly what they needed. It was a situation which did not make it easy for our staff to handle, but in fact often turned out to be just what the student needed in order to prise open a path to much deeper personal and spiritual maturity. In the event, during their time on the course, we were privileged to see our students develop in stature in the most glorious ways.

From the day of my arrival, I was determined not to collude with the expectations that we should turn our students into something to suit the establishment. Many were deemed to be square pegs for the church's round hole, but I saw our task as empowering them to bring their true selves to ministry. And if that meant that the church would have to change the shape of its holes, then so much the better. If God was calling a carpenter to ordination, then the church would have to make way for them. Dave was a case in point. When I paid a visit to his vicar, he almost pinned me to the wall! 'Dave is a thoroughly working-class bloke, so you're not going to give him a parsonical voice and turn him into something he's not are you? He has so much to offer as he is.' The vicar took a lot of persuading but it served to reinforce my commitment that our students should be helped to stay true to the person God had called. Training for ordination must undoubtedly concern itself with preparing for ministry the whole person, not just the intellect, and this is often referred to as priestly 'formation'. But I had seen some courses which interpreted this as priestly con-formation, 'conforming' the candidate by rejecting their true self and making them adopt an artificial persona which is felt more appropriate to the role. I had myself experienced an element of that so, on our course, I was having none of it.

We therefore designed our first year programme to revolve around the question, for the students as for the staff, 'Who am I?' And to start the process, even before each student actually began their time with us, I made it my business to visit each one in their own home and place of work to affirm the gifts and experiences with which they came. I'd learnt from Dr Günzburg at Monyhull Hospital, and from my parish experience, that if you had not visited someone in their home context, you would never really understand what made them tick or recognise the gifts with which God had already endowed them. On those visits, my abiding endeavour was to discern as far as possible, what it was about them which was sacred and so, why God had called them.

Since our students lived the length and breadth of Britain, my work therefore involved a phenomenal amount of travelling each summer before they began their course. I drove miles and became past master of the national train timetables. Each evening I would find a phone box and check in with Vicki and the girls to let them know how my journey was progressing. One memorable evening, however, I was alarmed to learn from her that the whole of our Handsworth district had been hit by riots, resulting in burning and looting all across the neighbourhood. As soon as I got home I went out on to the streets and learned that there had been an altercation in the adjoining neighbourhood of Lozells which involved two policemen and an incorrectly parked car. Apparently the abusive language led to violence which in turn had escalated out of all proportion to the incident. Local people had come out on to the streets to vent their frustration at the constantly provocative attitude of local police, but the whole situation had intensified, not helped by the throb, throb, throb of a police helicopter forever hovering overhead, its spotlight picking us out one by one from above.

PAK BUTCHERS AND GROCER

Glass, Bricks
and
Devastation

The national press were soon swarming all over our neighbourhood and the next morning had the temerity to interpret the event as a race riot, even though locals had always taken pride in the contented mix of cultures in our community. What made me so very sad was that from that day on, local people, having been taken in by the press headlines, began themselves to interpret the events as racially motivated. So an altogether unsavoury atmosphere of mutual mistrust appeared on our streets for the first time – yet another example of how our perceptions are manipulated by the powers that be. We noticed with dismay that groups of white tourists from other parts of the city now began descending on our area to take pictures of the damage and to snap the bemused local people for their own entertainment. For Handsworth, the whole business had been humiliating and alienating. I'd been writing about such experiences in my doctoral dissertation, and now here it was in my face – like the blood of Abel crying out from the ground (Gen. 4: 10).

I managed it through a packed first year of study weekends, course work and student mentoring, all based on learning from experience, climaxing in our Summer School to which all ninety students were invited. We invited wives and husbands into these sessions too, because we were very much aware that their lives, once their spouse was ordained, would never be the same again. We hoped to offer them at least a little preparation for that transition. The Summer School venues had to be large and flexible, and because we were catering for families and many young children, we were pleased to take over a residential college in Bognor Regis where we were given free access to the fun at the nearby Butlin's Holiday Camp. The downside was that the college buildings in which we were housed were as cheap as the fee they charged us, and one night Vicki and I awoke to hear our children screaming because their bedroom ceiling had collapsed on them! There was little by way of apology from the college authorities and so we never used that venue again. The year ended with a grand service in Chichester Cathedral, at the end of which Alec, Bridget and I returned to the vestry and fell into one another's arms overcome with relief – we'd made it successfully through a whole year!

We were now training no less than a tenth of all Church of England ordinands so it was obvious that we could not continue with only three central staff. I obtained, at a very low rental, a suite of small offices in the grounds of a Black Pentecostal College near our home which reduced our administrative costs significantly. This meant that it became financially possible to delight in the appointment of a new vice-principal, Michael Allen, with his speciality in human psychology and the wonderful Jeni Parsons who, with her astute mind and loving disposition, took on the new role of Director of Studies. The very able Patricia Fletcher now shared in the administration alongside Bridget, and soon we became a really close and happy band of five, eschewing our packed lunches and nipping down to the pub for a fish and chip lunch together whenever we had a less frantic day.

At the heart of the Aston Training Scheme style was small-group interaction, designed to build human sensitivity, interactive skills and a commitment to collaborative ministry. Our students were soon aware of how human creativity is energised and enhanced by working in groups when they found themselves tackling set tasks that would have been beyond them if acting alone.

Our residential weekends together would each have a particular focus, be it liberation, mission, what it is to be church, spirituality, and so on, and for our culminating eucharists each group would be responsible for designing and offering a particular section of the service. If they had done that individually we might have expected the usual verbal offerings, but instead our liturgies became dramatic, interactive and exceedingly moving. Often the group togetherness would empower a more reticent member to take a leading role which would wonderfully enhance their self-confidence. And it was their own personal reflection upon their individual and group behaviour, helped by each having a pastoral tutor from outside the course, which helped them analyse and own their development.

I couldn't help feeling at one with those students who came to us doubting their appropriateness for ministry. Steve, for example, told me how he had looked at himself in his hall mirror as he prepared to go for his first interview with his bishop. He saw his piercings, his tattoos and his leathers and said to himself: 'there's no way they're going to accept me!' It helped him to know that I had a tattoo myself, but above all it was the affirmation he received from staff and fellow students in those groups that freed him to become one day a wonderfully holy, down to earth parish priest. Given the homophobia in many sections of the church, it was also good to see our students able to speak openly at last and think honestly about their sexuality, although I was constantly attacked by those outside the course for allowing such honesty. Michael, a rather scruffy but adorable gay Belfast man, was already astonishingly vocal about his sexual disposition. It was humbling to observe how he and the straight, besuited Edward, a one-time Irish land agent, became so trusting of one another that they were able to talk frankly about those times Michael's Belfast home had been ransacked by British soldiers during the Irish Troubles.

I could also identify with those who had had negative experiences of school or study, but again, our task was not so much to impart facts as encourage self-confidence. I asked Alan at the end of his time as a student with us what it was that had made him suddenly throw off his reticence and steam ahead with his academic studies. He explained that it was when he heard me, quite by chance, mention that Jesus would have had dirt under his fingernails. Being a car mechanic with ever-grimy hands, he had experienced that simple observation as a huge liberation. We worked in close harmony with the Open University so that each student could undertake an OU module suitable to their needs at a centre close to their home. This both deepened their study skills and broadened their horizons, coming away with a basic appreciation of both the arts and social sciences. And time and again we found that if we could build self-confidence in this way, then students' innate skills and talents would be liberated. But this was not easy in a church which at that time radiated such blatant racist, sexist and classist attitudes.

Another great benefit of the course was that we were not like many of the residential colleges which set out to attract those students who wanted to be affirmed in just one understanding of church and theology. The sheer diversity of our own student body forced them to come to terms with the extreme diversity of the Church of England. Jon came from a strongly evangelical congregation, but an industrial accident had left him in constant pain and unable any longer to engage in manual work. With us he encountered for the first time colleagues who hailed from the very 'high' catholic church style. They invited him to visit the catholic shrine of Our Lady of Walsingham and whilst there they convinced him to be sprinkled with the holy waters. Jon was astonished that within a church tradition so alien from his own he then experienced instantaneous healing, to be later confirmed by his medics. He was overjoyed, but saddened to encounter real hostility from his home evangelical congregation who adamantly refused to believe that anything from another section of the church could have the power they claimed as their own. Our students had every reason to become generously inclusive of the great array of styles and insights to be found within Anglicanism. We were all learning, for example, from Eve's haunting gospel songs and her championing of an equal voice for Black British people like herself. Another student, Veronica, was adamantly flying the flag for the ordination of women to the priesthood – which many of our students were at that time still finding very difficult.

The predominantly sexist language then rife in Britain was significantly influencing the mindset of our students. We therefore worked hard at unpacking its implications whenever it occurred during our group sessions. We had groups look at the rife sexism prevailing in Jesus' time when, in the Galilean villages Jewish women were not allowed to study the Bible. Likewise, contemporary Roman legislation decreed that wives were the property of their husbands. Our students unanimously agreed that this was unjust, but it forced them to ask how far we had actually progressed since then. Jesus had stood up against those cultural expectations for although he chose twelve men to represent the twelve tribes of Israel, he had many female disciples too. Special mention is given to Mary Magdalene, chosen to be the first witness and apostle of the resurrection, and there was the wealthy Joanna, wife of Herod's steward, who with Susanna supported Jesus' mission financially (Luke 8:3). As very close friends of Jesus, John's gospel singles out Mary and Martha, the sisters of Lazarus. And Luke's gospel, chapter ten, tells us that on his visit to their home he affirmed Mary for her concentration on learning rather than Martha's insistence that her place was confined to the kitchen. Other examples show how the earliest Christians had learnt the lesson and had women take on leadership roles in the church, and only later did it fall away from the liberational trajectory Jesus had set. Until we in our day had righted this wrong, women's ordination was not going to get a foothold. But on Aston the case was vigorously made, led by our Director of Studies Jeni, who encouraged us all to do some deep soul-searching.

Many of the church's clergy were however so buttoned up that they were quite antagonistic towards the course's self-reflective methodology. I ventured into one rather palatial rectory to visit a priest who had a national reputation for strident disputation and, as I recall, an enormous stuffed bear dressed in a top-hat in his hallway. As I sat supping tea and explaining what the course entailed for his young ordinand he interjected: 'I've heard that the Aston thing uses groups and modern relationship training and such like. Can that be true?' I did my best to explain the truth of it in the gentlest of terms, but was completely taken off guard when he exclaimed: 'Excellent! I'm so glad to hear that, for that's precisely what my young man needs. He's so lovely, but must be helped to be at one with himself if he's to be of use to others.' I sighed with relief, supped my tea, munched another of his exotic biscuits and relaxed back on the chaise longue where he had perched me. Every visit had its surprises.

The Aston Community Summer

Students came to us only after going through the church's rigorous discernment procedures, but the criteria by which new clergy were chosen at that time included no reference to matters of racism, sexism or classism – three areas which we believed were of prime importance if ever they were to become Christian leaders. Our sessions were carefully designed therefore, not only to encourage spiritual and intellectual development, but to address the questions of unjust discrimination. An obvious way to tackle issues of ethnicity was for Vicki and I to invite them to our home in Handsworth where we helped them reflect on what they experienced there. Vicki would alert them to the Acapulco Café, a notorious drug centre where the owner often flashed his shotgun at any troublemakers, and she rather bemoaned the fact that in all the years we'd lived there she'd never once been offered drugs on the streets – unlike everyone else we knew! She didn't want any drugs, but she wanted to know how it was that the dealers could see that. Our visiting students often registered that our shops usually sold goods for which the best before date had long passed and it grabbed their attention that the dress of the locals, although bright, had obviously seen better days. Those students who before this had been adamantly antagonistic to Muslims and their faith, had to admit that they had never ventured inside a mosque before. Others were quite surprised at the glorious vibrancy of the life on the streets, despite the area's rundown state. Most visitors to Handsworth found things fearfully intimidating. But our students returned home with a very different understanding of the reality of poverty, marginalisation and ethnicity, having sampled something of the *joie de vivre* of this oppressed, multicultural community. It alerted them to the need for a more sensitive and respectful approach to the cultures and restricted opportunities of others.

The students themselves were such a diverse bunch that this diversity itself opened their eyes to the complexities of how our different cultures shape us. Coming from every walk of life, one would turn up with a brightly coloured Mohican haircut, another in biking gear and tattoos, while others arrived in their pin-striped suits, Caribbean shawls or 'Afro' hairstyles. But all learnt to work together in the commonality of very challenging academic studies, the exacting experiential group sessions and the constant requests for self-assessment. But all this was tempered by great fun and the very deep and lasting friendships that were forged among them. My rush to get to one weekend venue on time reduced me to asking our secretary Bridget to pop out to buy some underpants for me because I'd not had time to pack a spare pair. How this became public knowledge I'll never know, but from then on it was regularly referred to, however obliquely, in our regular student concerts. These were opportunities for the hidden talents of the students to come to the fore – we had singers, poets, actors, script writers, musicians and comedians aplenty! Our fun evenings and times of relaxation were tremendously important on a course which was so very demanding.

Moving the church on

What I particularly hoped for was that our students would come to appreciate that whilst God is revealed to us in the Bible, God is also revealed to us in our own experience of the world. I was by now thoroughly convinced that by bringing these two sources of revelation together, the Bible and our experience, we could make connections that would furnish us with much deeper understanding, both of our experience and of the Bible. We might, for example, be deeply immersed in the challenge of our present despoliation of the planet and be very worried about how it is bound to affect our family and nation. We hear that people in the poor majority world are suffering too, and we join our politicians in blaming their governments for not being willing to cut back on their escalating use of coal and gas as much as we are. 'We lead the world on climate change', is one of the mantras of our statesmen. But while we're working on that issue, we might happen to hear in church the story in which Jesus compares what the rich put into the temple collection with the paltry amount offered by a woman he notices. But instead of blaming her, he observes, 'this poor widow has put in most of all who are putting money into the treasury for they have all put in money they could spare, but she out of her poverty has put in everything she possessed, all she had to live on.' (Mark 12: 43-44) Then, when we return to our environmental concerns, the story prompts us to look afresh at the plight of today's poor widows of the majority world who are experiencing drought and hunger because of climate change, and we are now prompted by Jesus' observation, to reflect more closely on the link between their plight and our wealth. We therefore perceive the double talk of the wealthy nations and companies who say they are giving most to ease environmental challenges, when it's actually the poor nations who bear the heaviest burden and give their very lives as a consequence of our selfishness. As we research the matter in more detail, we see that the rich nations are in fact exporting our manufacturing needs to those poor countries, making them produce the goods we then import cheaply back for our own consumption, thereby turning the poor countries into smokestack polluters as a consequence. The Bible has thus emboldened our analysis, mandating and energising us to enter into prophetic engagement in the world. The correlation between Bible and today's situation has in this way demanded that the Bible scholar must become one who both thinks *and acts*!

Thus far, we may say, the process has been quite traditional, letting the Bible speak to our condition. But the 'Doing Theology', contextual method I was promoting, then asks the theologian to see how the situation in turn speaks to the Bible, for correlation is not a one-way process, but must be truly reciprocal. So, in our example, the scriptural passage about the generosity of the poor widow, which is usually wheeled out by the well-heeled to show how Jesus affirmed the widow for her generosity towards the establishment, turns out to mean something very different. It is an accusation of those power élite who put pressure on the poor, driving them into subservience and sacrifice. Such things become very clear when we let both the scripture critique our situation *and* we let our situation critique the scripture. For God speaks through both scripture and experience and by bringing these two forms of revelation together we see theology working its magic – and not just for scholars, but for any committed Christian who wants to live at that interface between Word and world.

But that understanding of how theology should be made to function, which seemed so blatantly obvious to me, was way out of line with what many of the professional academics at the colleges believed at that time. During one visit, a very influential teacher of Old Testament yelled at me: 'what on earth has politics got to do with the Old Testament?' He surely knew that much of the Hebrew Scriptures is in fact religious interpretation of the political events of the time, but his anger at my approach had got the better of him. I knew, however, that many of the colleges and non-residential courses harboured younger staff who were themselves keen to experiment with more experiential methods of training, although many were constrained by the rigidity of their institutions. They told us that when our students went through to their classes, their critical awareness was all too evident after their previous two years on our course. They were more mature, self-aware and theologically alert than their other students – a joy to teach, they said.

The conservative mindset of the church authorities angered our students so much that when John Habgood, the Archbishop of York, came to speak, they asked him outright: 'if a student at one of the theological colleges passes all the examinations, but is not much good with people, would that candidate still be ordained?' The Archbishop was a thoroughly honest man and gave them an honest answer and bemoaned the fact that, as things stood, such students were passing on to ordination without further difficulty. He was therefore very impressed to hear how holistic was our own

197

assessment process. At the end of each year, our students would produce a detailed self-assessment of their individual progress and then a visiting team of assessors would work with them to determine whether they should proceed to the next step of their training. This was a heavy burden for the students, but had astonishing results in terms of their developing personal maturity and spiritual growth. This rigorous assessment process did however have its funny moments. One year we set off with a group of students to the Berlin Kirchentag, where the issues of the day were addressed in the light of the Christian faith. The students were keen to relax on the beach by the lake, but realising on arrival that the German initials FKK signalled that the bathing was nude, they chickened out on the grounds, they said, that that was taking their student assessment just a shade too far.

It was important to share with the wider church what we were learning from our approach to training and so we were asked to publish a book about it. Norman Todd worked with us on it, but was not sure what the title of the book should be. He'd heard our Aston Scheme referred to by those who knew little about us as, 'a thing called Aston', and so we decided to use that somewhat disparaging remark as our title. The book turned out to have a wide circulation and I hear that it encouraged other educators to try our approach.

It was good to meet some college staff and a growing number on local courses who were altogether affirming of our approach, and were determined to introduce many of our practices into their own educational processes. In addition, many others from outside the academic world were keen to promote what they saw us doing. Among them were many of the bishops, one of whom, David Sheppard, Bishop of Liverpool, invited me to lead his final diocesan lay conference before his retirement. Another, the Bishop of Bristol, Barry Rogerson, asked me to run a conference on contextual theology for all his clergy. So whilst our students were influencing the colleges from within, I was campaigning outwardly for this approach whenever I had opportunity.

The theological method and style of working which I was championing were greatly influenced by Tillich's theory of correlation, and of course by the liberation theologians of Latin America, especially Leonardo Boff with whom I was in correspondence. In addition, my friendships with priests and nuns visiting from Peru and Brazil, who were working with Christian peasants and poor farmers in their own countries, were extremely important in influencing how our work developed. Boff had described his liberation theology as a pastoral cycle of reflection, but had written of it in such academic terms that I felt sure that, if it were to become more accessible, it would benefit from a more visual representation. Because diagrams had helped me so much with my own learning difficulties, I was also taken with some that had been used by the educational psychologists I'd worked for during my year at Monyhull Hospital and so I began to use those as my model. Other thinkers had similar ideas, but I could see that they were working theoretically rather than basing their suggestions on experience of actually doing theology this way. I was therefore prompted by many of my colleagues to present my method to the wider public, which eventually issued in publishing it in a book entitled *Let's Do Theology*.

I had confidence in the book because many friends and colleagues had already been working with my method. They provided me with helpful feedback so that I was able to refine many details and present the whole theological process as a thoroughly contextual approach. I continually stressed that the Bible was not the only Christian treasure that could offer spirit-inspired correlations with our present issues and experience. We were, for example, also served by a vast heritage of Christian writings, art, music and so on through the ages – and just as with our approach to biblical material, so we had to apply the same rigorous critique to each of them regarding the context within which each was produced. What all these treasures had in common was they were each an expression, offered from within the constraints of their particular context, of an experience of the one eternal God, the Ground of Being, and therefore offered insight in varying degrees into God's self-revelation. This was why they too could correlate with our own experience and issue in inspiring theological thought and action. Theology was therefore no longer to be thought of as an abstract thing, but as informed Christian action – hence the title, *Let's Do Theology.*

'Let's Do Theology' in English & Chinese

Little did I suspect that students would be using it as a basic textbook in colleges around the world even thirty and more years later. At least one mission organisation, Unlock, began to build its whole programme around it, and we now see that diagram cropping up everywhere.

I was really thrilled one day to receive a letter from Anthony Harvey, the same New Testament scholar with whom I had had such an altercation at Canterbury just prior to my ordination. His letter praised the work we were doing with our students, seeing it as a vindication of what he had hoped to achieve years before when he had had me as his student. He applauded our way of seeing education and training as an integrated process of growth for each student, offering experiences that would gradually build, brick upon brick, into a coherent and strong base for their continuing learning in life. This was another important principle that I'd picked up from Monyhull Hospital, where I'd been in on the development of 'process learning'. From the arrival of Anthony's letter to the end of his life we became very firm friends, with Anthony often helping me with my biblical enquiries and book research. It was a lovely experience of genuine reconciliation in which we both learnt from one another.

What I've more recently found so very encouraging is that, although our students had originally been deemed by many as second class ordinands, as the years have passed we have seen them become cathedral deans, archdeacons, directors of training and first class parish priests. They have brought to the church at large a more collaborative attitude to leadership, they'd helped towards the breakdown of clerical elitism and they'd played significant roles in the formation of clergy and lay training. When we consider that throughout the Bible there are accounts of people who were considered by their society to be of no account being especially singled out by God to play very significant roles in God's plan, then it's evident that we were on to a winner. The Hebrews remembered for example that their great king David, only a shepherd boy, had been selected to lead his people to freedom and unity and, most significant of all, Mary, a young, pregnant, unmarried lass was chosen to become the mother of Jesus himself! Was it this that had turned her into such a revolutionary that she sang, 'He has taken down princes from their thrones and raised up the lowly' (Luke 1:52)? Our course had obviously therefore had the hand of God upon it, for it turned out that we had been training not the also-rans, but the church's élite corps.

What next?

My initial contract as principal of the programme had been for a five year period, but the governors prevailed upon me to lengthen my term to seven, which I was more than happy to do. But the moment eventually arrived when it was right for me to move on to make room for the next chapter of the Course to be taken forward by new minds and allow my own ministry and thinking to develop elsewhere. We were certainly going to miss living in Handsworth with its heady texture of life and cultures, and neither were our two daughters pleased at the thought of moving to a new home. Vicki had, over the years, become quite an authority on how to empower young

Asian mums to manage life when caught in the vortex of cultural flows, and it was important that wherever we went that expertise should not go to waste. We'd lived in Birmingham now for nearly twenty years, we'd seen our children born there, we'd gathered hundreds of friends there, and most of my work contacts were there. In addition to my work with students, I was really enjoying helping to train social workers in Worcestershire, working with the local Diocesan adult education department, and was an admiring member of the Black and White Partnership of churches organised by Rostwith Gerloff. I was running the Birmingham Theology Co-op in league with John Vincent's Urban Theology Unit, chairing Ute Jaekel's Asian vegetable Ashram and still pushing hard for the Ordination of Women and church unity. If we had to move, I didn't want to say goodbye to all these passions of mine, but quite what was in store for us remained a mystery. But my contract was fast coming to an end, so time was pressing.

CHAPTER 9

BACK TO THE JELLIED EELS

Although I'd loved my seven years heading up the Aston Training Scheme, the heart of the Church of England is essentially to be found in the work of its parish churches across the nation. So I was pleased therefore that my next appointment was to an exciting and challenging parish back in East London.

Whilst in Birmingham I had submitted a contribution to the Archbishop's *Faith in the City* report, which, in 1985, was to take the nation by storm. It had opened up the Church of England to the challenges and opportunities of the urban and made strident recommendations to church and state. Perhaps it was seeing my interest in urban ministry which prompted Bishop Jim Thompson to invite me to his Stepney Area to become Team Rector of All Saints, Poplar, deep in the heart of London's East End. I went to have a nose round the parish surreptitiously, feeling somewhat like the Prodigal Son creeping back home, but I was very excited by what I saw. Before I drove home that evening, I fancied some fish and chips and, while it was good to chat in my native tongue whilst waiting in line, the terrible taste of the skate and chips almost put me off going for interview.

In the event, the interview proved to be a very enjoyable day-long process during which I was shown round the church building with its spacious Georgian grandeur, its statues, candles and intoxicating smell of incense. I met the talented staff team and was interviewed by some of the leading lights of the congregation, the Bishop himself, and an Oxford college chaplain. Apparently they agreed unanimously and invited me and the family to come down to Poplar and continue our lives there. I felt I was bringing my family home to where I first belonged.

When you look at a map of London you see the River
Thames curling southward in a great U-bend just east of the
Tower of London, and that loop creates what is known as 'the
Isle of Dogs'. Like sentinels guarding the top of each side of
the U stand two great churches: St Anne's Limehouse on the
west and All Saints Poplar to the east. During the Blitz, 'the
Island' formed the A1 target for the German bombers seeking
to destroy the industry and dockyards that were keeping
Britain alive. But during the 1960s those thriving docks had
fallen into decline and by the 80s were proving a millstone
around the economy of the region. Old run-down terraced
houses had been surrounded by concrete high-rise blocks and
small but comfy maisonettes built for the Festival of Britain by
the post-war Labour government. Poplar was really not much
to look at, but the people were simply magnificent. They'd
been cut off from the globalising changes that were now
impacting the rest of the capital city by what was reckoned to
be the busiest road in England. This was the East India Dock
Road leading into the Commercial Road, stringing itself across
the top of the Island. This isolation left the Island as a last
bastion of the old-time cockney East End of my childhood,
making me feel immediately at home.

If you emerge from the Blackwall Tunnel and turn left, All
Saints, with its fine spire, is easily spotted on your left. Around
the area cluster some of the best Chinese restaurants in
London since the original Limehouse China Town is nearby.
One senses the ghost of Moriarty, Sherlock Holmes' great
rival, lurking in the alleyways. Opposite the church still stands
Chrisp Street market where, in 1933, my dad had bought
mum a pair of gloves, his very first gift to her. So this was their
home territory, and sure enough, when Vicki and I arrived
with the removal van, mum and dad were waiting on the
doorstep to welcome us into the rectory with a warming cup of
'Rosie Lea'.

The Georgian rectory stood proudly opposite the parish church and presented us with no less that nine large bedrooms. It also had a basement big enough to accommodate the parish offices, a print-shop and youth club rooms which still boasted a full-sized, but battered, snooker table. The house was separated from the road by a high chicken wire fence so that the garden was open to the many passers-by who loved to stop and inspect the All Saints peacock! We inherited the bird along with the house, but on hearing that he had never been given a name, I decided to call him Dudley in honour of the region from which we'd just come. I was a little taken aback, however, on noticing one day that Dudley Peacock was sporting a series of large lumps in his long neck. But passing parents assured me not to worry because it was simply that Dudley was still digesting their gift of boiled sweets that their children knew he loved. But Dudley was a tough old bird and took it all in his strut. The rectory was not a quiet house. It had the docklands railway running behind it, the fire station and ambulance centre round the corner, the flight path from London City Airport overhead and the busy East India Dock Road clunking by. So we were pleased that the heavy Georgian shutters could be pulled across our windows at night. In all the time we lived there we were burgled only once, but the locals were soon knocking on the door to assure us that they would find the culprits and make them pay. Unfortunately, the intruders had come from out of town so our missing belongings were never returned.

The church was packed for the service at which I was made the new Team Rector of Poplar. The choir processed, the incense ascended, the great organ swelled and a contingent of my old students joined the congregation to sing the rousing hymns. Bishop Jim presented me with the legal documents and preached a riveting sermon, after which we all gathered for the bunfight and the speeches. The churchwarden, Sid, who had worked in the music halls years ago, invited everyone to give me a big hand, at which point the most enormous model hand I'd ever seen appeared in the crowd. To follow that, I could only play things for laughs, so explained that when vicar in my previous parish, I'd been known as Laurie the Vic, so here as rector I was obviously going to be labelled Laurie the Rec. At that, Janice, my new parish secretary, turned to John, her husband, and said: 'He'll do.' When I heard that remark, I knew I was back home.

The population of Poplar Parish was just under twenty-nine thousand and had recently been recognised as one of the most deprived areas in the country. But I had joined a large and very talented team of clergy to serve it: the young, charismatic Irish priest, Niall Weir, a fountain of generosity, Peter Bristow, an insightful ex-Roman Catholic priest and Marion Palmer, our deacon. Two retired parish workers, Grace and Daphne, worked tirelessly despite their age, and finally Father Bill Shergold, the legendary 'Ton-Up Vicar' of the sixties, who'd retired back to the parish where his ministry had begun, was now a gentle and stabilising presence. As members of the team moved on, others such as Veronica Hydon, John Hawkins and Eddie Carden joined us. The editor of the *Newham Recorder*, Tom Duncan, headed up the laity as our parish Reader, Brian Hagger was our brilliant Director of Music, whilst Sid Langely, the born entertainer, along with Peter Draper, were our trusty churchwardens. The wonderfully gregarious Janice Milbank supported us all as the parish secretary, and happily agreed to move her office across to the church so that she could keep the church doors open to the community on a daily basis.

The huge Poplar Parish was the outcome of the amalgamation of nine former East End parishes, including St Frideswide's, the church where the events of the television series *Call the Midwife* had actually taken place. But the TV series told stories about the sisters that were only half as exciting as those told by the locals. During my home visits I'd sometimes spy sections of stained glass built into the bathroom décor, the explanation being: 'We took it from St Matthias' Father, cos we don't like seeing the old place turn into a ruin.' Their love for this second of our redundant churches spurred me to open

206

negotiations with the council to see if it could be turned into a community centre. St Nick's church to the north was now rented out as a record storehouse, but what was still visible of the ceiling delighted the eye, for it had been decorated by the famous artist, Hans Feibusch. So I began legal proceedings to move the record company on so that the building could return to its proper use. To alert Bishop Jim to our needs, the parish invited him to a community party on the open space in front of the building. He marvelled at the fact that we had managed to power the amplifying equipment without a generator. We assured him that the people of Poplar had learnt the hard way how to overcome little problems like that, but I suspect that the lads had wired us into a local lamppost.

Our church school's modern building stood just round the corner from the old St Saviour's church, which was now leased to the Celestial Church of Christ, an African Pentecostal congregation with a special connection to Benin. I was warmly welcomed in and proudly directed to observe the biggest inflatable banana I'd ever seen, suspended above the altar. It reminded me that our own All Saints church itself housed some interesting ornamentation. I was once asked by Patrick Appleford, who'd been a Poplar curate years before: 'is that old cow still in your church?' I was somewhat at a loss to know how to answer when he explained that when our *Call the Midwife* church had been closed, they removed the large statue of its patron, St Frideswide. She had established the cathedral in Oxford, and so her emblem is the ox, and her statue which was removed to All Saints church shows her with an ox at her side – not quite an old cow!

Father Niall was housed in the old vicarage of St Michael's church, originally called St Leonard's, which had once been home to the legendary East End 'slum priests'. Niall hosted wonderful free concerts there for the locals, and used his theatre connections to bring in such celebrities as Fascinating Aida, and Larry Adler, the then famous classical harmonica player and raconteur.

The great church of All Saints had appeared on the scene in 1821, adorned with Corinthian decoration and topped by an elegant steeple. Our worship was of a high catholic style, but quite unfussy, which proved very attractive to the bustling families who made up the bulk of the congregation.

All Saints
Poplar

All around the community there was an exceptionally strong sense of belonging, reinforced by the stories of their devastating war experiences, still vividly remembered even after forty-five years. But their present experiences were shocking in themselves. I suggested to one small group that we each share our life stories, but it was not long into the exercise before we were in tears on hearing each participant tell of their life experiences. And yet, these same people gave very little evidence of despair. Often they were more vibrant, carefree, bombastic and ebullient than you would dare believe. Although not everyone was a saint, each was a fascinating character worthy of a biography. Wonderful friendships and unaffected fun were everywhere, their inner strength clearly underpinned by their shared sense of place. The people of the Bible felt a sacred devotion to their promised land, and here too I wanted to say: 'Take off your shoes, for you're on holy ground.' The people here were the cleaners, drivers, artisans and office workers who kept the city ticking, but who were rarely noticed or valued. This disregard reminded me of our creator God's preparedness to hold everything together, enabling others to function, but without being noticed, and rarely thanked or applauded. For me, God was obviously in this place.

But that's not to say Poplar was all sweetness and light! These same loveable characters could swear, curse and lash out, even at their dearest friends. Sometimes the workplace could become fractious, with grudges harboured and the weak isolated. There were racist groups and the occasional civil servant or social worker out to seek their own petty aggrandisement, but even then, I still felt God within it all, but now yearning and suffering with his children. Some will see this as romantic idealism on my part I'm sure, but there was so much gritty realism about the place that it was difficult to harbour romantic fantasies about much of it. I suspect that it was not so much the place itself, but the profound emotions it conjured up, which made me know the place was holy.

Religion in Poplar

Many Poplar people believed there was a God, but the nature of that god was another matter altogether. George came only to the annual All Souls service, and despite his lonely life, would always say to me afterwards: 'God is good, God's always good.' On the other hand, the pressure of misfortune made some reject the god they still believed in. On a tombstone in our graveyard someone had scratched in heavy crayon: 'God is a bastard', as if to cry out: 'my God, why have you forsaken me?' Since I wore my cassock on the street I'd sometimes be stopped and pulled into a discussion about God. There I learned that many had already thought long and hard about matters of faith, and even prayed a simple prayer each night – but they were certainly not going to church! They would tell me they were spiritual, but not religious.

In Poplar I also found that people had a very keen appreciation of the realities of sin and evil, although they would rarely have used such terms. Many of the personal sins were, to some extent, a consequence of not being able to withstand the structural evil which was constantly being visited upon them. I have never had to wait upon the whimsical decisions of someone else in order that I could have the chance of a reasonable existence. But that was the predominant experience of many of those I lived amongst. Many lived in homes too small to allow them to get away from an abusive family member, whilst some relied for their weekly income on the complications of a demeaning benefits system. Jacky had been violent towards those he loved, but I had heard that in his childhood he had himself been abused in some way. He'd repeatedly battered his mother, and would come to the rectory late into the night and demand that I take him into the church to say some prayers. There he would stand in front of the altar screaming obscenities at God, shouting: 'look at my mother! God, look at my mother!' It would take ages for his anger to subside, after which I'd say a quiet prayer with him, we'd light a candle and we'd leave in silence. Often those who were suffering at the hands of another or from their unjust circumstances would turn the guilt inwards and say: 'I must have done something wrong to be punished like this.' Sin and evil are everywhere, but were more sharply focused in Poplar than in more sophisticated communities where people can sometimes be better shielded from the consequences of their own faults or the faults of others.

Getting physical

Despite the harsh architecture and the intense challenges of daily life, the vibrant and gloriously vivid personalities of the people made Poplar a thrilling and joyous place to be. Their spirited physicality was in your face: the loud behaviour, the blaring music and the brassy fashions reminded me that we can find God not only in silence, but in the vivid actuality of life, and that the spiritual is in no way limited to the nonmaterial or super-natural sphere. The Christian faith is firmly rooted in the very physical experience of the life and death of Jesus, a human being embedded in the earthiness of history. My friend, Austin Smith, had posed the question: 'is crucifixion a religious experience?' bringing home to us that we dare not shunt God off into some ethereal ghostly siding, for even within the harsh physicality of torture, God is there with us.

Some today labour under the illusion that Jesus was not a real, physical person in history at all, even though it's confirmed by contemporary evidence. Roman historians like Tacitus (Annals 15.44.3) and lawyers such as Suetonius wrote about the Jesus whose followers were causing so many problems for their Empire. Records left by early Jewish rabbis follow the Romans in being disparaging of him – surprisingly, even claiming credit for his death. But in addition, we still have letters and documents which were written by the earliest Christians themselves, a few becoming part of our New Testament. So the brash physicality of the people of Poplar was a vivid reminder that Jesus was a real historical man, reinforcing the truth that God is not in some distant Never-Never-Land, but fully engaged in our world, for as the Gospels have it, Jesus is Emmanuel – meaning 'God is with us'.

But just as different newspapers today will report the news from their own perspectives, so likewise we have to remember that the Gospel accounts of Jesus' life were written by those who wanted to impress on their readers just how their experience of Jesus had impacted their own understandings and changed their lives. So the gospel accounts are not a straightforward recounting of historical fact, but reflect how Jesus was *experienced*. Luke feels it's particularly important to show how Jesus liberated people from oppression, and so includes many stories and events to demonstrate that point. Matthew, on the other hand, is dead keen to tell us how Jesus was there for his own Jewish community – although to keep the balance he also includes a story about three eastern wise men, non-Jews, coming to worship the child. Whether

Matthew's three wise men actually existed was not the point for first century readers, but they would have understood Matthew's spiritual point that Jesus was saviour for the Jews, but not exclusively so. Likewise, the virgin birth story was introduced into two of the later gospels to press home the fact that the birth of Jesus was all in God's hands, not ours, even though in today's world of modern biology that story may sound decidedly troubling. That's why biblical scholarship has developed the very advanced tool of biblical hermeneutics to unravel how these texts would have been understood by contemporary readers and therefore what their meaning and veracity is for us today. If we then add the tremendous advances we've made in our archaeological research, we see that we really do know that Jesus was a real human being in history whose impact was earth shattering. We recognise too how biting was his critique of the issues of his day and what an astonishing teacher, sage and social analyst he was. The historian, Tom Holland, has shown us how the emergence of Christianity has been the single most transformative development in western history, and how it has shaped our norms and culture. Britain would not be as it is without the life and teaching of this man Jesus.

Some of the issues Jesus critiqued were obviously evident in Poplar too. In our own congregation were many highly-skilled manual workers who had been reduced to life as security guards or supermarket shelf-stackers by the forces of globalisation. They were just like those Galileans who once took pride in their own small family farms, but had been made, by the cash-crop requirements of the Roman trading system, to sell up and stand in the marketplace, alongside day labourers. They now hoped to be hired for a day on the very land they'd once owned – hence the parable of the labourers in the vineyard (Matthew 20). Again, although our church was still not ordaining women, Jesus had welcomed many female followers, even selecting Mary Magdalene to be the first apostle of the resurrection, sent by him to tell the other disciples he had risen from the dead. Even so, men soon claimed church leadership, and have been hanging on to that privilege for two millennia. In All Saints Poplar, the women were very feisty cockney characters whose gifts were of real consequence. They initiated many of the projects, and were keen to play their part. Indeed our curate, Veronica, who had been a student on the Aston Scheme, continued to be one of the leading lights in the fight for women's ordination.

The more we look, the more relevant Jesus becomes to the fundamental issues of our society's woes, and the more radical and subversive the historical Jesus becomes. There was no doubt in my mind that this extraordinary man would have been very much at home in Poplar today.

All Saints faces the challenges

The people of Poplar were certainly in the direct line of fire when it was decided to redevelop the dock area around Canary Wharf so that it could serve the needs of the new global economy by becoming a centre for financial services. Foreign money was poured in, and the Isle of Dogs became the biggest and dustiest building site imaginable. All our local television signals crashed as a result of the massive iron structures that were rising into the sky, and as we coughed our way through each day, house prices began to rocket. Local tenants were given notice to leave their homes to make way for a new, young, wealthy and tech-savvy labour force.

All Saints' church had had to decide how to respond to this transformation of the south of its parish, especially when it was offered a large sum of government redevelopment money. They could have refused it as being a sop to buy them off, but eventually they had decided to accept the grant so that they could use it to create a parish centre in the crypt space below the church as a way to relate to the incoming workers whilst serving the locals too. When I arrived, this refurbishment was almost complete, but a very significant debt remained. Even the labourers on site were saddened that the standard of refurbishment was not what they themselves had hoped to see in a sacred building. Eddie Carden set about designing a full programme of concerts, conferences and the like, but as the Docklands development picked up speed it became apparent that our crypt was never going to compete with the facilities being offered in the new luxurious company buildings. We therefore reverted to focusing on serving the local community, and in doing that, the crypt really came into its own. It offered the space for wonderful Christmas parties for the homeless and housebound, and the serving of nourishing hot meals throughout the year. Social events were always popular, and gave the congregation's remarkable talents a chance to shine, and the high-calibre staff team now had space to lay on an exciting programme of worship, Christian education and pastoral engagement.

At my appointment, the Bishop had made it clear that an important part of my responsibility as rector would be to put the parish back on its feet financially. So I set about negotiating with our local general practice for them to buy some of our land which was situated next door to the rectory. Our older members remembered that the Queen Mother herself had visited the site during the war to meet locals using the bomb shelter that was then under the site. Remarkably, to mark her ninetieth birthday, she agreed to visit us again to view our now refurbished crypt where years before she'd met other cockneys sheltering from the bombs. Sid laughed at the sight of armed police patrolling the grounds, remarking: 'if anyone even tries to touch the Queen Mum, the locals love the old gal so much they'd tear them limb from limb.' She was safer here than anywhere else in the world.

The vast interior of the All Saints church itself had seen better days, and was in dire need of a coat of paint. But that was easier said than done for, being a church, it was not only impossibly high for us, but it required a special church faculty before the work was allowed to begin. In typical East End fashion, a husband and wife team turned up one Saturday morning and just got on with it, week after week, as best they could. Quite by chance we were visited by a middle-aged couple who, having noticed that the church had only been decorated up to stepladder level, offered to send a crew round with scaffolding to finish the job in a professional fashion. It turned out that having grown up in Poplar the husband's small business had flourished, so he now had the money and the wherewithal to offer his services for nothing. His only stipulation was that he begin the work immediately whilst his paint crew were between jobs. But I knew that the required faculty would take months to acquire. A couple of weeks after the work was completed, the Archdeacon came to preach and was astonished to see the church interior looking so glorious now that the high walls and ceiling were all newly painted, with even the florets of the Corinthian capitals delicately picked out in gold. Being the church officer responsible for making sure the clergy kept to all the regulations, he asked how it could be possible that all this had been done without permission. I apologised profusely, and told him that I thought an angel must have done it, and promised to have all this new paint scraped off if that were his wish. It was as clear to him, as it was to me, that I would never make a good archdeacon.

It was fortunate that the refurbishment was completed before the visit of the pioneering anti-apartheid campaigner and friend, Bishop Trevor Huddleston, who came to conduct our confirmation that year. Father Niall had built up a prodigious confirmation programme for local young mums, and after their own confirmation each of them was expected to bring a friend along to the next year's confirmation classes. I had vastly underestimated the energy of this aging revolutionary bishop, who won the hearts of all, and when they gave him a great cheer at the end of the service, he raised his clenched fist in response – the age-long salute of solidarity and resistance. That day spent with Bishop Trevor was an experience never to be forgotten. Our kids just loved that he treated them as respected adults. Such a large number of women were confirmed over the years that they decided to form a club along the lines of the Mothers' Union. However, we were all startled when one of their outings turned out to be a trip to the West End to see the Chippendales – a male strip show that was all the rage across the country. I don't think that any other church could boast a Mothers' Union quite like ours!

On arrival in Poplar, our daughters had immediately fallen in with friends at their new school in Bethnal Green, and within a few weeks had dropped their distinctive Brummie accents and fast developed a cockney twang. They were, however, appalled by the head of the Religious Education department, who was drumming into her pupils her belief that to be a Christian they must treat abortion and homosexuality as unforgiveable sins. She had even called them both out for wearing their tiny earrings which, she said, were unbefitting of a clergyman's daughters. They rebelled by wearing increasingly outlandish, goth-like outfits, and quite right too!

One of the things that Vicki and the girls found fascinating was to look out at the church from the rectory when the horse-drawn hearses drew up for funerals. However impoverished the family, saying goodbye to a loved one had to be done in style according to East End tradition. The magnificent black horses with their billowing head plumage clearly enjoyed showing off to the crowd as they trotted proudly into the church drive, drawing the ornate glass carriage bedecked with an avalanche of bouquets. To match the occasion, I would select from the church's vast array of liturgical copes, a voluminous black silk number with an exquisitely embroidered Sacred Heart of Jesus on the back. Once, when a fight broke out among the mourners, it was immediately quelled by the sight of me turning from the high altar and swooping down upon them with black cope flying wide. Brian, our organist, said I looked, 'just like a bat out of hell', and I wondered if any priest before me had been described in quite that way.

Our girls loved to look out at the weddings, not only to check on the bridal dresses, but because they knew that when it came to the photo shoot after the ceremony, Charlie, our graveyard resident, would on occasion emerge in his army fatigues with a plastic bag over his mouth from which he inhaled glue vapours. He would manage to smuggle himself into the photographs, which must have set each family wondering who on earth the other family had invited along. We had been concerned about booking one wedding, because the church organ was being repaired that week, so we had to borrow an electric organ for the occasion. The happy couple were quite content with that arrangement. But on the day, just as the bride was being escorted up the aisle by her father, the organist realised that the organ volume was far too low and so pressed hard on the foot pedal, assuming it to be the volume control. But to everyone's alarm it triggered one of the organ's pre-set recordings: a ranting rendition of 'Robin Hood, Robin Hood, riding through the glen'.

Despite all the fun and the close friendships that we were developing in the area, we were never blind to the reality of the dangers around us. Vicki had not been in the vicinity long before she was invited to work at Bonner Primary School in Bethnal Green where, as their Family Support Worker, she continued to help families from other cultures to enter into the English educational system. Each day she was busy visiting homes around her school, in the evenings often climbing the stinking staircases of very unpleasant tower blocks all by herself.

Vicki with
some of
her mums

We knew also that, although our daughters were street-wise, they too remained very vulnerable. I, like many inner-city clergy, repeatedly suffered abuse and threats. One evening, I looked in at a local pub where I'd planned to meet Smokey, who'd asked to talk a problem through with me, but as I searched around the crowded bar, a group of very tough, unpleasant young men grabbed hold of me, forced me on to my knees and battered me with sexual taunts. They'd seen the dog-collar, and therefore assumed me to be gay, which to them was something to be scorned and jeered at. Luckily I got away, but what hurt me most was that others in the bar who knew me were too frightened to come to my aid. In retrospect, I was grateful for the experience because it made me more aware of the insults which gay people suffered every day in our homophobic society.

The staff team were very proud of serving in a parish where they'd had so many acclaimed predecessors, including many of the legendary pioneers of the Anglo-Catholic movement such as Fathers Dolling, Bartlett and John Groser, often referred to as the East End's 'slum priests'. However, these great priests of yesteryear are in some circles almost revered as indomitable saints of the past – a very difficult act for us to follow. It therefore came as something of a relief to read in Eileen Baillie's contemporary account of those times, *Shabby Paradise*, that her priestly father had suffered a breakdown under the pressure of it all. It gave us hope that when we ourselves felt weighed down by the heavy odds against us, even those revered saints had had to cope with that feeling, long before us.

Every Sunday after mass I was expected to turn up at the Greenwich Pensioner wearing my black cassock, where I'd be directed to a table just inside the pub door. On the table would stand a pint or two, the glasses acting as a virtual confessional queue, with each one indicating that someone wanted to have a private word. It was in the Pensioner that I heard about a local chap who'd been paid to commit a murder, but only afterwards remembered that he'd need a way to dispose of the body. He therefore decided to burn it, sections at a time, on his balcony barbeque. Stan told me that it was the smell that had given him away, adding dismissively: 'he just got in over his head'.

This left me with a dilemma, for whilst the murder itself obviously warranted earnest condemnation, how was I to react to what sounded like Stan's casual acceptance of it? Stan was a good man, and soon retracted his remark, but he had raised, for me, an ongoing concern that there will always be some aspects of any culture which do not conform to what is acceptable for the Christian. Because Christians have a name in society at large for being over-pious and puritanical, many dismiss the faith altogether for being prudish and narrow-minded, and I was loath to reinforce that false picture of Christianity. So rather than pick up on it every time something fell short, I would go with the flow but be careful to seek out the presence of God hidden within the culture, and focus awareness on that presence with all my might. I understood my role, and the role of All Saints, not to stand there constantly passing judgement on the local culture, but to seek out where God was at work in it. It was then up to us to get alongside God in that mission, looking for the good, encouraging the best, and letting it outshine the dark recesses in which evil might hide. Jesus had told a story of land workers discussing how to deal with the weeds in their field, the master deciding, that for the good of the whole crop, it was better to leave them there until harvest, in the hope perhaps that the healthy plants might overwhelm them (Matthew 13:24–43). Not for the first time, one of Jesus' simple stories forced me to think hard and long about my present actions. What I took from this was that whilst Jesus was the embodiment of justice, he was also the bringer of mercy and grace, which tempered justice and sought ways to understand by being alongside his people. In Poplar I would wear my cassock almost everywhere I went, and that was a strong symbol of where I stood. But also, it allowed me space to stand alongside and show understanding. I tried to tread a careful line and follow the example of Jesus, but that was certainly no simple matter.

God and Jesus?

This overflowing generosity of Jesus was in a way mirrored in one of the most engaging characteristics of people in Poplar; their astonishing generosity, giving freely from what little they had to help friends and those in need. And that helped me to address the greatest conundrum of all – the question of who Jesus really was. Christians believe that he participated in the very being of God, and they use such images as 'Son of God' and 'The Word' to picture his total unity with the Divine. But how can the man Jesus possibly be God?

I've mentioned before Rudolf Otto's great classic, *The Idea of the Holy,* in which he spoke of the numinous experience, in which we can suddenly be aware of a mysterious depth and presence all around us. I was particularly struck by the fact that such an experience can take us off guard, for it seems to come at us, rather than being something of our own making. There is definitely a sense of being confronted, of being reached out to, in those moments of ultimacy. This must mean that the Absolute is generously intent on reaching out to touch our lives and bring us a deep sense of joy. It's a joy which can go way beyond mere happiness, for happiness is very dependent on circumstances, but this joy is an inner sense of completion, meaning and most of all, of being overwhelmingly and generously loved, whatever our outward circumstances. It's an experience which unfortunately does not come to all, but if it does, it's a moment to be treasured and never forgotten.

Such experiences of being reached out to can turn a life completely around, just as the Bible story of Moses seeks to show. Moses sees a desert bush which appears to be alive with fire, and he is so blown away by what happens there that it impels him to lead the Exodus liberation of his people from Egyptian slavery. But in the story, he has the presence of mind to address the bush and ask the name of the presence within it. He asks the name of this force which is reaching out to him and is given the name YHWH, Yahweh, a mysterious name that defies precise translation. It is quite close to the Greek word, *ginomai*, and that can be translated as 'I happen', a word with a dynamic immediacy. And the Hebrew additionally carries a sense of intentionality and relationship.

The New Testament makes even clearer the relational and personal character of this Holy Presence reaching out to us, for those disciples who were encountered by the historical Jesus were, like Moses at the burning bush, similarly aware that they were in the presence of ultimate meaning and holiness when with him. They sought to picture this in their story of the Transfiguration, where they see Jesus alongside the two Hebrew characters who had 'seen' God – Moses and Elijah. In the story, these two were now seeing God who was once again reaching out to them, but this time in the person of Jesus, and at that moment he too was becoming like that burning bush, as radiant as the sun (Luke 9: 28–36). The resurrection events present the same truth, but in a different way, for when his followers experienced Jesus after his death, once again it was an undeniable experience of the God who was generously reaching out to them in love. At the burning bush, and at the resurrection, humanity is confronted by the very presence of God. The resurrection showed that Jesus would *always* be with them as the one who, just like a burning bush, always 'happens'.

There is, of course, no way to 'prove' that these stories actually represent historical happenings, except that it has proved possible for others, through generations long, to experience exactly what those first disciples experienced – the radiant presence of Jesus as the generous expression of the Ground of their Being. And proof always comes down to experience, whether that be experience in the science laboratory or experience of those profound moments in our life of being confronted by God's presence. In both cases, it is only our experience that convinces or 'proves' anything, and I count myself one of the joyful billions who have experienced that Presence seeking us out – although I find it as hard as did those first disciples, to explain it or describe it to others. I've known many who have had this experience come at them quite unexpectedly as an encounter by the Ground of our Being, almost out of the blue. Many will talk about that as 'meeting Jesus', which sounds wacky, but it is their way of describing an experience of deep personal encounter and assurance, which is all part of the Jesus thing. The way in for others can be through what some call mysticism or deep contemplation – mindfulness often being a first step along that path. This is not so much the personal encounter experience, as one of being taken up into an experience of unity with all creation and with the Ground of Being. It is the experience of God which the fourteenth century mystics called the Cloud of Unknowing. If we're lucky enough to be gifted with both of these ways in – both the personal encounter with God *and* the mystical integration with the Fount of Being – then we're really motoring! It often takes work on our part, often in the form of prayer, when we seek in one way or another to put ourselves in the presence of the Presence of God. But when prayer turns from being the old shopping list of wants into a love letter to God, then prayer is real at last. And in Poplar the generosity and openness of the people was opening me up to an even more profound sense of the generosity of the God who reaches out to us in such self-giving and generous ways.

In for a big surprise

Poplar's generosity gave me lots to think about, but walking home from the Greenwich Pensioner one Sunday lunchtime, I had another sudden realisation too. It dawned on me that my anxiety which had haunted me through the years about who I was – the cockney lad or the middle-class college student and churchman – had now been overtaken by a sense of calm fulfilment. Poplar had allowed me to own both sides of myself and to accept my hybridity, so that these two aspects of who I was no longer battled with each other – I was one fulfilled person. There was an integration, a new integrity, of personality within. Churchwarden Sid summed it up when one morning he greeted me with, 'Hello Father, how you doin' son?' Later that day, I happened to read once again, the gospel episode where Jesus had put a question to his disciples at Caesarea Philippi: 'Who do people say that I am?' (Mark 8: 27–30) Perhaps at that moment he was wrestling with the realisation that there were two aspects of himself within him – the human and the divine. And his disciples helped him relax in the acceptance of his integrity as one integrated presence. In my own very small way, I too was grateful to those around me in Poplar, for allowing me to relax and at last accept myself for who I was.

Some of my conversations at the Greenwich Pensioner were, indeed, intensely serious, but, on occasion, were tinged with naughtiness. Two students had been assigned to me by their college principal because he thought they needed more exposure to the tough realities of the world if they were to be ready for priesthood. I therefore took them along to the Pensioner, where the locals had obviously got wind of the fact that they were staying with me. When I arrived in the pub, sure enough, the pints were waiting for me at my usual table, but this time accompanied by Big Maureen. She wanted a chat but, encouraged me first to have a word with the landlord. I left my two charges with her, and came back a little later to see them ashen faced and anxiously looking to me for help. Maureen had apparently told them that her partner had left her, which was quite untrue, and that she was therefore taking out a contract on him, either to have him kneecapped or topped, and she had been asking the pair which of the two options they would advise. When I heard this, I castigated Maureen for being so naughty, but it was difficult to do so with a straight face when the whole pub was curled up laughing. A large part of the old cockney humour consisted of setting friends up, and that morning, they'd done it wonderfully well. I really should have seen it coming.

No such thing then as 'closing time' at the Pensioner

I felt very much at home in the midst of this thoroughly cockney culture; I loved the people, and had already learnt so much from them about how Christ could be vibrantly present, even in the depths of the stresses and strains, and I looked forward to seeing where that awareness would take us next. With the help of our Reader, Tom, I was near to paying off the huge shortfall that the refurbishment of the church had left in the parish finances, and I had in my mind plans to turn the overlarge rectory into a parish centre, and for our own family to move to a much smaller house at the other side of the church. To enable the plans for the resurrection of St Nick's Centre, I was in process of moving the record company on, and so that we could house one of our clergy, had already fought a long legal battle to move a wealthy couple out of St Nick's clergy flat, knowing they had another home abroad. Thankfully, the judge summarily dismissed them for taking the church for a ride for so long. So now that we had most of the major parish affairs back on track, I felt liberated at last to concentrate on what I took to be the real business of ministry: encouraging our laity to use their many talents to discover what were God's wishes for the next stage of our parish journey.

Through the years, I'd continued my explorations of urban theology, publishing a number of articles and a booklet entitled *God in the Inner City*, and I looked forward to taking this further with the congregation. The Archbishop of Canterbury had invited me to join his Urban Theology Group, whose task was to follow up the *Faith in the City* report with some companion volumes of urban theological reflection. It was a very exciting group to belong to, with Peter Sedgwick chairing and Professor David Ford, Michael Northcott, Sister Margaret Walsh and others on the team. We worked together over a number of years to produce two large volumes of urban theological studies, *God in the City,* edited by Peter, and *Urban Theology – a reader,* edited by Michael. After a hard day's writing in Liverpool, I was waiting at the railway station with David Ford for a delayed train home, when I remembered that my secretary, Janice, had sent a message through, asking me to phone her as soon as possible. I therefore found a nearby public phone box and dialled through, to hear Janice say: 'you've received an important letter with "strictly confidential" all over it. So I opened it! And you'll never guess what it said!' It turned out that I was being asked to become a bishop in Essex, the county just to the east of London. At first I could not believe that the Church of England would think of choosing as a bishop someone with my background and unconventional views, and so I assumed it to be a typical cockney wind-up. But Janice was adamant, and kept repeating that she did not want me to leave Poplar. I was absolutely stunned, not knowing what to think. It made for a strange train journey home.

* * *

CHAPTER 10

DONNING THE MITRE

Janice as ever, took it all in her stride, remarking casually, 'well, things always come along in threes.' Poplar Parish was, after all, well used to having its clergy plucked from them to become bishops, for Mark Hodson had left in 1955 to become Bishop of Hereford and John Eastaugh had followed him to the very same place in 1973. I had always wondered why it was that there was a spare mitre in the vestry drawer at All Saints – was it there just in case?

I was not at all sure, however, that this move was right, for I'd hoped to stay in Poplar for a long time. I was worried that being a bishop would obscure my concern to work for the marginalised in society, and I was also anxious that being a bishop would bind me too closely into the institutional church. I prayed hard about it, and went to talk it all through with the writer of the letter of invitation, Bishop John Waine, who assured me that as a bishop I'd have even greater opportunity to champion my causes, and it would even carry more weight. My life had always been charmed by having wonderfully wise mentors, but Bishop John was to prove one of the best and a very close friend into the bargain. But now it was time to decide. Was I to follow in the footsteps of so many of my cockney family and move out to Essex?

Finding my way

When I was asked to become the new Bishop of Bradwell, my immediate response was not as virtuous as perhaps it should have been, but rather, 'where the hell is Bradwell?' I checked the map and saw the name marked right at the extreme edge of southeast England. So I jumped in the car and headed east into the Chelmsford Diocese, where they were asking me to serve. I was soon into terrain I knew very well. I drove down the main road through the East Ham of my childhood, and as I crossed the M25 motorway, I was into the Area for which I'd have responsibility, including wealthy Brentwood, the sprawling housing estates of Basildon, the poverty-stricken Tilbury Docks, Southend and on out to the deeply rural Dengie Peninsula. This is where at last I found the village of Bradwell-on-Sea. To get to Bradwell Chapel itself I drove even further east, then parked the car and walked out towards the windswept coast. As I walked alone in silence, the open fields to my right, a ditch and hedge to my left, I spied in the distance the primitive stone chapel, tall and gaunt, standing out against the broad sky and open sea beyond. There was something strikingly numinous about the whole atmosphere – what mystics call a spiritually 'thin place'. I leaned into the wind, made my way up to the weather-beaten wooden door, pushed it open and peered in, to see a broad flagstone floor, just a few wooden benches and some kneeling stools. In the distance I spied the simple altar with the great cross of St Cedd on the heavy stone wall beyond. The building seemed to draw the visitor in, and promised to reveal its heart to those who would sit and listen to its stones. As I sat on one of the wooden benches with my shoulder resting against the ancient wall, I could imagine St Cedd and his monks arriving by sea from Lindisfarne in 654, rolling up the sleeves of their habits, and manhandling the stones of the old Roman fort that had been there long before, so as to build this simple but inspiring structure. They gradually transformed the Roman fort of Othona, that symbol of imperial domination, into a place of prayer and sanctuary. I could feel the prayers of those monks of old, and the devotions of the generations since, penetrating my very being, radiating out to me from the huge granite stones as if they were mystical storage radiators of prayer and holiness.

I was unaware of the passage of the hours as I sat there, lost in the vibrant tranquillity of this place, when suddenly I became aware that it was late, and all around me had become quite dark. This holy place had allowed me one of those exceptional life experiences, when the presence of the Absolute invades the moment. It was difficult to fathom how I, once a young East End tearaway, then a cantankerous student, and now an unorthodox priest, could possibly inherit the mantle of Cedd, that saint of old who came at such personal risk to build these walls and spread the good news of the Christian faith to this part of the world. However, despite my doubts and fears I now knew I had to say 'yes'. I tore myself away and walked silently back up the stony path for the long drive home. I had just experienced the power that was Bradwell.

Bradwell Chapel - Place of pilgrimage

A number of hurdles had to be cleared before the appointment could be made public, the first being a thorough health check. I was given the address of Dr Angus Blair, who saw all the bishops regularly, and so by virtue of this service, knew us all more intimately than any other human being, especially because he performed the routine check for enlarged prostate at each visitation. My friend Michael, then Bishop of Wolverhampton, had given him a rather appropriate gift at his latest appointment – a bottle of ale labelled Bishop's Finger.

I had good reason for feeling daunted by the task ahead, for I would be responsible for a third of the Diocese of Chelmsford, the second most populous diocese in England. Being one of its three Area Bishops, I would have a whole rack of legal responsibilities, including the appointment of clergy within my Area, of whom there were about one hundred and eighty, plus some twenty others who were unpaid. There would be lots of TV and radio work, mission planning, confirmations and ordinations, and other special services to attend to. I'd also be in charge of the selection of candidates for training for the ministry, the consecration of new churches and the general overseeing of the life of the churches in the Area – an Area which I now knew was geographically daunting. I was to be the bishop of an extraordinarily diverse part of the country, with the recognition that I would never have a dull moment in all the eighteen years I would be there.

In preparation for my new rôle I spent time shadowing my friend, Bishop David Bentley, Bishop of King's Lynn. One day I went with him to the annual national gathering of fairground people where he was expected to inspect and bless the first fair of the year and, as David explained, take a ride on one of the rigs. Without thinking, he selected the big wheel, but as the two of us clambered into our seats, it struck him that this could have been a foolhardy choice. Sure enough, the operator put the great wheel into motion and rapidly increased its speed until we felt its force was going to fling us off into oblivion. As we clung desperately to the handrail, each time we neared the ground, we heard the howls of laughter from those in the know. David yelled to me over the sound of the rushing wind that we'd better be smiling next time we were down there, because the newspaper photographers would be delighted to capture us exhibiting terrified grimaces. We managed with some difficulty to fight back our alarm and smile for the cameras, but were much relieved when the wheel slowed to its normal speed and eventually came to a standstill, allowing us both to disembark with as much gravitas as we could muster. We were greeted with great cheers, but Bishop David's wife whispered to me: 'wasn't that taking work experience a little too far?'

The Church Commissioners offered a grant to buy a cope and mitre and the regulation purple shirt. Their outdated ideas became evident when they expected Vicki to relinquish her own work and become a hostess, for which they would equip her with a very large oven and enormous sets of tableware. They really had no idea! My brother-in-law, Ted, made my bishop's crook in his workshop at Ford's, and the silversmith, Michael Bolton, almost exploded with joy, explaining that: 'the one thing that every jeweller dreams of is making a real bishop's ring.' Its large size made me feel self-conscious at first until, when visiting West Ham dog track, I saw the men sporting rings much larger than mine. So from then on I wore it to remind myself of my cultural roots. Our daughter, Becki, had by then taken a weekend job spraying cars and had acquired a very alternative Goth look to suit her artistic nature, but when Michael Bolton took her under his wing, jewellery design became her passion. My new boss, Bishop John, took my new silver ring into his chapel to be blessed, and then turned to Vicki and me and said, 'of course, you do realise that you're about to embark on a very busy life. You won't have time, Laurie, even to pop out and buy a tube of toothpaste.' I had no notion, then, of how right his prediction would prove to be.

After the waiting, the reality

The service of consecration was to take place in Westminster Abbey on 23 Feb 1993, St Polycarp's Day and, as is the custom, I was invited to bring my immediate family to spend the night before, as guests at Lambeth Palace. The girls just loved it, and the next morning appeared in the abbey in their heavy Doc Martin boots and all the gear – I felt so proud of them. It was such a joy to see the abbey filled with friends

231

from each period of my life, including a coach-load of parishioners who had motored all the way from Birmingham, some who'd made the journey from Germany and even folk-singing mates from my early years. The drawback of the abbey is that if you have to sit behind a pillar or monument, you don't see much. But the splendour of the ancient building, the sonorous swell of the organ and the magnificence of the procession all joined in praise of the Holy Spirit of God whose presence made us all tingle with anticipation. We wove our way through the complexities of the splendid liturgy towards its key moment, when first, Graham James, who was bound for a bishopric in Cornwall, and then I, knelt before the altar for all the bishops to gather around. It was then that they laid their hands on my head for that special prayer which asks the Holy Spirit to inspire the new bishop with the necessary gifts of grace. My sister, Babs, had brought her granddaughter, Laura, along with her and, although still very young, she'd remained quietly attentive throughout the worship. Babs asked her afterwards what she'd liked most about the service and, in her own way, got it exactly right. 'My favourite was when they played "we all pat the dog" with uncle Laurie.'

The service of ordination as bishop, sometimes referred to as a consecration, spells out for all to hear exactly what being a bishop is about. It pictures the role as that of a shepherd, guarding and guiding the church with care - the giving of the crozier, or bishop's crook, symbolising that style of servant leadership. The service also tells us that bishops must know and be known by their people, especially confronting injustice as a friend of the poor and marginalised. It lays a lot of stress on the bishop being the 'principal minister of word and sacrament,' teaching, leading worship, confirming new members and ordaining the clergy. We have to take a lead too in training and commissioning lay and ordained ministers, and ensure they are doing all that they should in their parishes or areas of special responsibility. The word bishop comes, by way of Old English, from the Greek *espiskopos* - one who 'oversees' everything and keeps things on the right course - so it's our job to act as a focus for unity and strategy. All this means it's a very wide and tough brief, but it's worship and prayer that lies at the heart of it all, and without which the whole thing would career off the rails – and we bishops would certainly lose the plot!

After the service in the abbey, lunch for all my guests was provided by two gay friends I'd met at a special conference, to which I had graciously been invited, where gay priests could share their concerns confidentially. The service at their conference always remains in my memory as the only time in my life I'd had my bum lovingly squeezed during the sharing of the Peace.

Later in the afternoon of the consecration, all were invited back to All Saints Poplar for a final farewell, where we were astonished to see that the parishioners had somehow managed to wrap the vast rectory in episcopal purple ribbon and affix a gigantic purple bow high above the front door. My dear Indian friend, Nadir Dinshaw, had given me my bishop's pectoral cross for the consecration, but the parishioners had also had Michael Bolton make another to match my ring, and they now presented that to me to wear on high festival occasions. As always, the speeches were hilarious, Arthur quipping that since I was a bishop, it was only right that I now be equipped with the proverbial actress. I was then invited to address the huge gathering, and although I had nothing prepared, I amazed myself when I began speaking spontaneously and eloquently. It was the first time in my life that I had had the confidence to do so without notes. What had happened when I knelt down in that abbey I'll never know, but thereafter, and in all sorts of ways, I found myself able to accomplish things which beforehand I would never have dared to attempt.

The very next morning I was a working bishop, but without much idea of what I was supposed to do or how to do it. It was then that a guardian angel appeared on the scene in the person of Pat Howes. Throughout my ministry, I'd been blessed with amazing secretaries and PAs and Pat knew exactly how to organise my diary, what my responsibilities were, where I had to be and when. She guided me along, as did Philip Need, the diocesan bishop's chaplain, who presented me with a map of Essex and reminded me that I would now have to answer to the name Laurie Bradwell and that my initials on documents would henceforth be +LB, the plus mark being the Christian cross that all bishops add at the beginning of their signature. Bishop Bob Hardy told me that once, on his way home from a late night service, he had stopped off at a café and on learning that he was a bishop, the waitress had asked for his signature. He took a paper napkin and carefully signed it, +Bob Lincoln. She was overjoyed and thanked him saying, 'Oh, and look, you've put a little kiss for me too.'

The first caller to our new house was a local churchwarden, who wanted to know why on earth his parish was still without a vicar since, as of today, it was my responsibility to find one. I made a feeble excuse, assured him I'd get it sorted, made myself a strong coffee and sat for hours reading up on the law relating to the appointments procedure. It was ridiculously complex, and I wondered why the Church of England had saddled itself with such a ponderous way of doing things. What really made me angry was all the talk about the rights of the patron of the parish, when in any other walk of life 'patronage' was considered a dirty word. Because of ancient history, it was still the patron who held great power in the matter of appointing a parish priest, even if they knew little or nothing about the parish. It seemed to me that the parishioners and the bishop could just as well share the decision together, but the C of E was mired in history and so, despite it feeling so alien, I had to learn to work with what the law demanded.

Despite living close to the sprawling housing estates of Basildon, my study window looked out across the Essex countryside. For the first time in my life, I would observe from that window the coming and going of each season, and from time to time, I even snatched a brief moment to walk to the end of the garden and back, enjoying the scents and sights of the natural world around me. I think this was the dawning, for me, of an awareness that nature was not there merely to be subdued and exploited, but that it cared for us and we in turn had a responsibility to care for it. I owed it to God and to the next generation that I repent of my old mindset and think again: for I had been as complicit in overconsumption as the rest of my generation. It made me conscious that, although the meerkat might look caring and cuddly from the outside, it has one great flaw, in that it eats its own grandchildren. It occurred to me that my generation think of ourselves as very caring of our families, but by consuming their future, we too are, in some ways, eating our grandchildren. The whole business is as macabre as that!

Sharing the workload

Each day I would be at my desk at seven, leaving tape-recorded letters and instructions for Pat to deal with during the day and then, after prayers, I'd usually be off on the road. The final event of the day would often be a confirmation, the licensing of a new vicar or a speaking engagement. And then I'd sink into the car seat exhausted and spend an hour or so driving home. Getting home at well gone ten, I then had to deal with absolutely piles of letters and emails, the many notes that Pat had left for me, and prepare scripts and so on for the next day, before I could hit the hay. The sabbath rest was instituted for very good reason and I was aware that round the clock working and spending sixteen hours a week driving, offered both a very poor model to the clergy and a blatant invitation to poor health. How to arrive at a balanced life-style was just one of the concerns I would talk through with my new spiritual director, Abbot Stuart, and with my work consultant at our regular meetings.

David Jennings was my newly appointed archdeacon, with whom I worked very closely. We hit it off immediately, for we recognised that we had similar values, but complementary gifts

– his, the most remarkable memory and head for detail. We were both very new to the roles, so we definitely felt this was a fine example of the blind leading the blind. Our major difficulty was that the Church of England has grown through the centuries into a church that is impossible to lead or manage. Perhaps it had been like this from the beginning, when Elizabeth I attempted to put paid to England's inter-party religious strife by forging a Church of England which was so broad it could include everyone. But trying to hold this unruly C of E together in a mutual bond of love takes some doing, especially now when institutions themselves are no longer held in high esteem. I learnt, however, to love the extreme diversity of the parishes of my Episcopal Area, for each was seeking to offer an honest expression of their own particular experience of the mystery of God – but, of course, no one way was sufficient to capture the all-encompassing reality.

Across the world about eighty million other Christians have modelled themselves on this inclusive approach and now comprise the Anglican Communion. The Anglicans in each country decide things together for themselves, but feel an accountability to all the others in the Communion through meetings and friendships across the globe. Well, that's what is supposed to happen. But, of course, the differences sometimes overwhelm such an enormous and varied global family that relies on goodwill rather than central diktat, and that can issue in all sorts of unsavoury exchanges, especially on those topics which have psychological and emotional resonances. Not everyone has what it takes to be a real Anglican, but I believe it's a calling well worth the challenge.

It seemed to me that my first task was to get to know the people of my own Area, for I'd noticed that many bishops rely on taking confirmations and special services in order to get to know their parishes. The drawback is that at such special gatherings we don't see the reality of a parish's everyday life, and at them the bishop will often meet many occasional visitors, but not so many who attend on a normal Sunday. I therefore kept confirmations to the evenings, which freed up my Sunday mornings to be in parishes and see something of their usual congregation. I also invited Archdeacon David to join me for a few months touring, staying in local homes, preaching at church services and getting to know our people. Just to make it great fun for everyone, we challenged them to invent crazy ways for us to travel from place to place. We found ourselves being transported in wheelbarrows, hearses, steam cars, tanks, helicopters and even in the back of a skip which had been ingeniously furnished with two armchairs and a standard lamp to make us feel at ease. One minute, I was taking the reins of a gypsy caravan, whilst hearing from the Romanies all about their life and culture, and the next I was being sped up the road in a racing Ferrari. Everyone loved the fun, and students from one of our universities videoed the fun and games. Each evening, we addressed large gatherings, explaining the Christian faith and answering questions put to us by groups as different as town officials and politicians, dock workers and industrial and commercial leaders. We ended our journey with a great service in the cathedral, mixing old and new music with riotous colour and calm tranquillity, eventually arriving home, both feeling that we had at least begun well the task of engaging with the people of our Area.

Every year, ecumenical pilgrims from far and wide would converge upon our beloved Bradwell Chapel. Through the years, our guest speakers included Cardinal Basil Hume, Michelle Guinness, John Bell and Archbishop John Sentamu. Tents and marquees would house activities and presentations, whilst the ancient chapel offered a space where pilgrims could venture in and sit quietly in that holy place, away from the noise and bustle of the crowd. Now and again they would hear a harp being played by Annie Mawson, who each year, travelled all the way down from the Lake District where she ran her Sunbeams Trust (a music therapy charity for those suffering severe difficulties). She and her seafaring partner, Michael, soon became the most eccentric and talented friends we've ever had, the four of us enjoying holidays together, one even taking us to Ireland, where Annie and I gave riotous musical concerts together. To tell of our other extraordinary family adventures together would require a book of its own!

Back at home, life was never dull. By now, Rebecca had become a fine silversmith and sped off round the world to explore life's extremes by swimming with sharks and tasting the spiritual calm of Thailand. Hannah had fulfilled her yearning to become an actor, landing the dream role of Shakespeare's Juliet at the famous Hull Truck Theatre. It was on stage that she met Matt, who turned his role as Romeo into the real thing, the result being their marriage some time later in our local parish church, followed by a reception in a fairy tale setting, which the locals had created for them in our garden. The local community had indeed welcomed us all into their hearts, Vicki becoming a regular at the lively parish church, and me enjoying the occasional gig at the village folk club at the Swan Inn. Vicki would travel with me to some of the many special events at which I presided, and on our journey home, shared with me some of the gossip she'd heard in the congregation, including what they thought of the bishop! It was not, at first, easy to be myself whilst inhabiting the role of bishop, where one becomes the recipient of other peoples' wild projections. It was helpful to remember how some Greeks, eager to be introduced to Jesus, had come, presumably with their projections of celebrity, but Jesus had countered their expectations by talking instead about his impending humiliation and death (John 12: 20ff). But it takes perceptive self-awareness and astonishing honesty not to be hoodwinked by others' adoration or censure, and simply be the person you are. It was very easy for me to fall into the performer's trap of fulfilling onlookers' expectations of how a bishop is supposed to behave. Even now, I'm not sure, given all the baggage that goes with the bishop's role, that I made a very good job of it, but it cheered me if someone remarked, 'you're not like a normal bishop.'

Although the media like to concentrate on church pomp and its high profile shortcomings, the church's real treasure is to be found in its parishes, where ordinary Christians work away at making the world a happier and more just place. And these were the people I was there for. To support the parish clergy, we invited them in small groups for residential times away for recuperation and discussion, and I also began publishing a monthly journal that I called the *Bradwell Papers*, inviting clergy and others to join me in offering articles of theological reflection and pointers to good practice. I was just as keen to support lay parishioners, so one year I determined to spend four full days in each of my nine deaneries, shadowing our people in their places of work. I found myself working on farms, stacking Tesco's shelves at night, in town planning offices, banks and engineering works, hospital storerooms, heavy industrial sites, driving trains, and lots more besides. At the end of each week, we would hold large gatherings to talk through the issues that had surfaced. Jesus 'the carpenter' had shown that creative work can be wonderfully meaningful, but the laity were telling me that they found their church attendance stressful. This was because they heard sermons there about acting ethically, knowing that this was simply not allowed to them at work, where profit was put before people on pain of dismissal. Some were told to lie in order to gain orders, many were overworked or made to work shifts that crippled family life, others had repetitive and boring work, others were bullied or had no proper contract and so could be laid off at a moment's notice. If the church doesn't speak out for just and rewarding employment, we are clearly not honouring our lay people. I found those conversations extremely helpful when I had invitations to speak at employers' gatherings, and also they prompted me to remind our clergy to address these issues in their sermons and liturgies.

What we clergy really love is getting away from the desk, and instead visiting and engaging with people in their daily lives, and therefore whenever I visited a parish I'd always ask them if I could accompany the vicar on an ordinary home visit. Odd things were apt to happen, however. On one occasion, the priest took me along to visit an elderly woman who had recently become housebound. She'd asked her carer to stock up with cakes and biscuits of every sort so that she could entertain the bishop in style. When she asked me if there was anything else I fancied, I mistakenly asked if she had some sugar to add to my tea, only to see her face cloud over with anxiety. Then she suddenly remembered. 'Yes, on my very last Saga holiday, they had lots of sugar packets in the hotel foyer, so us old dears stocked up on them.' She had her helper get them down from a top shelf and offered me a packet. At that point my embarrassment became very evident. 'Anything wrong with it, bishop?' I inquired if she remembered an AIDS scare occurring at the resort at that time, because what the elderly ladies had been stuffing into their handbags, to the amazement, no doubt, of the onlooking waiters, were not packets of sugar at all, but condoms!

I loved the fact that as a bishop I was in touch with non-church people to an enormous degree. I'd always bemoaned the fact that as a parish priest, most of one's preaching was to the converted, but I was now constantly invited to appear on local TV or radio, to speak at the universities, professional conferences, business gatherings or even football matches! Mixing with the likes of judges and the rich was a new experience for me, and it came as quite a shock to receive one invitation to a dinner party which noted that, 'tiaras may be worn on this occasion'. At first, I worried about having to speak at such gatherings, given my Christian socialist views, but in time, experience taught me that they much preferred me to be challenging and critically constructive, rather than just to beam and bless. I was pleased to meet some, like Ian Marks, who really wanted to see radical change in society and those that did became firm friends. Ian became aware that I'd worked with a Community Foundation in Poplar, and was keen for me to join the Foundation he was setting up. Despite initial opposition, it grew through the years, so that the Essex Community Foundation is now one of the largest and most respected fundraisers and distributors to local voluntary projects in the country. Ian never shouted about his Christian faith, but like so many other minor saints, just got on with it.

I had come into office in 1993 just as the legislation which allowed women to be ordained as priests at last became law. There inevitably remained pockets of strong and often vociferous opposition, not least among the older bishops. They had been so shocked at the end of the previous year when the church's national parliament, the General Synod, had decided that women's ordination could go ahead. They therefore called all the bishops together to prepare a paper offering priests who opposed the measure all manner of very generous supportive arrangements, including the creation of what were nicknamed 'flying bishops' who would offer alternative sacramental and pastoral oversight to those against the decision. This meant that the concept of unity, represented by the bishop, was destroyed at a stroke, for those of us who ordained women were, by some illiberal priests, often targeted with insults and derision. What many of us also found questionable were the very considerable sums of money handed out to those who preferred to leave their parishes rather than accept women. One priest came to me saying he'd read the terms and decided to use this arrangement to take very early retirement, having spotted a loophole that allowed him to take the money, even though he didn't much mind the women as long as they stayed away from his parish. I count myself very lucky, therefore, that I also had a number of very fine, sincere priests who, although against the new ordinations, remained honest and true, remaining my close friends, even to this day.

Despite those painful episodes, there was jubilation and overwhelming joy throughout most of the church and I'm proud to boast that I was among the first to ordain women in

England. There were so many in waiting that we had to have three grand services in our cathedral on that day – as we said at the time, we were ordaining morning, noon and night! It all turned out well, and proved so successful, with the Church of England becoming all the better for it.

After waiting for many years! An emotional

The Church International

I'd been five years as a bishop when I attended my first Lambeth Conference, the global gathering of all the bishops of the international Anglican Communion of churches. This involved some seven hundred and forty-nine bishops in all – plus wives and just a few American husbands. Vicki and I were housed with a couple from Sudan, who opened our eyes to the extraordinary deprivations and dangers which beset the Christians of that country. I'd just published a booklet on the biblical concept of debt and Jubilee, which sought to highlight the West's iniquitous financial exploitation of countries like Sudan, so I was keen to learn all that I could from our new friends. Nevertheless, as important as that issue was, it was the church's old obsession – that of sex – which overtook the conference.

In the debate on the issue of homosexuality, the carefully drafted and moderate resolution was swept aside by a flurry of procedural motions. In its place, an alternative draft was introduced which was harsh and pitiless in its refusal to accept gay people, let alone gay relationships. Just before the amended motion was put to the vote, the Archbishop of Canterbury, George Carey, stepped forward, took the microphone and began to applaud this defamatory resolution, which had the effect of further steering the vote in favour. An overwhelming show of hands, including many from English bishops, voted it through, and so I left the great hall and immediately headed for the now empty chapel, where I sat silently for a couple of hours wrestling with whether I should now resign my post as a bishop. As I walked back to our rooms in despair, the Bishop of Edinburgh, Richard Holloway, came rushing up to me to tell me that he had just been in heated conversation with George Carey, who had tried to assure him that when he had spoken so persuasively in favour of the resolution he thought the vote had already taken place. Richard and I found that extremely difficult to believe, but by then there was no way to reverse the damage that that Lambeth resolution would do to the lives of so many gay people.

For me, the best thing to come out of that Lambeth Conference was resolution II.7 which a small group of us had drafted. It recommended that the church around the world should now study very seriously the issue of modern urbanisation with a special emphasis on what it was doing to the lives of the marginalised and excluded. Andrew Davey and I joined forces to give a presentation on the issues, Andrew being the Church of England's authority on the subject, and the driving force behind the initiative. The project was destined to take the two of us on many international journeys together, but right now I already had plans for a personal visit abroad.

I'd been offered a three months sabbatical break during which I planned to visit Michael, our first lodger, now living in Brazil.

I had already booked my flight when I was then offered a bursary to undertake some study at the Episcopal Divinity School in Boston, Massachusetts. I hastily reorganised my schedule and was so glad I did, for on arrival I was bowled over by the beauty of the city of Boston and the forests of New England. I became determined to see as much of the Eastern Seaboard as possible and take weekends out to visit the old friends I'd made during my student days in New York. My supervising professor, Christopher Duraisingh, became a good friend, and constantly presented me with ever more exciting intellectual challenges. I also sat in on Professor Ian Douglas' course on global Anglicanism on the understanding that I could skip the assignments and concentrate my time writing up my research into a small book entitled *The Impact of the Global.* This was then translated into other languages and sent to Anglican bishops around the world. It was designed to explain what was then the new concept of globalisation, and after some theological analysis, to encourage them to address the pressures that global urbanisation was exerting upon the marginalised.

I made some wonderful American friends in Boston, including Ed Hanson, who later followed me back to England to be ordained in the Lincoln Diocese, Elizabeth, who readily allowed me the use of her car so I could enjoy driving through the streets of Boston, and Stefani and Joe Duggan, who later invited me to join their international consultations on Postcolonial Theology. But by now my plane ticket to Brazil was burning a hole in my pocket so I had to bid farewell to new friends and journey south.

It was only whilst flying for what felt like hours over the Amazon, and looking down on the magnificent forest below, that I grasped for the first time just how immense was this great country of Brazil and how fragile the planet. I landed in São Paulo, to find Michael now happily settled into the Brazilian culture with a family of his own, and living in a small, gated community with armed guards on the gates – a very necessary expedient in that dangerous city. Michael worked at the vast São Paulo Hospital where I was overjoyed to see him so highly esteemed as head of his own prosthetics department. I was escorted into one of the vast rambling slum favellas, and there chatted with some of the most oppressed and marginalised people in the world, their lives dominated by drug gangs, automatic weapons and grinding poverty. I had a long discussion about it with their primate, Bishop Glauco Soares de Lima, who was rightly proud of his church's socially inclusive policies, declaring that its welcoming attitude to all, regardless of their poverty, their sexual orientation or race, was an expression of the 'essence of the ministry of Jesus'. It was a real tonic to hear this truth so powerfully and overtly expressed by a person of such consequence.

On our way home our car was surrounded by a vast crowd of dancing people of all ages slowly making their way to the nearby stadium where, to judge by the pulsating choruses charging the humid air, a great Samba festival was evidently already well under way. The exhilarating rhythms were so infectious that we were soon gyrating joyously in our seats as our car crawled happily along with the thronging crowds. It is Samba music which expresses the very soul of the poor of Brazil, and the best bands are from deep in the heart of the poor favellas. Michael translated the words of one song to me. 'We have nothing. No money, no homes, no good clothes, no good food! But that is because God has been saving for us what no one else has – the Samba!' I once heard a Latin American bishop say, when encouraging us staid Englishmen to move while singing hymns: 'Let your bodies feel the music! Be like us. We worship God with our hips!' His words reminded me how the physicality of Poplar had exemplified the words of St John's gospel – 'the Word became flesh and dwelt among us' (John 1: 14) – and now, amidst this powerful Samba soul music, our souls soared as our bodies leapt to be at one with our fellow dancers in this visceral experience of physical joy and heightened spiritual togetherness.

Our team leader, John Waine, retired as the diocesan bishop in 1996, to be followed by John Perry. But by the time I returned from my sabbatical, another John had taken his place; Bishop John Gladwin. I knew we were kindred spirits from the word go because Vicki and I had invited John and his formidable wife, Lydia, to spend their first night at our home after they'd done as much unpacking as they felt able to cope with. They arrived late, still dressed in jeans and dust, but when Vicki invited them to have a cup of tea, I whispered to John that I had a nice malt whisky he might prefer, at which he beamed with enthusiasm. So the two of us withdrew to share in the spirit. We chatted into the night, and by the time we went to bed, between us we'd solved all the problems of church and nation.

As the different diocesan bishops came and went, so also came the time for David Jennings, my archdeacon, to move and become the Bishop of Warrington. As my next archdeacon, I was blessed with the appointment of yet another David in the person of David Lowman, a man of superb talent and vast experience. We were once attending a very grand occasion together in Liverpool Cathedral and, dressed in full fig, were seated together on the dais in full view of the huge congregation. The service, however, was taking much longer than anticipated, prompting a very attentive verger to creep up behind us to explain that if we did not leave before the end of the service, we'd miss our last train home to the south. He disappeared for a moment and then came forward with great solemnity to escort us down the aisle, his head held high to convince the seated masses that our exit was a very special part of the proceedings. A taxi driver, seeing two clergymen sprinting down the cathedral drive, screeched to a stop and guaranteed to get us to the station in time. He careered through the city at tremendous speed, jumped a light and tore down a one-way street in the wrong direction in full view of four police officers who, on spotting our clerical garb, with remarkable Liverpudlian affability, did not bat an eyelid. We arrived with time to spare, but not a little traumatised, the taxi driver assuring us that he felt that on that evening he had done a good work for the Lord.

I was always keen to spend time in the parishes, but there were many institutions and issues which required additional attention from our teams of specialist chaplains. I had two prisons in my Area, one of which had been transformed out of the blue from a women's prison into a holding prison for refugees and asylum seekers. Our new prisoners were often people of other faiths needing specialist support, but luckily I'd already established close relationships with the Jewish community in Southend and with the mosque in Basildon. The mosque had been firebombed, and because of the friendships we'd already forged, I was invited along to Friday prayers to speak to the brothers and sisters and reassure them of our keen support. With the gracious help of the Basildon rector, Esther McCafferty, I'd also had the opportunity to act as a broker in connecting the Muslim community more directly with the town authorities. They were now more ready than ever to help at the prison, and had soon created good working relationships with our specialist prison chaplains.

With Mr
Salwar
after the

It turned out that our hospital chaplains were struggling with rather different issues. For many years the enormous Basildon hospital had benefited from the free services of the local parish priest, Canon Lionel Webber. Lionel was a larger than life character who had famously been interviewed one

Christmas night on local radio after having done his evening round at the hospital. He'd obviously had a drink or two on the wards, because when asked to share a Christmas prayer for the listeners he gently began: 'and now let us pray for all the poor buggers who are stuck in hospital this Christmas.' After Lionel's retirement the hospital authorities were trying to get away with offering no chaplaincy provision at all until I created a stir, and with the help of some knowing advisors led by Annette, our own Archdeacon of Colchester, managed to reintroduce a chaplaincy team. We also had a fine team working alongside deaf and hard-of-hearing people who taught me to sign the phrase 'the Peace of the Lord be always with you,' for use at the cathedral when presiding there. The next week I gave it a try, but noticed a few of them giggling in the front row. After the service I asked them what I'd got wrong. They explained that I had not quite signed the word 'peace' correctly. Apparently I'd signed to the whole cathedral congregation, 'The sausages of the Lord be always with you.'

Down by the River Thames, the cement industry had gouged out now empty chalk quarries and left the land derelict. A new housing development was under way in one such quarry, and we struck up a good relationship with the developer, raised the money with the help of the Essex Community Foundation, and established a multi-purpose church building to serve the new community. In an adjacent quarry they had developed one and a half million square feet of retail space at the new Lakeside Shopping Centre where we were also determined to set up a chaplaincy. The owner's manager had offered us what I thought was a rather disappointing space right next to the public toilets. I came back to the office and complained about it to Pat, my PA, who immediately recognised it as a godsend. 'If I were in trouble by myself in Lakeside, the loo is absolutely the first place I'd head for so that I could get some time alone. If the chapel was right there, I might well pop in to sit quietly.' Pat was absolutely right, and so Jill Edwards, the inspirational lead chaplain, therefore bagged the space and gathered around her an ecumenical team who soon established a very thriving ministry from their new base. If there is any pastime that is simply not for me it's shopping, so when I was taken to see some of the two hundred and fifty Lakeside outlets, I was pleased that the chaplains could shepherd me round. I shuddered to learn that coaches would leave the city of Southampton at the crack of dawn each week, packed with families who would take the three hour journey up to spend their day shopping at Lakeside. It was a sad reminder of what our consumer society is doing to people.

Being with the chaplaincy teams in our two universities, the docks, hospitals, prisons, retail outlets and so on, kept my mind alert to the complexities of the world in which the church seeks to serve, whilst the parish system, which is the bedrock of the Church of England, was seeking to maintain a Christian presence in every community. We had one hundred and eighty churches across my Area, so trying to visit everyone regularly and hold it all together in my mind was a mighty challenge. All this would have been quite impossible had it not been for the Area Team I had around me, with their specialisms in young people's work, Christian social action, mission, IT, fundraising and so on. I had the assistance, too, of a series of quite brilliant chaplains, Ian Jorysz, Audrey Cozens, Christopher Cunliffe and then Chris Mann, who each kept me on track, offering background research and organising the complex liturgies. But perhaps the greatest support of all came from the parish clergy and laity, who appreciated the impossible pressures and forgave me my shortcomings and mistakes.

A few of the Bradwell specialist team

I found the rural regions of my Area totally fascinating, and I enjoyed visiting farms and smallholdings, where I learnt about the challenges and joys of rural affairs and agricultural policies. But the vast majority of our south Essex population lived in the urban centres, the sprawling social housing estates, and the new or dilapidated towns. This complexity brought home to me that although we readily categorise areas as rural, urban, inner city, suburban and so on, we should not allow those catch-all labels to blind us to the unique particularity of each human community. At that time, the church still usually regarded the neglected housing estates as merely another aspect of the inner city, ignoring entirely the fact that most were situated at the fringes of our towns and cities. I was glad therefore when, at a conference on so-called inner city ministry, Anne Morisy gathered Andrew Davey, myself and a few other friends into a side room, and suggested we set up a separate national network to serve the forgotten housing estate churches so as to encourage mutual support, training and research. We toyed with different names, and eventually came up with the National Estate Churches Network (NECN), with Anne acting as its secretary and me in the chair. We soon had hundreds of members gathering in small mutual support groups across the country, and from that base we lobbied and cajoled the church at large to pay attention to this frontline ministry, which was always being forgotten or side lined. On behalf of the Network, I wrote a letter to the new Labour government just as it was about to produce a Parliamentary White Paper on urban issues, pressing them to include policies for the outlying housing estates as a special concern. I published the letter as a booklet which included a more extensive theological rationale and critique. We were thrilled to see that, as a consequence, the White Paper, when it was put before Parliament, had a healthy section on housing estate problems, perhaps for the first time in such a document. It was not long before Jane Winter joined our steering group, and what with well-attended annual national conferences, a lively newsletter, the ongoing life of the regional groups, and an informative website, we began to make good headway in turning the church's attention at last to these poorly resourced areas.

One disappointment for me during those years was that I always found the national meetings of bishops disconcerting. Here were really close friends, whom I deeply respected, but when we were all gathered together in the same room, some strange metamorphosis came over us. I'd never been to a public school, but it certainly felt like an overlarge gentlemen's club to me. We had our fun times though, especially when during a residential meeting, one bishop woke in the night, and thinking he had found the door to his en suite loo, found himself instead standing naked in the public corridor without a key to get back into his room. At breakfast the next morning, we were all swapping cartoon captions to suit the event. What made the bishops' meetings worthwhile for me were the conversations over meals or in smaller groups, because it was there that we shared ideas and were at our most creative. It was the national bishops' gathering which appointed me as chair of their Urban Strategy Consultative Group, and commissioned me to produce a substantial paper for the bishops, setting out a strategy for the church's engagement with our British urban issues. They set aside a whole session to discuss the resultant fifty-page document, but I soon realised that it was going to turn into yet another one of their reports, destined for the shelf. I therefore decided to develop it into book form, and in 2003 published *Urban Ministry and the Kingdom of God.* It received another 'book of the year' accolade from the *Church Times,* but my failure to energise the bishops sufficiently about my concerns helped me to appreciate that I did not perhaps have the skills required to operate in those particular corridors of the institution. It was best that the gifts I did have were utilised elsewhere.

I had better success, for example, by continuing to offer guitar concerts in various venues, where I'd sing and tell stories, and then answer questions from the audience – everything from why I never wore purple socks to why I thought God existed. We called those concerts 'An Audience with the Bishop', and they proved to be an inventive way to meet non-church people on their own terms. Meanwhile, the publishers of my book, *Let's Do Theology*, asked me to write a new preface to mark its twentieth year. But when I reread it, I realised just how out of date the book had become, especially since its advocacy of contextual theology had at last been widely accepted. I therefore rewrote the whole thing to bring it up to date. A year later I received, out of the blue, a book in Chinese, and it took me some time to realise that it was in fact a translation of the new edition. Apparently my contextual theology method was now catching on well in Hong Kong – no one had warned me!

The world was now suddenly awash with investment capital as a result of the new global order, and this money, looking for speculative investment opportunities, was being ploughed into urban regeneration. Old areas were refurbished, or else demolished, to make way for brash new office blocks and leisure centres, catering for young high-earners based in the new electronic technology or the financial sector. Bishop John, seeing the dangers of all this impacting unfairly on the poor, appointed me lead bishop on urban development for the diocese. I therefore brought Steve Williams on to our team to help me address the government plans for the redevelopment of southern Essex into what they called the Thames Gateway. Carol Richards worked alongside us in East London, whilst a number of parish priests played crucial roles in addressing the issues in their own parish settings. Alongside this diocesan programme, I teamed up with Chris Baker, an old friend from the William Temple Foundation. We decided to pull together a number of urban community practitioners from across the country to produce a book, *Building Utopia,* which critiqued this urban regeneration and spelt out how fragile the whole regeneration craze was. Sure enough, shortly afterwards came the 2008 financial crash, which brought it all to a thumping halt.

Grace abounding

It's wonderful that the Church of England and the Romanian Orthodox Church are so closely aligned, and that's why Bishop John took a small group of diocesan colleagues to visit our link Romanian Orthodox archdiocese of Iasi, right on Romania's far eastern border with Moldavia. The church hotel in which we were billeted had been confiscated by the previous communist regime, but had now been returned. But the elitist lifestyle of the old government officials continued to hold sway there, so the bishops among us were singled out for the finest rooms. At breakfast the next morning, I inquired of the others if they'd managed to find the air conditioning control in their rooms. They looked surprised that we had air conditioning at all, for they had lain sweltering through the night. Another bishop explained that he had found the controls in his en suite TV lounge, at which the others looked aghast. Apparently, mere archdeacons and deans had to make do with cramped little hen coops. The next morning, I came down to breakfast graciously offering to share with them my extra luxury-wrapped soap and toilet rolls, since they'd complained that there was little to none to be had in their rooms. Once back home, we bishops had great fun telling our colleagues how we admired the Romanian church and its sense of appropriate deference.

I was especially glad that we were invited to visit a Romanian inner city congregation who had been thriving under the leadership of their very saintly priest, who appeared at the door in his long black robe and flowing beard to greet us. After we'd enjoyed the congregation's convivial welcome, he invited those priests among us to go with him behind the iconostasis to see that part of an Orthodox church which is only ever seen by ordained clergy. He pulled the heavy curtain back, and ushered us into this holy of holies, where were situated the altar, and upon it a bible, a cross and the holy relics. It conveyed a visceral sense of the numinous presence

253

of God's Spirit all around us. In the midst of explaining the extreme sanctity of this holy place, the priest suddenly paused, and asked why the other priests from our group had not joined us. We had to explain that knowing the fierce traditionalism of the Orthodox church, out of respect for their host, the women priests among us had assumed they were not included in his gracious invitation. 'But you must bring them in,' he exclaimed. When we had all gathered, he reminded us that not one of us was a priest because of any human decision, but only by the grace of God, and he therefore counted God's women priests to be one with us. As we all gathered in that Holy of Holies to pray with him, the graciousness he had shown in this sacred setting clearly began to overwhelm us, and eventually one of the women began to sob. Soon we were all fighting back our tears of joy. I could only wish that some of our traditionalists back home could have been there to experience the incisive wisdom and grace of this holy man of God.

That Orthodox priest had used the word 'grace' repeatedly, a word which for me goes to the heart of the Christian message. From the start, the Hebrew Scriptures acknowledge God as the God of Justice, ensuring that we all receive what we deserve according to God's Law. The problem was, as St Paul much later pointed out, that if we really all got what we deserve, then God help us! The pages of the Bible therefore stress that the God of Justice is also a God of mercy. We can understand mercy to mean that we do *not* always receive the punishment we deserve. But grace is something much more special. As that Orthodox priest perceived, unlike justice and mercy, grace has nothing to do with us having deserved anything according to any law or formula. It's just the free gift of God. It's like the air we breathe and the gift of life itself – it doesn't depend on us at all, but on the overwhelming generosity of a God who freely bestows. So justice is wonderful when we see it, as long as it is tempered by mercy, but grace takes us into another dimension altogether.

My second Lambeth Conference was certainly an experience of grace after my first one, ten years before. This time, the atmosphere was altogether more profitable and enjoyable, with the highly gifted Archbishop Rowan Williams presiding. Many of the traditionalist bishops on the other hand had decided to meet separately as an alternative organisation they called the Global Anglican Future Conference (GAFCON). This time there was a wonderful sense of love and mutual respect at Lambeth where differences were aired within a well-managed listening process. We therefore came away from this grace-filled gathering with a deeper appreciation and understanding of one another's circumstances, and confident that the Anglican Communion had a strength and purpose worth working for. Although the conference participants had represented a vast array of cultural, linguistic and ethnic backgrounds, we had been able to meet with such openness and mutual attentiveness, that by God's grace we now knew ourselves to be one, even given all those profound differences. We now yearned to find a way by which both we, and those who had absented themselves and instead attended the GAFCON gathering, could join together in the same way. But at least we felt we'd touched base once more by remembering that our unity was to be found only in gracious listening to one another, and to God, the Holy Trinity of difference within unity.

Enlarging my responsibilities

Back in Essex, my PA and now close family friend Pat, retired, after whom the wonderful Amanda Robinson took over my office. At the same time Bishop John Gladwin announced that he would himself now retire, and hand over his work to me until the appointment of our next diocesan bishop. My new responsibilities as acting bishop of this immense diocese were, of course, to be in addition to the workload I already carried as bishop of my own Bradwell Area. Without making time for prayer, and without that free gift of God's grace, I doubt that I would have managed it at all, let alone enjoyed it as much as I did. I was therefore glad that, in a field next to our ancient chapel at Bradwell, stood the buildings of the Othona Christian community, which had been founded at the end of the Second World War to foster peace between what had been the warring nations. The community had made me their joint president alongside the inspiring Professor Frances Young, and my visits there often provided me with the tranquil environment within which I could reflect prayerfully upon all the responsibilities I was now carrying, and recharge my batteries.

I was particularly concerned about the recent changes in the church's regulations. For a long time I had hoped to see better employment rights for all the ordained, and more accountability for us all. When at last the new regulations were issued, however, they totally unbalanced the relationship between bishops and their clergy, expecting that the bishop act more like an employer than a spiritual colleague. This new gulf was aggravated by the way appointments to parishes were turning into a marketplace, with some dioceses even training their clergy to advertise themselves so that they could bag the parish of their choice. But this meant that some very fine priests were passed over who did not believe that they should 'sell themselves' as better than others. I was also dissatisfied with the now preferred understanding of mission as church growth. It was worrying to see attendance declining, but I did not believe that that concern should overtake the church's responsibility to put others first and serve the community. As has often been said, the church is there primarily to serve those who do *not* belong to it. As my misgivings mounted, I was becoming aware that I might be growing into a grumpy old man, but all my life I'd been out of sync with the institutional church, so I was content to let my reluctance be known. I was just grateful that I was now of an age where it would not be long before I was due to retire. I see now, twelve years after my retirement, that the church intends to think again about some of these issues, so I live in hope.

Those eighteen months overseeing the whole diocese brought home to me however just how grateful I was never to have been made a diocesan bishop. I'd often in the past wondered at the incompetence of some diocesan bishops, and hoped I might one day be appointed. But now I could see that my own limitations would never have suited me for that job at all! It required an immense capacity for work, a brain that could see issues in a trice and formulate strategy, a memory for faces, facts and figures, an ability to think on one's feet and speak eloquently off the cuff, the courage always to put the marginalised first, and all this in addition to having a oneness with ordinary people, and a depth of holiness to keep you on the right track. It was just too much to ask of me, and my admiration for those bishops who have those gifts rose exponentially during those tough months. I enjoyed the work immensely, but could now see that only a superb bishop could ever hope to lead the vast and complex diocese of Chelmsford so I went to see Archbishop Rowan, to impress that upon him. The friendship between Rowan and myself went back many years, so after I'd said my piece, he asked me about my own future. I only had a few months left before the usual age for retirement, and so asked him if, once the new bishop had been safely installed, he would think it right for me to retire from my role in Essex. I felt the need to set about a useful retirement and give some time at last to the ever-forgiving Vicki.

A friendship of many years

Rowan helped me considerably, by assuring me that when the name of the new appointee was known, he would share with them that I was now due for retirement so that they would not think it disloyal of me to leave soon after their arrival. 'See the new bishop in and then retire,' proved to be counsel that not only relieved me of anxiety about the future, but also gave me fresh energy to see my last months of work through on full throttle. Being the Bishop of Bradwell had been a great honour and blessing, a privilege beyond all imagining, but clearly my eighteen years in Essex was now drawing to a close, and I needed to begin preparing for retirement.

CHAPTER 11

THE LIFE OF RILEY

It was late in November 2010, that we invited the great and the good of Essex and East London to gather in the oak-panelled county council chamber to welcome the new bishop. Hiding all the while from the bevy of reporters and onlookers, I led him and his wife along the back corridors of the building and stepped out on to the rostrum to ask the audience to stand and welcome their new Lord Bishop of Chelmsford, Stephen Cottrell and his wife, Rebecca. I'd been elected to the national committee that had selected him, but now our clergy, too, expressed their delight with thunderous applause. For Stephen was already known as a bishop of very high calibre, with a gift for oratory and spiritual integrity. He was very bright, a local boy, and to cap it all, he was big enough to tackle this huge job. At our first private meeting, Stephen had told me that he understood that I would be staying only long enough to bring him up to speed on the current diocesan issues. As soon as he was in post it was clear that I could now retire a happy man, knowing that the diocese would be in good hands. Rebecca and Vicki had also become firm friends, so all was set fair for Vicki and me to turn our minds to the business of making the final plans for our retirement.

Getting ready to leave

During our final months we erected a huge marquee in the garden, and invited clergy and folk of all ages and from all sectors of life to say 'thank you' to them for giving so much of themselves in serving the Bradwell Area. They came in great numbers – during one exhausting week, as many as two thousand!

Before her own retirement, Vicki had been travelling up to east London to undertake her school work, taking the opportunity to pop in to see that my parents were both OK. In their old age, Rosanne, their lodger of many years, had suffered a debilitating stroke, but rather than despatch her to a nursing home, they had the grace to take on the caring role themselves. Despite her lack of speech and confinement to a wheelchair, they gave her a full and happy life, for as long as they could manage.

Our daughter, Hannah, was settling into married life with Matt in their tiny Sussex cottage, but we were overjoyed when they announced that they would have to move to a larger house, because Hannah was expecting. And soon we were rejoicing in the birth of our first grandchild, Robin, who has since proved to be very creative and accomplished, full of deep understanding and thoughtfulness. She fills our retirement with happy visits, and long conversations about her favourite subjects, classical history, artistic design and literature. She was later joined by a brother, Tom, a whirlwind of energy and fun. He became ever more interested in military history, spending untold hours devising games of strategy, whilst evidencing a growing sensitivity and caring heart alongside his bright mind.

Hannah, Matt, Robin & Tom

Their dad, Matt, had meanwhile moved on from theatre and into post-production TV, film and then management, playing a leading role in his company's Oscar-winning success, *Gravity*. Later, he set up his own business consultancy, while

Hannah had become manager of the prestigious specialist plant nursery at Marchants Hardy Plants in Sussex.

My eighteen months as both Bishop of Bradwell and acting bishop of the whole diocese, had left me no time to prepare myself for a different sort of life, so I had booked myself in for a clergy retirement conference, looking forward particularly to the session on the theology of retirement. I'd already been pondering John the Baptist's rejoinder when asked about Jesus' developing ministry. 'I must diminish', he said, 'so that he can increase' (John 3:30). As we get older, there are definite reminders of our diminishment as our bodies become less energetic, our minds less sharp, our hair drops out, and instead of lifting the loo seat we men take it as an excuse for a sit down! We gradually find ourselves having to stand aside to let others take centre stage, and many don't manage that as generously as John the Baptist. But as we grow less able, ever more reliant on tablets and prayer, it dawns on us that all this diminishment is just a prelude, a preparation, for the final relinquishment of our powers, when we hand over all that we have and all that we are to the God who made us. We have, quite literally, to make space for those who come after, and let the next generation take the reins, so that they can grow and mature as we hopefully have done ourselves. And all this can be done gracefully – full of grace – or reluctantly, with resentment or even terror. Our present culture fears death so much that it's swept under the carpet or presented on our screens as either quite exciting or altogether unreal. We say to ourselves, 'death happens to the old and I'm not old so that's OK!' And so we fill all our time with diversions, until one day it finds us out, and we are unprepared.

Christians don't, as many think, believe in human immortality, for when we die we die. And we make that belief clear when, at a funeral we say, 'ashes to ashes and dust to dust,' but then we go on to speak of our 'sure and certain *hope* of the resurrection to eternal life though our Lord Jesus Christ.' The philosopher, Heidegger, was surely right to say we fear death because it promises our 'not being there' – the absolute denial of what it is for us to be and exist. On the cross, Jesus, in all his humanity, shares our human fear of obliteration as he yells: 'My God, my God, why have you forsaken me?' But he is also so shot through with the presence of the eternal God that even death cannot deaden his being. And so he does not cease to be. The very heart of who he is cannot be defeated by non-being. And this is his promise of what is called Eternal Life for those who follow him. For even our final diminishment, our death, need not be a negation of our selfhood – our being – for if we too are truly overwhelmed and possessed by God, the Ground of our Being, then we too will continue to be *who* we are, even when we have ceased to be *as* we are.

As we get old, we already have the experience of no longer being *as* we once were, but hopefully we know that we are still *who* we were and still are. It is to be hoped that we might see diminishment as the emptying of all our internal clutter to make space within ourselves, and for some this proves to be the space where Christ's eternal being can find us and fill us. John the Baptist managed to deal with that experience of diminishment gracefully, but that did not mean that he was bound to 'go gentle into that goodnight'. For, like Jesus, he died as he had lived, a courageous outspoken champion for justice. I hope that my demise is not as traumatic as his, but I do pray that I'll have the courage for justice to the end.

On the Saturday of my retirement weekend, the cathedral was ablaze with colour and movement, echoing to music old and new and crowded with relatives, friends and those who represented my past years. It was then that I had that opportunity to share with the congregation the one sermon that I'd been preaching in so many different ways – that God is that mystery in all things, and if we delve into that mystery, we become aware of how much we are loved. My dear friends, the Roman Catholic bishop and the Greek Orthodox abbot were there, and from the Swedish church, Bishop Bengt had journeyed over from Stockholm to thank me for the international partnership we had forged between our dioceses. Under one of the many mitres on parade was Edward

Holland, formerly the Bishop of Colchester, who, during the Peace, spotted Vicki's sister in the congregation. He steered his way through the throng to greet her with arms outstretched, and hugged her most lovingly, telling her how sorry he was to see her go. Gini explained that he had made an understandable mistake because she was but one of three sisters, first Carol and then the identical twins, Vicki and herself. My wife Vicki, she pointed out, was seated elsewhere and dressed in a brown coat. At the end of the service Edward, therefore, approached the twin in the brown coat and repeated his hugs and best wishes, at which Gini once again had to explain that she'd totally forgotten that she too had a brown coat with her, which she'd only now put on. Poor Edward was very apologetic, but it was a lovely way to make friends.

Saying
goodbye to
dear friends

The following day saw Vicki and me back where it had all begun some eighteen years earlier, at Bradwell Chapel. It was a very simple, meditative service, at the end of which, I placed upon the altar my Bradwell crozier and cope in readiness for whoever was to come after me as bishop. Then Vicki took my hand, and we walked back down the aisle surrounded by our friends and stepped out into the open air, to face the next chapter in our lives. But not before Lawrence, the local parish priest, with his typically Irish hospitality, held out a silver platter whereon stood a bottle of special Irish whiskey and a glass, to bid us both a long life and abundant love for our retirement years.

A home of our own

Our new life was to be in Bexhill-on-Sea, where its open sky and sea gave Vicki the natural space she craved, whilst in the town and surrounding areas were all the issues of urban life which were life-blood for me. Spike Milligan, who had been stationed in Bexhill during the war, had suggested that, 'if you look out from Bexhill beach, you can see the Continent, and if you turn around to face the town you will see the incontinent.' It was true that in the 50s and 60s the town had been home to large numbers of the elderly, but now it was alive with young families, many charity shops and homeless beggars. In a music shop I came across Jay Myerson, a fabulous guitarist who soon became my music tutor and good friend, accompanying me at many a guitar concert which I continued to offer in aid of charity. I was determined, too, to use my retirement in trying my hand at veggie growing, so I dug out a patch in our new garden, and following the instructions on the packet, dropped the tiny carrot seeds into the ground. It was then that a paralysing conviction stopped me in my tracks: 'this will never work! How on earth can I expect carrots to grow from such tiny little seeds?' It dawned on me that I'd been preaching about the parable of the sower, and about seeds growing secretly all my life, but I'd never actually got the point! The carrots turned out to be delicious, and now I read the parable with new conviction.

As soon as we'd moved our furniture into our new home we took the holiday we had dreamed of for years. First we stayed with dear friends, John and Linda Vrahimis, in Cyprus, who took us to the northern part of the island to view their ancestral home, now occupied by the Turks after their invasion in 1974. It was from there that they had both escaped through a hail of bullets with their newborn child in their arms. We flew from there across to Israel/Palestine where, on an earlier occasion, I'd unknowingly travelled through a terrorist stronghold where a European face could easily become a literal hostage to fortune. My Arab friend had made me duck down out of sight, so that thankfully we arrived without incident, but it had certainly put the wind up me! This time, Mones and Sally drove us safely north to Nazareth, the town in which Mones had grown up, and where his Arab Christian family now lived. The food and hospitality were without equal, and we loved looking through the photographs of their grandparents' earlier life in a village which had suddenly and unexpectedly been demolished by Israeli bulldozers. We later visited its ruins, now masquerading as a picnic spot for unknowing tourists. After an equally eye-opening conversation with the mayor of Bethlehem, I realised that a European could live in this country for decades, and still never fully comprehend the subtleties and complexities of what is happening in that land. But Mones took it all in his stride, and was working hard to sow peace and harmony in his ancestral homeland.

We returned home, only too aware of how safe and privileged our lives had been by comparison, although our life from now on was to be very different from anything we had experienced through forty years of ministry. We now sat through meals without me once being called away by phone or the front doorbell, and for the first time I understood what people meant by saying 'have a relaxing weekend'. Oh to be normal at last!

One of the greatest joys of retirement, for those who are blessed with them, is to see your children grow and develop in their own distinctive ways. Becki, now back from her meditations in Thailand, and her conservation work diving with sharks in South Africa, had met Paul, a naturalist who looked after Mitcham Common, and so they settled down to life together in South London. They chose as the venue for their marriage ceremony a little house in a tree – as you do – followed by a short service of blessing under a bower in the cottage garden below. After a further year or two, we were able to welcome young Oscar Alexander Moorhouse into the world, and Ozzy was soon another toddling miracle in our lives. Like his dad, he adores caring for animals and the creepy crawlies in the garden and, like his mum, loves dressing up in outrageous costumes.

Becki & Paul
with Ozzy

We were looking forward to joining our local church, so I went along in mufti, unaware that the vicar had recognised me. At the door he accosted me with: 'you're not here to cause trouble, are you?' He'd obviously found out that I'd been one of the first bishops to ordain women, and that had put me right out of court as far as he was concerned. I didn't know that he was due to retire, so instead we looked elsewhere and soon found a new spiritual home. After being licensed as an Honorary Assistant Bishop in both Chichester and Rochester dioceses, I also began taking occasional services, being invited to confirm and ordain and license clergy, which was always a joy.

A personal breakthrough

I had not anticipated how my retirement would give me time to think! I remembered that, on beginning my doctoral dissertation, the events of my life had looked like so many disconnected pieces of a jigsaw, which I then hoped to piece together. As I now reflected upon my many and varied experiences, at last the pieces were coming together into a coherent picture – although not quite the picture on the original jigsaw box because, as in every life, quite unexpected things had made my life unique. I was now in a position to look back and contemplate a more completed picture, and ask what I had got wrong and could have done better. I should, perhaps, have been more thankful for all that the institutional church had given me. Institutions are, after all, our human attempts to work together in cooperation, to further those best endeavours which would be quite unachievable if we all went our own way. On reflection, had it not been for institutional religion, I would not have been introduced to the Christian faith in the first place! The very best of our institutions, even the BBC or the NHS, can let us down, and sometimes so can the Church of England, and working so closely to it had certainly alerted me to its many shortcomings. But it had also allowed me to work with some of the most inspiring and caring people imaginable.

In my reflections upon the internal workings of my own past life, I was now able to recognise that the aggressive anger which had so marred my adolescent years had, over time, been given new creative purpose. The result of this was that I was no longer always destructively critical, but now more positively able to critique injustice and work hard to combat it. But the one thing that I had never really sorted out was my abiding negativity and anger towards *myself,* born partly from my continuing word-blindness and fear of failure. I suspected that it was my vulnerability that had led me to distrust life and to be overly defensive and manipulative. I'd absolutely adored people, but sometimes used others around me to make me feel more secure. At heart, it was what so many of us experience – that we're really not very loveable. We say 'God loves us', but do we truly and honestly believe it?

Soon after retirement, I'd begun to visit Crawley Down monastery to experience the beautiful liturgy which the monks had based largely on the Greek Orthodox service. It encouraged me to begin reading all about the Orthodox icons that I had always loved, and one evening, on turning a page of Rowan Williams' little icon guide, *Ponder These Things,* I was blown out of my chair by a very simple thought. Rowan was explaining the meaning of the *Eleousa* icon of Mary holding her child Jesus, or perhaps it's more accurate to say that she is trying to hold him, for the icon portrays him as clambering up his mother's lap to kiss her cheek as any baby might. In my life I'd desperately been trying to earn the love of others, and here was Rowan saying: 'If we begin, as most of us tend to, with a notion that God stands at a distance waiting for us to make a move in his direction, this image should give us something of a shock. The Lord here does not wait, impassive, as we babble on about our shame and penitence, trying to persuade him that we are worth forgiving. His love is instead that of an eager and rather boisterous child, scrambling up on his mother's lap, seizing handfuls of her clothing and nuzzling his face against hers, with that extraordinary hunger for sheer physical closeness that children will show with loving parents ...' The icon pictured, he said, 'the love of God in search of us, as unselfconscious and undignified as the clinging child, as undignified as the father in the story of the Prodigal Son running down the road to greet his lost child, an image of the immense freedom of divine love, the freedom to be defenceless and without anxiety. God, we could say, does not care in the least if his love makes him look as if he is dependent on us, as if he needs us: that is our problem, not his.'

All my life I'd been trying to convince God, others and myself, that I was somehow worth loving. And here was a picture of God who didn't care about all that, but instead had always loved me, just as I am. That's what love does, and that's what God is. Just to be, to let God love us, can be a way to taste a little of what in old-fashioned religious language they call salvation. And at that moment, as I contemplated that lovely icon, I felt a great weight lifting. I'd been loved by God, and by others, all this time and I had not been able to see it, or accept it, because deep inside I was still convinced it depended on me rather than them, when love isn't really like that at all. I'd often rehearsed what my dad would always say about love, that it's 'what runs up your back and knocks your hat off', and that's how I felt at that moment as I read those words. It was as if a new dawn was lighting up the landscape of my life. I was loved for who I was, and was accepted, even though I'd always thought myself unacceptable. I was, at last, back in touch with the Ground of Being – not as an abstract concept, but as a profound experience of being loved. Was this what Jesus meant when he said that he yearned for us to become one with him, just as he found himself at one with the Ground of Being, so that 'just as, Father, you are in me and I am in you, so they also may be in us'? (John 17: 21)   From then on, although those old anxieties still occasionally rumbled around within me, I felt liberated now to look to the rest of my retirement less driven, more relaxed and newly energised.

Three fulfilling initiatives

It was my former mentor, Bishop John Waine, who well before my retirement had offered some sage advice. He warned that as soon as I left office, I would be inundated by letters and phone calls, asking me to take on responsibilities for some initiatives which were not necessarily what I would have chosen for myself. John strongly advised that well before that happened, I should select just three areas that really did excite me, and set up ways in which I could engage those issues during my retirement years. I could then politely, but firmly, decline those letters and calls by explaining that all my retirement time was already spoken for. I diligently followed his advice and found it easy to name the three areas which really did interest me. The first was to become more fully engaged with those who lived in our deprived housing estates. I wanted the second to have an international flavour, but still address issues of marginalisation, so I opted to give time to an Indian charity. And third, I wanted to play a small part in promoting peace, by fostering better relationships between people of different faiths.

I had a ready-made way into addressing my first retirement issue, that of engaging with our deprived housing estates, for I had, all this time, continued as chair of the National Estate Churches Network – the NECN. I now volunteered to take to the road for the network, visiting housing estates of all types, gathering data, learning first hand about the issues, teaching and generally flying the flag for this forgotten sector of British life and ministry. The horror was that these inspiring places were not appreciated at all by the church at large – indeed, often their work at local level only continued in the face of their own denominations' reduction of support, both in terms of finance and personnel. I therefore thought it would help if my five years of engaged research were made public, so I published it all in *Blessed are the Poor? Urban Poverty and the Church.* The question mark in the title was important, for it sought to wrestle with the question of what on earth Jesus meant by saying, 'blessed are the poor' when, on first sight, the poor appear to be anything but blessed.

The best way to unveil the real values of a nation is to see how it treats its poorest members and, if we listen to what they have to tell us, we can learn the truth about our society. It made me wonder if, perhaps, that was one of the reasons why Jesus himself had chosen to live and work among poor peasants and become one with them. It enabled Jesus to offer the most remarkable analysis of the condition of the poor in Luke's account of the Beatitudes (Luke 6:20 f). First he says, poverty means hunger – and on the estates, this can mean hunger for food, for decent education, good health care, good housing and so on. Next he says 'Blessed are you who weep now', for there's no doubt that marginalised people are often in despair at their chances of being allowed to make the decisions that will determine their life. Then Jesus says, 'Blessed are you when people hate you and exclude you.' And that is, perhaps, the worst part of being poor: you become marginalised, with unfair assumptions about your morality and your values being loaded upon you by people who have no conception of the sort of challenges your life presents. It all angered Jesus so much that he attacked the hypocritical scribes and pharisees, calling them 'white-washed tombs' and 'a brood of vipers', for using their power to weigh down upon the peasants in such self-righteous ways. With its focus on themes of this nature, I should not have been surprised that the poor rejoiced at my book, telling me that they felt it was telling their story and exposing the reality of their predicament. The powers in the church institution, however, did not embrace its ideas until that is, an ally appeared in the person of the newly ordained Bishop Philip North. He was a persuasive speaker, and urged the General Synod to invest more resources in our housing estate parishes and vigorously supported the contention of my book that, in addition to offering help, the church needs to listen to what the poor have to teach us.

By the time the book was published, I'd already served for twenty years as the chair of the National Estate Churches Network, and I knew that I now needed to stand down and bring in some fresh young leaders. I was, therefore, delighted that Andy Delmege, a Birmingham parish priest, and the remarkably talented priest, Lynne Cullens, agreed to take it over, and so the two of them worked together to bring fresh vigour and perspective to the whole show. It now continues to go from strength to strength.

The glories of India

Andrew Davey and I had launched our global urban initiative at my first Lambeth Conference, and so we journeyed to New York along with Bishop Roger Sainsbury, where we were invited to meet with the Under-Secretary General of the United Nations, Mr Nitan Desai. He was glad to see the Anglican Church involved in what he took to be one of the fundamental problems confronting our newly globalising world. I was, additionally, invited to offer a lecture tour in the urban centres of Texas and, in the following year, to lead the Toronto Diocesan conference, where they were keen to look at the implications of globalisation and urbanisation for their own country. We then held a major seminar in South India. It was here that Vicki and I had previously toured with four sizeable Indians, all crammed into a tiny dilapidated car in good Indian fashion, driving for hours at a time on dusty unmade roads in stifling heat. It was a very fair introduction to the realities of India. Its casual unpredictability struck us later, however, on a visit to a highly prestigious college, when being shown round by the principal, I happened to notice a poster advertising a lecture to be given that very evening by a visiting European specialist on international development. On seeing me look up at the poster, the principal remarked: 'Yes, we're looking forward to what you have to say.' It came as a total surprise to me, and so I quickly had to knock something together in my mind ready for that evening as we continued the tour of the campus!

Despite that, I was enthralled by all the wonders of this ancient and vibrant culture, and readily agreed to go out to India once again with Andrew Davey for a follow-up conference. Although we were both appalled by it, Andrew and I had, over time, become accustomed to the ubiquitous corruption in Indian society and particularly its presence among the church hierarchy. On a later visit, however, I was having breakfast with a group of Indian friends up in the mountains when in walked the first white face I'd seen for some time. Chris Brown turned out to be another Anglican priest who had just retired from being chief executive of the children's charity NSPCC. He knew India extremely well, and suggested that, with his brother Philip, we might together establish a UK charity to raise funds in support of two projects where we'd seen none of the corruption which was endemic elsewhere.

And so it was that *Friends of the Poor in South India,* came into existence. We were keen to install some toilets for one project, but noted that because bank computers limited the number of letters allowed for a title, they had unfortunately, but appropriately, registered us as 'Friends of the Poo'! We later renamed the charity *Building Better Futures International*, the work taking me into some areas where most Indians are still terrified to go, staying with tribesmen and women in tiny communities in the hills where they, quite literally, live in Stone Age conditions. In one battered home made of sticks, leaves and tarpaulin, Mr Muttupandi proudly showed us his television which, he explained, had been provided by their local politician just before election day, even though she knew full well they had no electricity to make it work! The village community were reliant upon earning a pitiful income by collecting lichens and fruits in the snake-ridden forest, but had now, annually, to acquire a government permit to do so. The officer would only authorise the permit if he were offered the young girls from the community each year. I took my own daughter there some years later, and although a tough lass, on seeing those conditions, she cried herself to sleep that night. We would never have believed it when we first set the charity up, that over the years, *Building Better Futures International* would help thousands of marginalised and abused women to receive skills training, employment and a safer future.

I was to learn that Indian rural tradition forbids women to remain in their home during menstruation, so each month they have to sleep outdoors at the mercy of snakes and male predators. We were keen, therefore, to build a training centre with safe overnight accommodation for as many as could squeeze in. It's also there that the women receive training in sewing and the like, and are then provided with machines so that they can earn enough to provide their families with the basic essentials of life. Many other projects also now take place in the training centre, and it is there that the children receive essential supplementary education from our team of teachers. We've even managed to raise the money to provide a coconut plantation, which provides work for more women, and thus an income to help sustain all the training. All this goes on under the indigenous leadership of Jesuran Stanley and Raja Samson and their teams. And, in addition to all this, my spirits have been lifted to see ordinary folk in the UK dig deep to give their fellow human beings at the other side of the world the chance to take control of their lives and create a meaningful future for themselves.

A warm welcome from Jesuran & his

I was sitting on a veranda in the heat of the morning sipping from my cup of chai and saying my prayers, when I found myself reading Jesus' story of the rich man, Dives, and the poor man, Lazarus. Dives had lived a life of luxury, ignoring the starving Lazarus on his doorstep, but on finding himself in Hell, looked up to Heaven to see Lazarus, and began his feeble pleading for release. It had only taken me a few hours in the air to reach these impoverished people from the UK – they are on our doorstep! So we truly are that rich man, Dives.

A world full of religions

The majority of human beings are followers of a religion, each faith proclaiming peace, but sometimes resulting in quite the opposite. My third retirement endeavour was, therefore, to engage more meaningfully with people of other faith traditions, so that more mutual understanding might prevail. And as a consequence, I learnt more than I could have imagined, and gained many friends besides.

On a city pavement in Chennai, previously known as Madras, I sat on a low wicker stool, once again drinking my beloved chai, conversing with Nallini Chettur, the owner of Giggles, 'the biggest little bookshop in the world'. Nallini asked me all about myself and then said, 'I know the book that you need.' She ordered her diminutive assistant into the tiny shop which was piled so tightly with books from floor to ceiling that even he had difficulty squeezing in, yet he eventually emerged clasping the designated volume. Nallini took it and described it to me in great detail. It was, she said, an admirable account of the real nature of Hinduism. It is important to realise, she explained, that Hinduism is not a faith at all, but a culture, its own devotees preferring to call it a *dharma,* a dutiful life. And the variety of ways in which one can lead that Hindu life is bewildering; there's the path of *Bhakti,* or devotion, the path of *Jnana* or knowledge, and even the path of *Karma* which is the life of good deeds, words and thoughts. A very close friend, who belongs to the priestly Brahmin caste, later took me to Banashankari Temple in Bengaluru, to explain it further to me. But I never quite fathomed how it was, that on asking him which Hindu god he himself prayed to, he was able to answer that he had no idea at all. I had studied Hinduism and Islam at university, but I soon learnt that the theory was far removed from the lived reality of these great world religions.

I was particularly pleased to find that back in Bexhill a new Islamic mosque was just being opened and so I gingerly ventured in to learn more. As I took off my shoes in the foyer, a very rotund figure came bouncing down the little corridor, all smiles and expectation. He was intrigued to know who I was, and welcomed me to come and sit at the side of the prayer hall whilst the brothers prayed. As the voices sang out verses from the Qur'an, I decided to recite silently the Christian Magnificat, for I knew that Muslims honour Mary, its author, and revere her son, Jesus, as the second prophet after Muhammad. The imam was keen to read the New Testament and learn about Christianity and so in return for his English translation of the Qur'an, I presented him with a copy of the Holy Bible. My friendships with our Muslim community have been blossoming ever since. The chairman of the mosque invited me to join the local interfaith forum, which turned out to be exactly what I had been looking for, and it was there that I was to meet many representatives of other world religions.

The forum immediately jolted me out of one of my early assumptions. In the 1970s all I'd heard about 'Moonies' from the media was that they were a dangerous, brainwashing cult founded by a Korean multimillionaire, Sun Myung Moon. But to my surprise, Tim, a member of their Unification Church, was the thoughtful, sensitive and caring driving force behind the interfaith forum. Liz, a local Baha'i, shared her faith with us and Kai-Sang Lamar, from our Bexhill Buddhist centre, introduced me to the great Buddhist thinker, Thich Nhat Hanh, who had written, 'God as the ground of being cannot be conceived of. Nirvanas also cannot be conceived of. If we are aware when we use the word "nirvana" or the word "God" that we are talking about the ground of being, there is no danger in using these words.' He went on to say that we can connect with this Ground through, 'dance and drumming, in walking and running and sitting on the earth, in swimming, playing and planting things in the earth.' This phrase, the Ground of Being, was very important to me as a Christian, and seeing it used in this Buddhist context made me recognise the similarity of the quest which all religions have in common – the search for that which is the ultimate, the beyond that is within everything around us. There is much to distinguish one religion from the next, to be sure, but it was astonishing that when in the company of a friend from another religion, I was always struck by a sense of being with a kindred spirit – a searching spirit. My Christian experience, however, taught me that it was more a matter of being searched for rather than searching.

At the Bexhill Quaker's hall they maintained a superb interfaith library. But what I learnt, above all, was that it's one thing to study a faith from a book, just as I had done so often, but an altogether different experience to enter into dialogue with its loving and inspiring adherents. The deeper our friendships became, the clearer it was to me, that if the different faith traditions are distanced from one another, there's little hope for the security and wellbeing of the world.

Exploring the beyond

I had an extremely odd experience whilst organising my next trip to India. Out of the blue, I received an email from a chaplain in the United Arab Emirates. He'd just had an unsolicited message telling him to warn me about a possible computer virus. How it had been directed to his screen we never found out. He asked if I might be the same Laurie Green he remembered from his days as a priest in the East End. He now headed up the chaplaincies in Dubai, but because there was no bishop there at present, they'd been praying for a bishop to come and confirm their new members. I looked up Indian flights via Dubai and saw that it would save me two hundred pounds on my ticket, so it was a win-win situation all round. Neither of us could see any sign of a computer virus, and we remain puzzled about it all to this day, but from then on I often stopped with John on my journeys to and from India. He took me to see the impoverished foreign workers who were being shipped in to build the towering skyscrapers for the rich to inhabit. He smuggled me into one of their work camps, but when I saw the conditions I became quite subdued. John nevertheless brightened my spirits by explaining that he'd formed close working relationships with the Dubai government, and that some of the workers' long hours and risks to safety had lately been reduced. Visitors to Dubai see none of this, and experience very few restrictions upon their behaviour, but none of those privileges extended to the workcamps.

Some years later Chris Mann, my former chaplain in Bradwell, became chaplain in Al Ain, also in the UAE, but situated in the eastern desert very close to the Oman border. After visiting the local camel market one morning, we drove off into the appropriately named 'Empty Quarter', one of the most inhospitable deserts on earth. For a brief moment, we got out of the air-conditioned car to experience the beauty, isolation and searing heat of the desert, but we could not stand that environment for long. The tribesmen who had, until recently, inhabited deserts like this surely had to be hardened individuals, savage fighters and totally committed to their tribe if they were to have any chance of survival. It made me realise that the nomadic patriarchs of the Hebrew Scriptures would have lived in just such desolate environments. Perhaps that's why they interpreted their experiences of God in such harsh and primitive terms. Nevertheless, we're thankful that we still have a record of those times in the Hebrew Bible.

As I stood in the desert museum, learning about the ways of these people, little did I realise that back home in Britain, my dear mother lay dying. It was whilst waiting in the airport for my flight back to the UK that I managed to contact home at last, and was told the news. Only two years before that, despite her dementia, we had all celebrated her hundredth birthday. But more recently she had been curled up in bed like a baby, unable to communicate except by holding my finger and bringing it to her mouth. The dementia had begun to creep in some years before, and had slowly inhabited the whole of her body, and yet our visits had, until very recently, still had their moments. On one occasion, she had looked at her granddaughter, Becki, and remarked: 'I don't know who you are dear, but I know that I love you.' It seems that the spirit which binds us together in love is quite independent of our mental capacity.

Vicki and my sister, Babs, had been constant visitors at her bedside whilst I was away and the nurses had been angels. But I had arrived back in something of a daze, unable to register the reality of the loss of my mum. At the funeral, David Tudor, the local priest, spoke of mum's life with great delicacy and grace and, since many of his congregation haled from the East End, he understood something of the meaning of my mum's courageous cockney life. He spoke of her meeting dad at the local ballroom, dancing their first waltz together to the 1930 hit, *I'm dancing with tears in my eyes, for the girl in my arms isn't you.* David ended his tribute with the words, 'now at last she's dancing again with her beloved Len, but the words this time will be, *I'm dancing with tears in my eyes because the girl in my arms is now you!* At the end of the service, with the coffin still in its place, our parents' favourite tango tune began to play. I looked at my sister Babs as she looked at me and we knew what would please mum and dad most of all. So we danced the tango, their favourite dance, all around her coffin, and as we did so, at last, I could remember my mum as she really was, and could recognise that the frail shell I'd seen in the hospital had simply been waiting to be filled with eternal life. Funeral services can do all sorts of important things for us.

The overwhelming depth of it all

Despite the onset of a lung weakness, I managed to plant more veggies, produce a CD to help fund our Indian charity, have great fun with our grandchildren, and even offer a little help at the night shelter which my friends Leslie and Andrew Crighton organise. Bishop John Waine's sage advice to choose only three interests saved me from other requests, until that is, I did receive that inevitable request to take on a further task, and ironically, it was from John himself! He had just completed his ten year appointment as the Bishop Visitor to the nuns of Malling Abbey in Kent, and told me that they would like me to succeed him in that capacity. He explained

279

that I would be expected to learn all about the enclosed life of the Anglican Benedictine sisters, and be of service to them individually as well as to the Community as a whole. Mother Mary David had quite recently been elected as the abbess, so it was particularly to her that I became a sounding board and confidant, and, much later, to Mother Anne, her successor. The welcome I received from them all was so very loving and warm, and in time, although never allowed before, I was even welcomed behind the forbidding doors of the private enclosure where only the nuns themselves normally ventured. They even invited me to share with them the silent meals in their refectory, which was a joy. The fifth century Benedict was the inspiration for the Order of Saint Benedict, to which all the sisters belonged, and he wrote for them a Rule of life, of which the very first word is 'listen!' By the porch of Norwich Cathedral is an imposing statue of him, with his Rule in one hand and the index finger of the other across his lips. The nuns move quietly, and speak only those words which are essential, so that all their attention may be fixed on serving one another and on listening to God. It's an infectious quietness, that seeps into us, making us realise that a lot of the noise in society is there to save us from listening to deeper things.

Some of the sisters had lived this communal life away from the common round for as much as fifty or even sixty years, but they were anything but uninformed or lacking in intellectual bite. The simplicity of their lives at the abbey is a witnessing challenge to a world fraught with worry about getting on and owning more, and their constant joy at finding the presence of God within every second of time and every centimetre of space, serves to magnify the truth that so much of the 'stuff' in our world is there just to divert our gaze from what's really important.

The prayer at Malling Abbey is serene and all-encompassing, the manual work strenuous and rewarding, and the studies regular and fascinating. But despite all the beauty of their lives, I began to hear from the sisters that the abbey buildings themselves were causing difficulties, because of their immense size and their own reduced number. They therefore, after much prompting from me and the strong lead from Mother Mary David, undertook a complete reorganisation of the abbey, allowing them to vacate the western section to create there a welcoming centre for spirituality and retreat, and to play host to a new theological college on that part of the site. When we consider how these same nuns remember when there were grilles on every window and only Latin was used for the daily round of services, it is remarkable that they were able to negotiate the extraordinary upheaval of this reorganisation and face the changes with the same tranquillity and stability of community life as steadfastly as ever. They proved to the world that even after Covid lockdown it remains possible to live life ever attentive to the Presence. The jewel in the crown at Malling Abbey is, without doubt, the beauty of the daily Office of sung services and prayer. Their great church echoes round with their simple plainchant recitation of the Psalms and biblical passages and transports the visitor to new depths of awareness and realisation. One visitor remarked that, when he attends the Divine Office of prayer at Malling, he doesn't bother to follow the words in the book, but just sits silently as he is plunged into 'a spiritual sauna' of transforming song and spiritual Presence.

With the sisters of Malling Abbey

It's tragic that many of us are so limited by our western culture that we miss out on any awareness of these divine depths within human experience, and only live a one-dimensional life filled to bursting with the illusional diversions of acquisition and the lure of status and power. Western society has not been helpful to those who want to touch the depth of the mystery of life, but it is there for those who refuse to be bamboozled by the glitter. And I speak as one who, having been touched by that deep mystery throughout my life, has nevertheless been diverted from time to time by my own selfishness. But that Ground of Being, that God, has been constantly popping a head through the window at me until at last I've begun to get the point. It's as if God's mystery has a gravitational pull upon us which constantly reaches out, granting to each of us the gift of being, and an existence full of challenges and opportunities to love, to learn and to be loved to eternity. But behind all this, in order that we remain free beings, God remains hidden in a cloud of our unknowing, putting no pressure on us, giving us many clues, but letting us unravel the mystery for ourselves. A love that deep is overwhelming. We can only respond with awe and wonder, and then seek to love one another for all we're worth.

CHAPTER 12

AFTERTHOUGHTS
– WHAT'S BEEN ESSENTIAL?

So here I sit in Bexhill, God's waiting room, having written these pages of reflection on my life, trying to make sense of how a cockney kid from the East End, with a jellied eel factory at the end of the road and a Stalinist granny upstairs, got to be a bishop in the established Church of England. Lack of space has meant that I've had to leave out from my narrative, many extraordinary events and beautiful people who have been a strong influence upon me. But they've been in my mind and in my heart as I've scribbled and typed away. As I've reflected on my life I have, in some senses, had to relive events in my mind and that's made me search for what it is that makes me 'me'. I still carry the same genes that I had way back in 1958 when I became a teenager, but my cells have long since been upgraded and downgraded through the years. I'm not *what* I was, but I do feel that I remain *who* I was and, hopefully, *who* I will always be. I'm now well past my seventy-sixth birthday, and it will soon be my turn to make space for others to come after me. To get out of their way and let them have their day. I'll become part of the forgotten cloud of those who have gone before, but I hope that sharing my story with you and those who come after, will prompt others to reflect on their own story – for I have, without doubt, learnt a lot from writing mine. So where does it all leave me?

A faith that makes sense

The central thread of my life has quite clearly been my Christian faith, so I've attempted to give a flavour of how that developed over the years. And now, perhaps, I should try to sum that up and say where I've got to with it so far. My friend, Ian, says that when people like me start explaining their belief it becomes so convoluted and confusing that we eventually vanish up our own exhaust pipe! But that's because in truth, seeking to use the limited means of expression available to humanity to talk about the mystery of God is bound to get us all tangled up. But I'm heartened by what the Dominican philosopher Herbert McCabe observed, that if, when we talk about God, we don't feel intellectual vertigo, it can't be the real God we're talking about. This chimes in with my deepest conviction about God. As I've said all along, this is a conviction that God is the ultimate mystery, and, to us, will always remain so – but perhaps it's the mystery that makes life so very wonderful. For to be frank, I love it that even though I know my wife Vicki better than anyone else does, she's still a mystery to me!

But since we can never actually know the full nature of God, we might well ask: 'then what's the use of all these theological words? Why try to say anything at all about God?' Anthony de Mello's answer to that question is simple. He replies, 'Why does the bird sing?' I find that when we've been gripped by the mysterious experience of God's presence, we just can't help ourself. My favourite philosopher, Paul Tillich, suggested that since our words are so inadequate when trying to speak of God, we should be wary of becoming addicted to them. Some people even find the word 'God' so overlaid with baggage, said Tillich, that it's best that they forget that word and find a word or symbol that works better for them. Some can't stand the word 'Father' to describe the loving relationship that God wants with us, and I can well understand that, especially if their father was a heavy presence, or they feel it excludes the feminine. In which case, said Tillich, why not jettison those words which don't do the trick for you and find others? So I do my best to sit lightly to some of those problematic words or even substitute others at times. But I still have one worry about it as a solution to our language problem.

If we're left to our own devices, making up words as we go along, we might end up inventing some wacky nonsense religion of our own – and there are enough of them around already! So rather than go our own way, it's best to take very serious account of the experience of others, and especially of the religious greats who have gone before us. They can often furnish us with words, music, architecture, liturgies, and so on, which help us to better understand our human experience of the mystery and give expression to it. And this is where religion comes in. It immerses us in the experiences of others so that we can learn from the very best of the past, and it guards us from making it all up to suit our own prejudices – although, as I hope is evident by now, I believe that everything should still be critiqued very carefully.

So let me try to recap what I've learnt thus far about the Christian faith as I've journeyed on my way. And I hope you will see how it all connects with the life story I've been telling.

The genius of the Christian faith

We miss the mark: You'll remember that my early years introduced me to the fact that the world isn't as it should be. My socialist family instilled into me the importance of doing our best to rid society of its injustices, its inequality and its lack of true freedom. For something is seriously out of kilter with the way we all are. Even though we have a sense of the potential that's in us to make the world a better place, we never seem able to become the society that we know we could and should be. We're always missing the mark. The religious word for this is 'Sin' – the state of creation's disjointedness. But there's also the word 'sins', in the plural, and that's to do with how we individually, and as groups, mess up the planet, fail to care for the marginalised, don't respect people who are different, and so it goes on. We're alienated from what we could be and try as we may, we don't seem to be able to put it all right.

I learnt to see this as the angst which was so well described by those Critical Theorists and expressed in Munch's famous picture, *The Scream*. That picture is of a face with mouth wrenched wide open by anxiety, but to set us right all human society seems able to do is stuff that open mouth with junk, with a striving for status, a promise of yet more commodities and a chance for celebrity. But these all prove to be illusory remedies which numb the pain for a while, but only serve to hide from us the nub of our inner problem. So whilst, even as a boy, I had a strong sense that things were not right, none of the usual answers seemed to hit the spot.

We glimpse the mystery: The genius of humanity is that we're not only able to sense that there should be more to it than just a stuffed mouth, that same human spirit is also able to sense something deeper. For most, it's a passing moment that is soon forgotten, but others have lingered long and thought hard about that sensitivity. I've mentioned the times I was introduced to Plato and Aristotle who talked about the being within existence, Meister Eckhart and John Robinson who spoke of the Ground of our Being, Rudolf Otto who sought to analyse what he called the numinous experience, and the Christian mystics who wrote of the Cloud of Unknowing. Moreover, billions of ordinary people have experienced glimpses of a mystery within, which seems to be reaching out to us in the most startling and most generous way. That can be experienced and interpreted as a personal encounter with God, and often people will express that by saying, 'it felt like God was speaking to me!' Others feel taken up by an invitation to a mystical union with the Ground of Being. I had to learn that you can't magic these experiences up, as some gurus would have us believe, because the real thing relies entirely upon the unique initiative of the mystery itself – what religion, and that Romanian priest, taught me to call God's grace.

God reaching out to welcome us in: Right from the start I'd met many wonderful people who were intent on helping others. But when I learnt about Jesus, it was clear that he was taking this to an altogether higher level. It was as if, in living for others, he was so emptying himself of himself that the resulting inner space was open to be filled entirely by God's mystery, the Ground of Being. That's why he spoke of God 'abiding' in him and he abiding in God. And by virtue of that reaching out quality of the mystery abiding in him he turned to those around him, and to us, and invited us to abide in him so that through him we might ourselves abide in God (e.g. John 17:21). So the mystery which most of us only glimpse momentarily, forever wants to come as close to us as the food we eat! The gaping mouth of our anxiety can be filled at last with something worthwhile and permanent.

The really magical bit is that when this 'abiding' happens for us, we experience ourselves no longer alienated from, but at one with life, at one with our innermost selves, and most important of all, at one with the Ground of Being. This experience of 'at-one-ment', is the 'atonement' that Christian theologians talk about, and from it comes the desire and the power to engage the world in a new way, knowing that alienation can never finally be victorious. We are invited to begin living Eternal Life right now, looking injustice, hatred, inequality and all the nonsense of our consumer society straight in the eye, refuting its ultimacy and powerfully confronting it. And how does this work?

The God who suffers: As I became more and more convinced that the Christian faith made sense, the more I had to address this man Jesus and what he was teaching us. I'd seen many a crucifix, but never stopped to register how clearly that figure of Jesus demonstrates a God far removed from any notion of a God who punishes us. On the contrary, here is the face of a suffering God who opens wide his arms for us on a cross – an instrument of torture, a symbol of total alienation. Look at it

287

long enough and it radiates the truth that it's that power of self-giving that lies at the heart of everything, and in the light of that, all our grasping after power, after owning things, after celebrity or status, we can now reckon as nonsense, or as St Paul so graphically labels it, a load of crap (Philippians 3:8). We are saved from reliance on any of it because it has been replaced with the truth which sets us free. It took me years to realise that this is the truth that we are deeply and unashamedly loved by the creator of the universe, and while hatred always destroys, it's in giving ourselves away in love, as God constantly does, that life is created and we participate in Eternal Life.

Transformation: Loving in the Jesus way is to play our part in transforming the world for the good of all. Even the smallest gesture of love can transform someone's life as I'd learnt for myself. Jesus therefore calls us to live the life he called the Kingdom of God – engaging with society so that God's will is 'done on earth as it is in heaven.' And those words mean, of course, that Christianity is inherently political, because it is intent on creating caring communities and abolishing injustices – the social transformation which is what politics should be about. Christian politics is one that acts out of love and never from a selfish bid for power. And that's why the Kingdom also demands our own personal transformation, made possible by allowing the mystery to abide in us. That's the way the Kingdom of God turns from being 'pie in the sky when you die', to 'skate on your plate while you wait!' But it demands a Jesus-style life, and that means we have to be prepared to suffer for it.

The mystery of suffering: Some suffering is clearly self-inflicted. I've had lots of experience of wicked people, and it's taught me that while wickedness sets out to reduce others, it also slowly eats away at the perpetrator. They become diminished, shrunken people themselves. Even if they remain bombastic and self-seeking, their whole personality becomes shrivelled up. They die never knowing what it could have been like to live. The word 'hell' signifies that they are no longer able to experience God's light shining into their darkness as love, but only as wrath and punishment, for that's all they know.

But what of those who suffer needlessly? Realising that the God of Love is a suffering God has alerted me to the truth that love and suffering are actually inseparable. I've learnt that offering love to someone leaves us wide open to having our love spurned or taken advantage of. And that hurts and we suffer – which is certainly what happened to Jesus on that cross. But the other thing that I've often experienced is how someone's suffering has elicited from me a love I didn't even know I had. And that makes me ask whether, in a world where no one could suffer, would anybody ever learn to love? It seems to me the presence of suffering in the world is as inevitable as is love – they are so bound together. I wouldn't want to live in a world without love, so it seems I have to accept the suffering that goes with it.

Knowing that God experiences suffering on the cross and is every day giving himself away to sustain us, does help a little to understand why suffering exists in the world God creates. But suffering will still always remain a mystery. Our unknowing about suffering becomes yet another ingredient of the mystery we encounter when we have those glimpses of the depths in all that's around us.

A dynamic God: Finally, from the first, I've experienced God as dynamic and relational in the extreme, reaching out in all manner of ways, apparently intent on being in, being with, being concerned for everything we encounter. Christians seek to express this dynamism by talking of God as the Holy Trinity. The way I like to think of it is that the Father is the Ground of all Being, the fountainhead of all possibility. God the Son, Jesus the Christ, is the practical expression of God's love. And the Holy Spirit is the relationality of the mystery, which reaches out and draws us in to God's love. Succinctly put, I talk of God the Father as the Ground of all Being and Love, Jesus the Son as the Logic of Love, the practical outworking of love, and the Holy Spirit as the embrace of God's love for the world, and each of us in it. Each of the three has a very different part to play, but all play an essential part in the one unified action of love. And what's more, it's fascinating to see how this dynamism of God is inevitably mirrored in creation, for it too is founded on relativity, interaction and interdependence.

Icon of the Trinity
by Mother Anne,
Malling Abbey

In my beginning is my end

I'm so glad that my life has had its downs as well as its ups, or I guess I would have learnt very little. And I find great solace in the words of the late Archbishop Michael Ramsay who observed as he grew older, 'I believe more and more in less and less.' I feel, as he must have done, that a lot of the stuff I thought so important when I was a young man, now seems to be so very unimportant – and yet my faith and my love for others seems to have deepened. I'll never cease to be a bishop, so I love being invited to share in taking services, teaching those preparing for ministry and offering spiritual direction to those who want to be more in touch with that Spiritual Presence. It means that whilst I still can, I continue to do a lot of running around. But all the time I keep drilling down to what is indispensable in the Christian faith and jettisoning the nonsense that the church can sometimes get itself all knotted up about. For I've learnt from my sixty and more years of churning around in theology and doctrine that, as the Latin tag goes, *'Ubi caritas et amor, Deus ibi est'*, which means 'wherever love is, God is there!' And I've seen this in all sorts of people and in all sorts of places, Christian or not, joyful or sorrowful. I've learnt that even my unacceptability is accepted, for we are all truly loved. And it's all because the mystery reaches out to us, and hauls us back towards who God intended us to become when God first loved us into existence.

Life is such a splendid gift and is not to be wasted. As I come towards the end of mine, I offer this, my story, to family and friends and whoever else might turn these pages, knowing that the only true account of my life is that told from God's perspective. One day then, perhaps I'll be told what really happened, what I really was, and who I really am. But I hope and believe that the truth about all my shortcomings and my failures will be shared with me with consoling compassion, as I sink into the loving arms of God, the Ground of our Being.

Some of Laurie Green's other writings

Let's Do Theology: Resources for Contextual Theology
Power to the Powerless: Theology Brought to Life
Urban Ministry and the Kingdom of God.
Blessed are the Poor.? Urban Poverty and the Church.

With Chris Baker, *Building Utopia.? Seeking the Authentic Church for New Communities.*

'The Body: Physicality in the UPA', in *God in the City*

'Global Urbanisation', in *Beyond Colonial Anglicanism*

'Liberation Theology and Urban Theology', in *Liberation Theology for Church & Nation.*

'The Urban Vocation' & 'The Persistent Presence of the Holy Spirit', in *Crossover City.*

Jesus and the Jubilee – the Kingdom of God and Our New Millennium (booklet)

The Challenge of the Estates: Strategies and Theology for Housing Estate Ministry (booklet)

<u>www.lauriegreen.org</u>

292

Printed in Great Britain
by Amazon

12232495R00169